SCATMAN JOHN

SCATMAN JOHN

The Remarkable Story of the World's Unlikeliest Popstar

Gina Waggott

BLOOMSBURY ACADEMIC
NEW YORK • LONDON • OXFORD • NEW DELHI • SYDNEY

BLOOMSBURY ACADEMIC

Bloomsbury Publishing Inc, 1359 Broadway, New York, NY 10018, USA
Bloomsbury Publishing Plc, 50 Bedford Square, London, WC1B 3DP, UK
Bloomsbury Publishing Ireland, 29 Earlsfort Terrace, Dublin 2, D02 AY28, Ireland

BLOOMSBURY, BLOOMSBURY ACADEMIC and the Diana logo
are trademarks of Bloomsbury Publishing Plc

First published in the United States of America 2025

Copyright © Gina Waggott, 2026

For legal purposes the Acknowledgements on pp. 207–211 constitute an extension of this copyright page.

Cover design: Sally Rinehart
Cover image © Iceberg Records A/S, photo by Michael Von Gimbut

Lyrics by John Larkin (Scatman John) and Antonio Nunzio Catania, except 'Shut Your Mouth and Open Your Mind' by John Larkin, Antonio Nunzio Catania, and Ingo Kays. © 1994–1996 the writers and their publishers: Iceberg Music Publishing, EMI Music Publishing, Tony Catania Music Edition, Edition Scales, and Edition K-Tracks Publishing. All rights reserved. Used by permission of the John Larkin Estate (Lee Newman), Iceberg Records, Antonio Nunzio Catania, and Ingo Kays.

All rights reserved. No part of this publication may be: i) reproduced or transmitted in any form, electronic or mechanical, including photocopying, recording or by means of any information storage or retrieval system without prior permission in writing from the publishers; or ii) used or reproduced in any way for the training, development or operation of artificial intelligence (AI) technologies, including generative AI technologies. The rights holders expressly reserve this publication from the text and data mining exception as per Article 4(3) of the Digital Single Market Directive (EU) 2019/790.

Bloomsbury Publishing Inc does not have any control over, or responsibility for, any third-party websites referred to or in this book. All internet addresses given in this book were correct at the time of going to press. The author and publisher regret any inconvenience caused if addresses have changed or sites have ceased to exist, but can accept no responsibility for any such changes.

Library of Congress Cataloging-in-Publication Data

Names: Waggott, Gina, author
Title: Scatman John : the remarkable story of the world's unlikeliest popstar / Gina Waggott.
Description: New York : Bloomsbury Publishing, 2025. | Includes index. |
Summary: "The inspiring story of a middle-aged, stuttering pianist who, against all odds, became a global pop phenomenon by turning his greatest pain into his purpose"– Provided by publisher.
Identifiers: LCCN 2025025474 (print) | LCCN 2025025475 (ebook) | ISBN 9798881807078 (hardcover) | ISBN 9798881807085 (epub) | ISBN 9798881867676 (pdf)
Subjects: LCSH: Scatman John | Singers–United States–Biography | LCGFT: Biographies
Classification: LCC ML420.S299 W34 2025 (print) | LCC ML420.S299 (ebook) | DDC 782.42164092 [B]–dc23/eng/20250606
LC record available at https://lccn.loc.gov/2025025474
LC ebook record available at https://lccn.loc.gov/2025025475

ISBN:	HB:	979-8-8818-0707-8
	eBook:	979-8-8818-0708-5
	ePDF:	979-8-8818-6767-6

Typeset by Integra Software Services Pvt. Ltd.
Printed and bound in the United States of America

For product safety related questions contact productsafety@bloomsbury.com.

To find out more about our authors and books visit www.bloomsbury.com and sign up for our newsletters.

For John

And for those still finding their voice.

*The deeper that sorrow carves into your being,
the more joy you can contain.*

-KAHLIL GIBRAN, *THE PROPHET*

Jazz is freedom. You think about that.

-THELONIOUS MONK

CONTENTS

Introduction – The Unlikeliest Popstar 1

Prologue – A Good Little Soldier 5

PART I

1. The Ever-Present Saboteur 9
2. The Sacrilege 13
3. Be Someone 17
4. Girls and Booze 22
5. Portrait of the Jazzman 28
6. The Misfit 33
7. Happy Birthday 39
8. Secrets Too Hard to See 46
9. Jazz on the Gig 48
10. Working-Class Hero 53
11. The Dance of John and Marcia 58
12. Speedball 63
13. Breath of Light 70

14 Going Out 75

15 Uncovery 79

16 Surrender Means Win 80

17 Oil and Water 86

18 On the Sunny Side of the Street 89

19 U-Turn 95

20 Don't Kill Me, But I Have an Idea 101

PART II

21 The Stutter and the Scat is the Same Thing 109

22 Popstar 116

23 Let it Go 120

24 The Old Newcomer 125

25 Message To You 130

26 Scatman's World 134

27 Joyous Wisdom 140

28 Welcome to Scatland 146

29 Johnny Jetlag 152

30 Journey of Fantasy 158

31 Everybody Jam! 162

32 One Confused Soul 169

33 Calling Out 175

34 Take Your Time 182

35 I'm Free 188

36 Can You Hear Me? 193
37 Whatever God Wants 197

Epilogue 201
Resources and Support 206
Acknowledgements 207
Author's Note 212
Notes 213
Index 247

Introduction
The Unlikeliest Popstar

On a cold February night in 1996, backstage in Tokyo, a middle-aged man checks his mic, adjusts his fedora, and braces himself. Out front, thousands of teenagers are screaming his name.

He's a month shy of 54. Two years ago, he was fired from a gig for not knowing enough pop. Now, he's outselling Michael Jackson.

He steps into the light, hands reaching for him, the chants of 'Scatman! Scatman!' so loud he can barely begin.

He grins, tips his hat, raises the mic.

'I'm guh-guh-gonna ssssing for you!' he says. 'If I c-c-can.'

That stutter had nearly destroyed him. Now, it was his greatest asset.

The man was John Larkin. The world knew him, for one unforgettable stretch of the 1990s, as Scatman John. He shouldn't have been anywhere near a pop chart. He should have been dead.

For decades, he'd scraped by as a jazz pianist, chasing gigs and chasing highs, dodging destitution, death, and jail. His stutter shaped everything: how he spoke, how he played, and eventually, how he sang. He could scat-sing better than anyone alive, grabbing and firing syllables like bullets. Yet he couldn't even say his own name.

He poured the words he couldn't say into keys and strings, channeling his frustration into a searing improvisational style. For years, almost no one noticed.

Until, against all odds, the world did.

At 52, encouraged by his wife Judy and a moonshot gamble by a small record label, he made a strange, hopeful decision: he'd confront his stutter by putting it in a pop song.

It worked.

'Scatman (Ski-Ba-Bop-Ba-Dop-Bop)' and 'Scatman's World' topped charts worldwide. In Europe, he was the most successful male artist of 1995. In Japan, his debut album is still one of the best-selling of all time by a foreign artist, just below the Beatles.

I first heard – and loved – Scatman John in a decade defined by grunge, gangsta rap, and bubblegum pop. Like many '90s kids, I was fascinated by this older guy in a suit, rapping about self-acceptance and hope in a culture obsessed with youth and cool. Back then, it felt surreal. Now, it feels necessary.

Why does a weird Eurodance artist from the mid-'90s still resonate with kids born after he died? Maybe because authenticity never goes out of style. John was real. He was funny, flawed, and fully himself, telling one of the most quietly radical stories in pop history: You are not your shame. You are not your fear. You are never too different, too damaged, or too old to matter.

Today, being open about a disability or a difference is widely accepted. But in 1996, when John stood on stage at the German Echo Awards and couldn't get a word out, people were shocked. When he spoke about depression and recovery, it broke taboos. When he sang about 'Scatland', it wasn't nonsense. It was a vision for a world where differences weren't just tolerated but celebrated.

Somehow, Scatman John pulled off one of pop's rarest feats: multigenerational staying power. NFL star Jason Kelce sang Scatman to his brother Travis on their podcast, saying the meaning behind his favorite song made it even better. On TikTok, John's music has become shorthand for turning pain into power, remixed by Gen Z fans who assume he's a new viral artist, only to learn he peaked before they were born. In the streaming era, his tracks have been played over half a billion times. Every second, someone, somewhere, hits play on a Scatman John song.

John belongs to a small but significant group of public figures who stutter – King George VI, Joe Biden, Emily Blunt, Ed Sheeran, Kendrick Lamar. But unlike many, John didn't outgrow it, so he embraced it. By stuttering openly and unapologetically, he gave millions a new way to see themselves.

For the seventy million people worldwide who stutter – around 1 percent of the global population – his visibility was crucial. He showed kids with speech differences they didn't need to be fixed; they just needed to be heard. Even now, for anyone facing a challenge, he is a symbol not of perfection but of possibility.

For this authorized biography, I had unprecedented access to John's unpublished memoir notes, personal archive, and private correspondence. Before she passed in 2023, his wife Judy entrusted me with some of these materials so that the world would know the true story of the man she loved. With the support of her son, Lee Newman, along with John's family, estate, and record label, I was able to piece together his extraordinary life.

What I uncovered was a moving and often shocking portrait of a broken yet brilliant man who spent most of his life running from himself, only to discover that what he'd been running from was exactly what the world needed.

After years of research and more than a hundred interviews, I discovered just how many John touched: the addicts he sponsored, the musicians he inspired, the outsiders who finally felt seen, and the fans who found hope in his words.

This is the untold story of how an aging, stuttering jazz cat unexpectedly shot to the top of the pop charts – and the remarkable things he did when he got there.

'All of a sudden, I'm a popstar,' John once said.

'Wait until they find out who I really am.'

Prologue

A Good Little Soldier

Twelve-year-old John Larkin watched Sister Eletta shuffle over to the blackboard. He knew what was coming. He'd been dreading it for weeks.

The elderly nun scrawled 'Current Events' in white chalk. Silence fell over the sixth-grade classroom. John's heartbeat pounded in his ears. He hadn't wanted to come to school this morning, but his father had forced him to.

Clutching her rosary, Sister Eletta began summoning children to the front. One by one, John's classmates stood and confidently recounted their choice of 1954's biggest news stories.

'USA A-Bomb and H-Bomb Arsenal Growing Rapidly'

'Record Wave of Heat Continues Across Nation'

'Eisenhower Raps Split of Viet-Nam'

John wasn't listening. Each passing presentation meant he was getting closer to his name being called, and the minutes were ticking by. His chest tightened. He had hardly slept, waking with the same panic he'd gone to bed with. Last night, his father sat across from him at the kitchen table, watching as John memorized every single word of his carefully chosen article so that maybe, just maybe, this time he wouldn't do it.

'The state department of motor vehicles …', he silently recited, the words flowing seamlessly in the safety of his mind.

The moment arrived.

'John!' Sister Eletta commanded. It was showtime.

John swallowed drily and made his way to the front of the classroom, a good little soldier of a punishing God. The hair on the nape of his neck prickled as he felt all eyes on him, waiting for the performance to begin. It was always as if his classmates had never heard him speak before. The horror was fresh every time.

John turned around to face his peers and drew a deep breath.

'Th-th – eth eth th – th …', he began. His jaw stretched out, groping for purchase. 'Th-th-th-th …,' he spluttered, tongue against teeth, trying to pluck a three-letter word from a vice of fear.

'Th-th-th-', John tried again. He stood there, trembling, trying to get something more than splintered syllables to come out of his mouth.

He gulped another breath.

'Thhhhh …' His cheeks were red, his mouth twisted. Time stretched, each second an eternity. Some kids snickered and nudged each other.

After at least a minute of futile attempts, John gave up, and fell silent. He looked at the floor. The familiar feeling of defeat washed over him. Someone laughed out loud. John burst into tears, and ran back to his seat.

He would be able to recite that newspaper article, word for word, for the rest of his life. As he sat there with his head buried in his arms, his shoulders hitching, he wondered if this was his destiny: to be forever imprisoned by his own voice.

PART ONE

1 THE EVER-PRESENT SABOTEUR

On the morning of 11 January 1949, in El Sereno, California, a six-year-old boy stared out of his bedroom window in silent joy. A carpet of fresh snow had covered the backyard and turned the distant hills white. There was a stillness in the air, and snowflakes gleamed on the rooftops and sparkled from every angle. His older brother joined him at the window before they turned and scrambled to get dressed.

The blizzard, the first in almost twenty years, had caught Southern California off guard. Orange growers cursed the frost, and lit smudge pots to swaddle their precious citrus. In the middle of its Golden Age, Hollywood came to a standstill as abandoned cars clogged up Beverly Hills, their radiators frozen solid. In March, Laurence Olivier's *Hamlet* would win Best Picture at the Academy Awards, shortly after Harry Truman was inaugurated. New York, a city that would scoff at the amount of snowfall that brought Los Angeles to a halt, would see the opening of Birdland, 'Jazz Corner of the World', by the end of the year, where Charlie 'Yardbird' Parker himself would play on the opening night.

McPherson Avenue, where the boy and his brother crunched out into their front yard, came alive that January morning with children dashing outside to throw snowballs, build snowmen, and slither around in the rapidly melting slush before it was time for school.

The boy's name was John Paul Larkin. He had arrived on 13 March 1942, by caesarean at the Stanley Hospital in El Monte. Despite being born on Friday the 13th, there was no inkling that anything was wrong.

He was cute and compact, with broad dimples, prominent ears, and a tuft of coal-black hair. His fingers and toes were counted, his blue-grey eyes treated with silver nitrate to protect against infection, and then he was handed to his mother, Harriet. From then on, she would always call him Johnny.

Bill and Harriet Larkin had moved to the Golden State from Massachusetts shortly after they were married. Their first son, John's older brother William, was born in 1940. Everyone called him Billy, to distinguish him from his father, who 'didn't want any of that Junior business'.

Harriet, a petite beauty with a warm smile, sang professionally at the Million Dollar Theatre where stars like Billie Holiday and Artie Shaw once performed. Wartime Los Angeles had swelled with servicemen and factory workers, and jazz and big band shows provided entertainment and escapism. Five thousand miles away in Europe, the Nazis suppressed jazz as a 'degenerate' art form and had banned improvisation, including scat-singing, denouncing it as 'Negroid' music. In the USA, however, it thrived. Bebop radiated outward from the East Coast, and Harriet sang it all.

She was talented and earned good money, but motherhood and late-night singing engagements proved incompatible. After Billy was born and John was on the way, she gave up her career to become a full-time homemaker in their tiny two-bedroom home in El Sereno. Yet music stayed with her, and she sang to herself, with her husband, or to her two boys, soothing them to sleep with Brahms' *Lullaby*.

She cradled John as he was nursing, humming 'Blues in the Night' to him. To her delight, he babbled 'da da da da' back to her using exactly the same melody.

John would later reflect on how sweet that fact was: that he spoke the language of music before the language of words. The latter turned out to be a cruel and relentless adversary. As soon as John tried to speak, there it was.

At first, hesitations. Then came the silent blocks (J ….ohn), repetitions (Juh-Juh-John), and prolongations (Joooooohn) that are the hallmark of one of the world's most misunderstood speech differences: stuttering.

John's childhood thoughts, beautiful and fully formed, were mangled by an invisible force as soon as his brain tried to verbally express them.

How had it happened? He wondered. *Why me?*

Years later, in therapy and under hypnosis, he searched for the answer. At the time, many people wrongly thought stuttering came from an early shock or emotional injury, so John trawled through his past, hunting for the inciting event. Two possibilities stood out.

The first was when he was still a baby, and the family lived in an upstairs apartment in central LA. Harriet heard a loud crash and rushed outside to find that Billy had accidentally rolled John, in his baby carriage, all the way down the back staircase. By pure luck, John had landed on a mattress, unscathed.

The second was when John was about two years old. Ditch diggers were clearing the creek behind the Larkins' new house in El Sereno, and Billy and John were up to no good, lobbing cans and bottles down to keep them busy. Billy wound up to throw a broken bottle and accidentally smashed his little brother on the forehead. Harriet screamed as John ran into the house, his face a sheet of blood.

She bundled him into the car, pressing a towel to the gash, mimicking ambulance noises to distract him. John felt woozy as he watched the towel slowly turn a deep red. In the hospital, he lay conscious under the bright surgery lights as a dozen stitches went in.

Neither event, he later learned, had caused his stutter. Science would later reveal the truth: that stuttering isn't psychological, but neurological. John's brain was simply wired differently – something he had no control over.

For a brief, blissful period, John was too young to register what he would later call 'the ever-present saboteur'. He spent his early childhood colouring pictures at Farmdale Elementary School, dressing up as a cowboy, or taking part in the May Day picnic at El Sereno Playground, where he'd run in circles around the Maypole, clutching papier-mâché strings.

Most afternoons, John raced straight home from school to explore the creek behind his house. Parents warned their children not to go down there, but it was irresistible. The end of the creek disappeared into a tunnel, and local kids dared each other to see how far they could go down it without turning around and coming back. Sometimes, they perched like crows on the lip above the water until someone either fell or got pushed, and everyone would laugh.

John and his friend David found a slow-moving stretch of the creek where it was easier to catch frogs. They collected them, squirming and hopping, in a bucket. John named their kingdom *FroggyLand, Jazz, Boogie and the Blues* after a radio show he liked.

He spent hours crouched at the water's edge, hunting crawdads, watching guppies flick through the shallows, marvelling at dragonflies and water spiders skimming the surface. One afternoon, he spotted seashells and pocketed them, thrilled by the find.

The freak blizzard of 1949 sparked a vigilance in John to look out for extreme weather. Every night, he would sit and watch the TV meteorologist point out all the storms sweeping down from Oregon and Washington. John scrutinized the forecast, willing the temperature to be conducive to snow. By looking out of his bedroom window, he learned to tell the time by the shadow of the moon on the other side of the creek. He daydreamed about what it might be like to stand in the eye of a hurricane. He also had a thing for frost, and would inspect it twinkling on the lawns after a particularly cold night.

These were John's most beautiful memories: the snow, the moon, the frost, and the creek.

Rarely indoors, John roamed around El Sereno's hills, often following the local kids to play where they shouldn't. Their favorite haunt was a ruin they called the White House. Nobody knew its real name, because it was never finished. Rumour had it that a wealthy investor began building a country club in the 1920s but ran out of cash when the Great Depression hit. Now it sat abandoned and rotting on the hill, with an empty pool, a maze of foundations, and twisting, narrow service corridors. It felt haunted.

John followed a group of boys up the winding pathways and into the building, creeping through tunnels and crunching over broken glass. He could smell something bad. He looked up and noticed giant dirty pictures drawn on the walls.

It was here, at the White House, where The Thing happened for the first time. Then it happened again, in the crawlspace under his house, and again, in the shadows of a neighbor's backyard. John didn't know what The Thing meant, but he felt its significance, a shift in his universe.

One evening, when his mother came to put him to bed, he decided to tell her about just one of the incidents, to see how she would react. He lay there and carefully explained to her about what had happened behind the neighbor's house. It was vivid, the memory still fresh. Then, he waited.

To his surprise, his mother did nothing, said nothing. The next morning, it was as if he had never told her anything at all.

John churned with confusion. *If it's all right with mommy*, he reasoned, *it must be okay*. But he couldn't shake the feeling that it wasn't.

He decided he had better not tell anyone else about it, ever. It would be his secret.

Only one thought bothered him: God must have seen The Thing, too.

2 **THE SACRILEGE**

When the All Saints Catholic School opened on 13 September 1948, directly opposite the church of the same name, Bill and Harriet enrolled their two sons there. *To impress the neighbors*, John thought glumly.

Billy started third grade and settled in fast, making friends and joining the flag football team. John started first grade and got instructions that made no sense.

'Don't think so fast before you speak,' the nuns scolded. 'Take a deep breath.'

Staffed by the Sinsinawa Dominican Sisters, All Saints drilled Catholic doctrine and virtuous conduct. Stuttering, as far as they were concerned, didn't get you off the hook.

It would take fifty more years before science proved stuttering was rooted in brain function. Until then, it was dismissed as a problem of nerves, weak character, or even moral failure – something one could 'overcome' through willpower alone.

Parents were told not to acknowledge it, leaving children to struggle in silence. Teachers ordered kids who stuttered to slow down, calm down, or try harder. Therapists sometimes recommended ignoring the stutter or even punishing it. None of it worked. It was like telling a blind child they could see again, if only they put their mind to it – and then blaming them when they couldn't.

Forced to read aloud and answer questions while the other kids smirked and traded looks, John soldiered on, surrounded by well-meaning but useless advice.

His first-grade teacher, Sister Tharla, a pianist, fascinated him. He loved watching her play, enthralled by her energy and gestures. But the other nuns frightened him, especially Sister Eletta. Her trademark was her ancient, threadbare rosary, tangled around her wrists like handcuffs. John watched her praying and shaking, as if trying to get rid of something unspeakably awful. Eye contact with her was to be avoided; it felt like she could read minds.

One nun, he swore, had a beard. Another, he caught peeking in the boys' bathroom. In second grade, he fell in love for the first time – with his teacher, Sister Carla, a younger nun. He stole shy glances at her across the hallway. It made him feel strange and vulnerable.

Through it all, he stuttered on every word.

He longed to disappear into the background, but his voice wouldn't let him. By third grade, he was labeled 'the weird kid', and the other children made sure he knew it.

Some enlightened classmates saw past John's speech and got to know the funny, observant, and smart boy underneath. One of them was Bobby Rivera, who was also mocked for his weight. The two formed a bond that would last all their lives, the fat kid and the stutterer' against the world. Bobby's distinctive laugh delighted John, and he lived to make it reach a jiggling crescendo when the two of them were together.

Billy, confident and athletic, moved easily through school. He knew John struggled, but couldn't always intervene – they were in different classes and had different friends. Bullies, then as now, preferred to strike outside of school where they couldn't easily be caught.

Word reached Billy one afternoon that John was being cornered down at the El Sereno Playground. He marched down to the basketball court and confronted the older lad tormenting his little brother. Not usually a fighter, Billy grabbed the bully and punched him, starting a brawl.

'I ended up beating the crap out of him,' Billy remembers. 'I pointed a finger and said, "Don't you *ever* talk to my brother that way again."'

After that, the bullying never happened in Billy's presence, but when neither Bobby nor Billy could protect him, John learned to answer taunts with his fists.

One day after school, some classmates lured John towards a house on his walk home. Then they slipped inside and disappeared. He was standing outside looking for them when he heard the first grotesque noise.

'St-st-st-stutterbug!'

John's head snapped around. Two of these so-called friends were dangling from a window, sneering.

John's eyes narrowed. He rushed to the front door and furiously tried the handle. They had locked themselves in. Cowards.

'P-P-P-Porky pig!' they screamed. 'Buh-buh-buh-buh!'

John hammered on the door.

'Duh-duh-duh-duh!' came the gleeful shrieks from the safety of the house.

John turned around and stormed home, heat rising through his clenched fists. *They can't stay locked in there forever.* He would wait. He would remember. And he would pounce.

Days later, John spotted two of the boys sauntering down his street. The pain came flooding back. Anger mounted to fury. This was his chance. He knew what he was going to do. He was going to kill them.

He burst out of his house, white-hot with rage, and rushed at his tormentors. Bill Larkin saw the look in his son's eyes and ran out after him.

John launched himself at one of the boys, knocked him to the ground, and started pummeling him with his fists. Bill bellowed as he hoicked his son off by the collar and slapped him, hard.

John was yelling and swinging, his legs pinwheeling. Bill spun him around and slapped him again and again, trying to get John to stop screaming.

The boys fled, and John was frogmarched inside, burning with hurt and injustice. It was the first time he tasted anger and pain of that quality. He would carry it as fuel.

Bill loomed over his youngest son and shook his head. *Not good enough.* A dark-haired, stocky Irishman with a short fuse, Bill was politely described by the neighbours as 'old school'. He worked as a shipping clerk at an aircraft company and valued order, discipline, and control – things his youngest son seemed built to defy.

'Wh-wh-why do I stutter?' John asked one evening at the dining table.

'Shut up and eat your dinner,' his father snapped. 'There's nothing wrong with you.'

Oh, but there is, John thought.

He cringed when he overheard people asking, 'What's wrong with this child?' *He's just hyperactive*, Harriet insisted. *He'll grow out of it.*

Catholic school only deepened a conviction that was creeping into his young psyche: he was obviously, pitifully inferior. God had somehow made junk.

Judgment, both real and imagined, weighed down on him. *Why is what created me out to get me?* He wondered. He concluded that God must be disgusted with him. He pictured God up there in heaven, looking down, shaking his head, as he had so often seen his father do.

Desperate for redemption, John came up with a plan. He would attend Mass every single day before school. Then, surely, God would notice and love him.

Early the next morning, John sat alone under the timber rafters of All Saints, legs dangling from the pew. He listened to the weighty, monotone Latin, squeezed his eyes shut in prayer, and poured his heart into singing the hymns.

Feeling better already, John watched a queue form at the front to take communion at the altar. *God will be happy if I take communion too*, John thought, so he walked up and put out his little tongue to receive the host wafer. They said it was literally Christ's body. *Ewww*, he thought. But as it dissolved, like magic, he immediately felt reverent. Jesus was entering his body to cleanse him of all the sins he was sure he had committed.

Hands clasped, he trotted back to his seat. He knew he would be doing this every day from here on out.

After Mass, John crossed to the school and approached the door.

'Stop!' a sister yelled. John froze.

'Did you eat breakfast?'

The words broke John in half. He had forgotten that he should never, ever take communion without having fasted first. The bowl of cereal he'd eaten that morning soured in his stomach. His heart fell out from under him, and he panicked, trying to get the word 'yeh-yeh-yeh … yes' out.

'Go see Father Nevin in the rectory immediately!' came the reply.

John trudged back across the street, tears streaming. As he had been taught, he might even be excommunicated from the Catholic Church. He knocked on the rectory door, and a woman answered.

'Is F-f-f-fahahather Nea-hea-heah-vin here?' he croaked.

When the man of God in the black robes appeared on the stairs, John collapsed at his feet, sobbing. He choked out apologies, begged for mercy, wailed about how sorry he was, that he hadn't known, that he hadn't meant to.

Father Nevin gazed coolly at the broken boy curled on the ground in front of him and asked 'Holy God almighty' to forgive him.

'I look back at this incident and realize what depth of an atrocity this is … to do this to an innocent child,' John later said. 'This single event probably did much to solidify my permanent sense of never being enough. I wanted God to love me more, and he loved me less.'

Later, he heard a saying for where he ended up: *You can't kill a man who is already blown full of holes.* One more wound wouldn't make any difference.

'My life', John said, 'was destroyed before I even started grammar school.'

Punch-drunk with humiliation and with his faith ebbing away, John would sit in lessons, his thoughts drifting. Everything began with 'if only'.

If only his parents had raised him differently.

If only he didn't stutter.

If only The Thing hadn't happened.

If only he were someone or somewhere else.

John yearned for another identity, something he could fold himself into. It wasn't long before he found it.

3 BE SOMEONE

It was too late to drop the cigarette. Something in John made him take a long, deliberate drag right in front of his father, making sure he saw it.

'Get home,' Bill growled from the car window.

John ground the cig under his heel and slid into the back seat without a word. His father and Billy had driven miles across East Los Angeles looking for him. Now thirteen, John spent most afternoons on the street with kids his parents didn't approve of.

One of them, Bernie, had taught him how to smoke the year before. Unlike most first-timers, John didn't choke or cough. He took to it. He called his smokes *frajos*, the Chicano slang, and until now, had managed to hide his new habit from his parents, even though he was stealing their cigarettes.

Walking home from school with his friend Tony, he'd chew leaves or rub them on his hands to mask the smell. Now he sat in the car, reeking of tobacco, the air thick with his father's anger and disappointment. He knew this would end like it always did – with him getting the strap.

'Wait until the army gets hold of you!' was a threat often bellowed into John's face.

Harriet had known for months. 'You're breaking your mother's heart,' she'd say, cigarette in hand. She tried guilt, bribes, and even getting the doctor to wrongly insinuate that smoking affected his speech. Now that John had been caught, she let him smoke in front of her, saying it was better than him sneaking around.

Bill didn't agree. He hated how she babied John, and the inevitable dinner table fights flared. John tried to tune them out, his stress knotting tighter under another brewing thundercloud.

Out of Bill's earshot, Harriet complained to John about their marital problems, including sex. It deepened the rift with his father and made him feel burdened by his mother. She had wanted a girl, she said, and got him instead. Maybe she was confiding in him as she would have done with a daughter, John thought.

John listened as Bill and Billy chatted and laughed about sports. *The Family Hero*, he called his brother, who had no idea how much John envied him. To John, it seemed like his father loathed him, except on the rare weekends when he crawled into John's bed and held him, leaving John in a state of perpetual confusion and longing.

By now, John had joined an exclusive club: the one per cent of people who stutter into adolescence and beyond. Most kids – around 80 per cent – grow out of it. But John hadn't. Sometimes, he couldn't get a single word out, and his jaw, mouth, and face contorted so much trying to speak that it scared him.

What little speech therapy he had focused only on the mechanics of fluency.

'They taught me about plosives, slurred speech, and about speaking in tempo,' John recalled. 'If you say everything in tempo, you probably won't have a problem talking – but you'll sound like a damn robot. Who wants to be like that?'

He refused to accept that this was it – this was how he talked.

'I always acted like, "I'm only having a problem talking right now",' he said. As if it might go away. But inside, it was eating him alive.

One afternoon in 1956 when he couldn't escape the house, John went alone into the living room and flicked on the television. The sound of jazz filled the air before the picture came into focus.

John's ears pricked up. He knew that piano. It was Dave Brubeck. The image sharpened, revealing Brubeck on stage with his quartet – cool, sophisticated and, sharp-suited. John turned the volume up. He watched Brubeck's foot stomping time, his head bobbing and swinging, his fingers jabbing and dancing over the keys.

John rolled up his sleeves and tapped along on the glass coffee table, eyes closed. He lost himself in the polyrhythms, the counterpoints, the unconventional meter of ONE-two-three-FOUR-five. He felt the improvisations deep in his bones, a language he had never spoken but at once understood.

Every day, he returned to that glass piano, playing records on the turntable, pretending to be Brubeck. By the end of each 'concert', the tabletop was smeared with so many fingerprints that nobody could see through it.

His record collection grew as he filled it with jazz musicians – what John called his 'feeling people'.

Louis Armstrong appeared on TV too, eyes alight, feet swaying, occasionally lowering his trumpet for a full-throated laugh. When he scat-sang, gravel-voiced and joyful, it lifted John's soul – pure emotion without uttering a word.

A music teacher heard John was into jazz and suggested he listen to Ella Fitzgerald. John dropped the needle on a live recording of 'How High the Moon' and heard her take off – a long, fearless, technically brilliant scat solo that climbed and darted like a bird in flight. John was agog.

'I bet you I could do that,' he told a friend.

But first, he had to learn to play.

Every week, as Harriet wiped his fingerprints off the coffee table, John begged her to buy him a piano. One afternoon, she took John along to visit a friend who had one. John wandered over to it, sat down, and let his fingers skim over the keys. Then he pressed down harder, feeling it vibrate through him.

Immediately, he knew. *There's something in here for me.*

Soon after, Harriet gave in, and an upright piano was wedged into the corner of the bedroom he shared with Billy. From that day on, John played nonstop.

He started where most kids start, with simple pieces like 'Chopsticks'. Then he taught himself chords. Billy remembered the sound filling the house constantly.

John didn't stutter when he sang, and the piano gave him an excuse to do so, sometimes with his brother, and occasionally with his mother and father, too. He didn't know it, but singing engaged the right hemisphere of his brain (which handles melody and rhythm), rather than the left, which controls language and syntax. For most – but not all – people who stutter, this is enough to bypass the neurological block interrupting fluent speech. Everything from breath control to how the vocal cords, lips, and tongue work changes when singing, a phenomenon that allowed John to sing fluently.

He would spend hours and hours practicing. He never had lessons, couldn't read music, and played everything by ear. A neighbor, Chuck Wert, had a baby grand piano, and remembers John showing up at their house often just to play it because he liked to hear the difference.

The 'rather silent boy' was beginning to make a hell of a noise.

That summer, before eighth grade, John got a job bussing tables at the Cheli Air Force Station cafeteria, as Billy had done before him. Harriet was the assistant manager. The role didn't require talking, which suited John just fine. He cleared tables, hauled garbage, and restocked supplies. Harriet's boss was a man named Johnny Peverada, whom John quickly worked out was in love with his mother.

'I liked it,' he said. 'I liked anything that was against my father.'

Johnny let John smoke, laughed and shared jokes with him, and treated him with warmth and kindness. John wanted to tell him everything, even about The Thing. But he never did.

Billy noticed it too, that Johnny did things for John that their father 'either couldn't or wouldn't do'. Johnny built an aviary for John in the backyard and filled it with parakeets. John bred them, raised dozens of hatchlings, and talked to them as he tended them. Like singing, many who stutter find they're more fluent talking to animals or children.

A new school year arrived, and so did John's eighth-grade teacher, Mr. Lofgren. John figured the nuns had decided the boys' class needed a role model. And they got one.

A recent graduate, Mr. Lofgren was young and 'loose and human', and John liked him immediately. 'Lofty', as the kids called him, noticed John's torment straight away.

'When I was called on to read, my stuttering had become absolutely horrible,' John said. 'It would take me sometimes five minutes to read a simple short paragraph. It was awful.' Anyone whose surname came after Larkin relaxed and set their books down, safe in the knowledge that John would still be struggling through by the time the lesson bell rang.

Lofty watched John spiral into panic each time he had to speak. He pulled John aside after class and talked to him. Whether he realized it or not, Lofty followed what is now the fundamental principle for interacting with someone who stutters. He just ... waited. He gave John time to say what he wanted to say without judgment or interruption.

Then he went a step further and scheduled an entire evening with Bill and Harriet to talk about their son. Whatever was said behind that closed door, John never knew. But it didn't matter.

'I was on top of my little world,' John said. 'He cared. I was so very happy.'

John's stuttering lessened. He started to raise his hand in class and even volunteered to read out loud.

But there was a problem. John had been smoking more, and nicotine ran his day. He'd fidget in class, counting the minutes until his next cigarette. He was allowed off-campus for lunch and used the time to smoke with a crew of boys he wasn't really friends with.

'All I wanted to do was be like the other kids and be accepted,' John said, so he participated in whatever they did, including stealing candy from the neighbourhood store. The group would go in, buy a small amount of candy as a cover, and then steal more.

Word got back to the school. One day, Lofty stood in front of the class.

'I've heard there's been some mischief happening at lunch,' he said. 'And it needs to stop.'

He paused. 'I'm not going to name names ... like Larkin.'

John's heart sank.

'I was devastated,' John said. 'He had made me the hero and then shot me down in front of the whole classroom as being one of the bad guys.'

He stopped sharing so much with Mr. Lofgren, knowing he'd lost his confidence. By the end of that semester, his special relationship with Lofty had deteriorated. 'He abandoned me,' John said. 'He picked me up to the highest mountain only to let me down to the lowest pits.'

John wondered whether his life could have gone in a different direction if he had been able to keep Lofty as a confidant and role model. But 'no such luck,' he said. He never forgot the lesson: *Don't trust anyone who wants to help you.*

High school beckoned, but he wasn't going to the same one as Billy. The two brothers' lives began to go in different directions. 'We were never really close,' says Billy, 'but I loved him. It was so hard to get into his circle, and him into mine.'

Having been caught stealing, a further attempt to tame John was made by sending him to Don Bosco Technical Institute in Los Angeles, a private all-boys

Catholic school known for strict rules and vocational training. Discipline, they hoped, would fix John.

John called it a boot camp. 'A place where they try to unjam your circuitry by jamming it up more.'

Half the day was academic, the other half was hands-on technical training, considered an unusual approach in the 1950s. John picked cabinetmaking as his special interest, though he was unable to concentrate much. All he could think about was his next precious cigarette; the only thing that slowed the now daily flood of feelings threatening to overwhelm him. Having made a habit of a lunchtime cig at All Saints, he was determined not to wait until after school to smoke.

At lunch, he found an indented part of the football field where he thought he couldn't be seen. He would saunter over, check to see if anyone was looking, then hit the ground, chain-smoking as fast as he could. 'None of the other kids were like me,' John said. 'I was addicted and alone with it.'

When his hiding spot was discovered, he hid behind the science building instead. Then the dumpsters. He didn't care how bad it smelled.

'By now, any ordinary kid would've stopped,' John said. 'But I had to have that cigarette no matter what.'

John's mind raced in lessons, and he struggled to retain any information. Later, he wondered if he had an undiagnosed condition that affected his learning.

One thing he had correctly identified, however, was that his compulsion to smoke had become obsessive. Although he liked cabinetmaking (he made a hand-carved shelf for his mother that he was proud of), John was too distracted to give the lessons at Don Bosco much of his time.

At year's end, students gathered for the roll call of results. John sat beside his father, not expecting much. He knew he wasn't on the honor roll, so he relaxed as those names were read out. He'd probably be on the pass list. Or the 'try harder next year' list.

But they reached the Ls … and kept going.

John's heart picked up.

'I died as they got to the M's,' he said, 'and I still hadn't heard my name.'

Bill turned to look at his son, frowning.

'I didn't hear your name called,' he said.

This couldn't be right. *There has to be one more category of names*, John thought. But there wasn't.

He had been kicked out.

4 GIRLS AND BOOZE

When the 'new boy' walked into Woodrow Wilson High's tenth-grade classroom in 1957, everyone looked up. Tall and broad-shouldered, he wore a sports coat and khakis, his summer tan still fresh, black hair slicked into a waterfall. *Who is this?* His classmates thought. Especially the girls.

To John's surprise, his father didn't lose his temper after John got kicked out of Don Bosco Tech. His parents finally gave up on private schools for their youngest son, probably suspecting John would do better surrounded by his friends, so, aged 15, he joined El Sereno's public school.

John had never attended a co-ed school, and the girls got his attention fast. Though he called himself 'heterosexual by choice', he knew he was messed up.

'I was a basket case internally,' John said of his adolescence. 'The fruition of what had happened in my childhood was going to manifest as depression, and feelings of being different and separate.'

Eager to fit in, John formed his first band after meeting Paul Ackerman, a talented guitar player, and his brother Chuck. Paul smoked, which cemented their friendship. John didn't know much beyond basic songs like 'Heart and Soul' at the piano, but spent hours at Paul's place, learning blues on a battered upright that had survived a house fire. Paul's 'house' was a burned-out, blackened shack with no electricity that Paul still lived in with his mother and brother.

Paul introduced John to heavy drinking and, underage and out of control, they would 'whoop it up' at weekends. For John, alcohol came with a double bonus: it both dulled his stutter and lit up his confidence.

At lunch, he and his friends snuck into the school's music bungalow to play and sing. After school, the band practiced cover songs – John on piano, Paul on guitar, his brother Chuck on sax, and another friend on drums. Years before portable keyboards were around, they sought out venues with pianos. A favorite was the rec centre, where John remembered the band going in just as the local Alcoholics Anonymous meeting was coming out.

John and Paul had a favorite spot under the trees at the centre of campus, where they'd smoke and watch the girls go by. Slowly, John realized: they were watching him back.

'He has the cutest little stutter,' a young woman whispered to her friend. John overheard it. *See?* He thought. *I can get girls – I'm not fucked up inside.*

The more relaxed environment of public school suited John. Once settled, he became unnaturally garrulous, spending many lessons talking to and charming the girls.

One of his classmates, Janet, sat opposite John in algebra. That semester was the first time she got a 'D' on her report card for not paying attention.

Another, Nancy Beck, remembered John making wisecracks about the English teacher. 'He had a wry sense of humor,' she says. 'Very bright, sharp as a tack, looking for ways to laugh. He was able to see the irony in a lot of situations in life. I wouldn't have even thought it at that age, but he had a lot of sexual charisma. The girls were quite taken with him.'

John and Nancy dated briefly after surreptitiously holding hands on a school trip to Las Vegas. He'd inherited Billy's '51 Chevy and drove to Nancy's house after school to 'hug and kiss'. John never brought girlfriends home, nor introduced them to his parents.

'I remember being in front of his house,' Nancy says, 'but his dad was inside, so we weren't going to go in. It was a separate world.'

Girls rarely mentioned John's stutter. But he'd already worked out that if there was a piano nearby, he didn't have to talk. Every time he sat down to play, one thought burned bright: *I may stutter – but watch this.*

His oldest friend from All Saints, Bobby Rivera, also attended Woodrow Wilson. Bobby and his siblings were raised by a single mother, and their house became John's refuge. He'd often go there to eat dinner, crack jokes, and do anything he could to make Bobby giggle. John would mime playing an invisible upright bass, making ridiculous *zoom zoom zoom* noises until Bobby couldn't breathe from laughing.

'They'd be in another room,' says Bobby's older brother George, 'and we'd just hear Bobby non-stop laughing. They were nuts.'

Another friend, Tony, remembers walking home from school with John, who would chain-smoke and scat-sing his way down the street. Occasionally, John flipped back to words and stuttered. Tony jumped in and tried to finish John's sentences for him.

'No, no, no,' John ticked him off. 'Let me finish.'

George, Tony, and others never saw John as shy or quiet. Around them, he was loose, quick-witted, and full of fun. 'He was free to be John,' George says.

His grades were now acceptable (in his father's eyes at least), but his attention span and impulsiveness were still a problem. In one chemistry lesson, unable to follow along, John simply got up and walked out.

But not all classes bored him. He discovered a love for math, especially algebra. His teacher once called him a 'power thinker', and John floated through the rest of that day in a haze of pride. He liked to lose himself in equations, or anything else that took him out of his own head.

'I was girl crazy,' John admitted. 'But when I wasn't chasing them or burying myself in math or algebra, I would feel how depressed I was, so girls and cigarettes were becoming my favorite drugs.'

On Saturdays, John and Tony met their girlfriends at the movie theater for two feature films and a cartoon, none of which they watched, because they spent the whole time making out in the back row.

After parting with their dates one evening, the pair took a shortcut home through an industrial district. A car started following them. They sped up and flagged down a police cruiser. The man driving the tailing car told the police he was looking for two young men who had just robbed his house, and Tony and John matched the description.

Despite their protests, the police called their parents and brought them in for questioning.

'What happened in the movie you just saw?' the cops asked.

Neither boy could remember. They hadn't looked at the screen once.

Under interrogation, John's stutter was so pronounced that the officers gave up trying to talk to him and drove him home.

It wouldn't be John's last encounter with the police. But it would be the only time he was innocent.

John entered eleventh grade with new confidence, thanks to his music, his friends, and the buzz of female attention, especially from one girl: Anne.

Along with almost every other sixteen-year-old boy, John had a crush on her. Anne was a senior. Eighteen, long brown hair, broad smile, elegant and confident. John watched a trail of suitors follow her around the campus. One lunchtime, John spotted her in the hallway, shadowed by a persistent admirer.

'You should get a leash for that guy,' he said. Anne smiled at him. He smiled back.

Soon he was at her house after school, much to the surprise and jealousy of other seniors, especially the football team. *What would she want with him?* But it was real. John and Anne were dating.

A few weeks in, they met at a friend's empty apartment so they'd have the place to themselves. They opened the pull-out bed and started kissing. Then Anne began undressing.

John lay there, stunned, watching her.

Naked bodies are wrong, his Catholic upbringing pinged his conscience. He was excited, but also ashamed.

When she told him to take his pants off, however, John didn't need to be asked twice.

Afterwards, 'I was the happiest guy the earth had known,' he said. 'I'd just made love to the most beautiful girl in the entire school.'

Then they suddenly heard a key turn in the door. They jumped up, and Anne dashed into the bathroom. John hadn't managed to get his pants on properly when the downstairs neighbor came in. He knew the apartment was supposed to be empty, he said, and had heard noises. John acted as if sitting on a bed with his pants half off was the most ordinary thing in the world, explaining that he had permission to be there.

The neighbour left, and Anne appeared from the bathroom, laughing. John embraced her. 'We were both ecstatic,' he said, 'so aware of what we'd just done.'

They kept seeing each other, but eventually the relationship fizzled out when Anne graduated, went to college, and started dating someone else.

John had only just started his senior year when Vic Cussia, the Varsity Team football coach, cornered him. The team practiced at El Sereno Playground, and Cussia had seen John there playing touch football with his friends Bobby and Paul. John was a gifted punter and could send the ball flying nearly the full length of the field.

The team needed him, Cussia insisted. They had no punter.

John wanted no part of it. 'Those boys played too rough for my bones,' he said. He was terrified, but couldn't find the courage to say no. Instead, he summoned what he thought was his most manly voice.

'Sure, I ain't no chicken shit,' he bluffed. 'You bet!'

All week, John was paralyzed with fear, but he showed up for practice in his shoulder pads and jersey. He ran around and did push-ups, trying to look like an athlete.

'Larkin!' Cussia barked. 'Get over here, let's practice a few punts.'

John, faking fearlessness, got off a good, solid kick.

'The next play', John said, 'would confirm all the reasons I did not want to go out for football in the first place.'

Jealous that he'd dated Anne, the players had a plan. Instead of protecting him during the next punt, the blockers would let the defence charge straight through. The ball snapped high over John's head. He went scrambling after it, and players started to slam into him from all sides.

'They hit me so hard I was seeing stars,' John said. 'They knocked the living daylights out of me.'

He got up, dizzy and bruised, surrounded by laughter. Humiliated but too scared to quit, John stuck with the team out of fear of being called a chicken. The night before game day, he couldn't sleep. But when the match came, he stayed on the bench.

He saw his opportunity and lied that if he wasn't going to play, what was the point? So he quit, and he was glad.

John and Billy didn't socialize much in their late teens, but Billy gifted John his Volkswagen Beetle – the first of many cars John would either wreck or run into the ground.

Billy had enrolled at East LA College and was now engaged to his girlfriend, Sharon. John and Sharon hit it off right away. 'I loved him from the get-go,' she said, and treated him like a brother, with Billy joking that John preferred her over him.

One of John's first Beetle adventures was picking up Bobby on 'trash day'. They drove around the neighborhood, clipping trash cans and laughing hysterically as they toppled over. But this low-level mischief would soon blow up into something far more serious, fueled by John's increasing drinking.

Midway through his senior year, John and his 'senior B' crew decided to get drunk and gatecrash the 'senior A' party at the old El Sereno Theatre. They all squeezed into the Beetle and headed for the only liquor store in East Los Angeles that would sell to them, before joining the party.

By 2 a.m. they were wasted. One of them, Ronald, had just been flunked by Mr. Kursinski, the music teacher. Fueled by liquor and teenage fury, the party of drunks decided to 'get even with Mr. K'. They drove to the school, parked next to the music bungalow and staggered out of the car.

'One of us threw a rock through a window,' John said, 'then all hell broke loose.' Ronald hurled a piece of timber through the room. John picked up a trash can and slung it through another set of windows. They got into a frenzy, glass raining everywhere as they tried to outdo each other, smashing everything in sight. For good measure, they tried to set the place on fire. Then they piled into the car and sped off.

The next day, badly hungover, John began to realize what they'd done. They had all but gutted the music bungalow. Every window was broken. The grand piano was almost destroyed.

'The building looked like it had been totally demolished,' John said. 'We were all sober now, and scared.'

The friends got together in private and decided not to say anything. But then the principal summoned the whole class to the auditorium, and Mr. Kursinski announced that the police were coming to fingerprint the building unless the villains came forward.

Backed into a corner, John and his friends got the local phone book, called the principal at home, and confessed. The principal praised their courage but only promised that the cops would be called off, and disciplinary action would follow.

After questioning, John and Ronald were singled out as ringleaders and were expelled from Woodrow Wilson. Because they had confessed, they were told they could come back and graduate – but only if they finished their senior year somewhere else.

John had been kicked out again.

He knew he was drinking recklessly, yet sobriety meant depression. 'It would plague me horrendously whenever I was feeling my feelings,' he said. 'It was the driving force behind all the hostility, including getting kicked out. Nothing on the outside could fix it, except for girls and booze.'

Already late beginning a new semester, John scrambled to complete his senior year by enrolling at Franklin High in Highland Park. He stayed out of trouble by registering for the choir and dance band, and he also met Bob Arkin, a bass player with a 'unique and creative' family. Bob's brother, Alan, who later became a famous actor, played piano and broadened John's repertoire. 'I started to learn some real jazz playing there,' John said.

Music, he realized, was a temporary cure for his severe depression. 'I could, in my music, say what I couldn't even begin to say with my stuttering,' he said. 'The music was growing, like a vine from the inside of me, out.'

After keeping a clean slate for his year at Franklin, John graduated from Woodrow Wilson and joined Billy at East LA College. John wanted Billy to get him into Sigma Theta Chi, Billy's fraternity.

'It was the hardest thing to do,' Billy says. 'A lot of the guys didn't want him in. He stuttered. That was a negative. They didn't think he was social enough. But I was Pledge Master – and that carried weight. I got him in.'

As the 'new Larkin' on campus, John became a 'frat rat', changing his clothes and adjusting his attitude. He fit in – for a while. But then he fell back on his favorite crutch of alcohol.

In January 1961, barely into his second semester, he found trouble again. At a Friday night party on Monterey Road in Pasadena, John and his friends Steve and Dennis got into an argument with a group of El Sereno guys who turned out to be gang members.

A fight broke out – one that John, Steve, and Dennis were losing, so they decided to leave and come back armed. They returned with .22 rifles, shotguns, knives, and clubs.

The brawl exploded. Dennis fired the shotgun twice, then someone called the cops. Four units of police arrived, and everyone scattered.

Dennis and Steve tried to run but were found hiding nearby. John leapt into his car and hit the gas, but the detective chased and caught him.

This time, there was no way out.

Along with his two friends, John was arrested and charged with attempted murder.

5 PORTRAIT OF THE JAZZMAN

John gave the cops the wrong house number – maybe because he was drunk, maybe because he stuttered, or maybe because he didn't want his parents to find out.

But they did. The police booked and processed him, leaving him in jail overnight. The next morning, Bill and Billy arrived.

Billy found his little brother sitting in his cell and walked up to the bars.

'Why are you doing this, Johnny?' he pleaded. 'Why are you doing this to Mom and Dad?'

All John could say was 'I'm sorry.' Then he started crying. It made Billy cry, too. They stood there, two brothers, separated by iron bars and life choices. John asked for a cigarette.

'I think he wanted Dad to bail him out, but Dad couldn't,' Billy says. 'So he stayed there. It was a horrible weekend. It hit my dad so hard. It just tore him up.'

A few days later, someone – Billy suspected their mother – posted bail. The charges were reduced to disturbing the peace, since John hadn't carried or fired the guns. He pleaded guilty, was released pending sentencing, and later received probation. He was free to return to college.

Back on campus, John floundered in every class except Choir. Although he'd long since given up going to church, hymns and sacred music still moved him. When he heard that the Santa Monica Civic Auditorium planned a 'song fest' with college choirs from across the south, he brightened. Each choir would perform solo, then join together for a grand finale.

John suggested Anton Bruckner's motet, *Christus factus est*, to his choir teacher, who loved the idea and shared it with the other choirs to learn for the closing performance.

John drank heavily in the days before the final show and was still drunk when he stumbled into the auditorium and took his place in the huge choir.

The choirmaster raised his baton and John began, his senses both numb and electrified.

'I couldn't believe what I was hearing,' he said. 'Two thousand voices singing *Christus factus est* at my recommendation, and I was standing in the massive choir, drunk, and loving every precious second of it.'

The powerful, soaring sound filled the auditorium, at first solemn, then triumphant. John wept at the sheer beauty of it. He looked around. Others were crying too.

Then, it was over; the final amen drawn out. It was one of the most beautiful moments John had ever experienced.

In his second year, John took Billy's old job at Pedrini Music, an independent shop filled with everything a musician could dream of, from gleaming grand pianos to tall stacks of sheet music. With regular access to both music and instruments, John formed The Johnny Larkin Quartet – or Combo, depending on who turned up. They played everything, from campus gigs and twist and stomp dances to background music for fashion shows.

One afternoon, bassist Jimmy Espinoza passed a college practice room. 'I heard this wonderful piano playing,' he says, and remembers walking inside and finding John. They realized they were in the same fraternity and into the same kind of music. They jammed, bonded, and began playing together. Another friend, Gus Angelo, remembers John as 'outgoing, bubbly, smiling' – and always in those practice rooms. 'If you liked jazz,' Gus says, 'he liked you.'

John's network and reputation grew because he welcomed anyone, at any level. 'He wasn't judgmental,' Gus says. 'As long as he got to play a lot, he didn't care. He would rise to the level of the people he was playing with. He was like a chameleon in jazz.'

At frat parties, John played piano while Gus blew his cornet. Beer flowed, and dancers swayed to 'Night Train' and other rhythm-and-blues tunes.

The Johnny Larkin Combo also gigged in coffee houses and restaurants on Sunday afternoons. One night, John was booked as a trio, but his saxophonist failed to turn up. Left with just the drummer, John didn't want to cancel, so he scat-sang the sax lines instead. The crowd loved it.

John realized he had an edge. The halting, broken syllables in his speaking voice influenced his melodic jazz phrasing. 'Freed stuttering,' he called it. 'As a person who stutters, scatting came along real easy, because they're real close,' he said.

Scat-singing, or simply 'scatting' – improvising an instrument using wordless syllables – had been a vocal jazz technique for decades, but rarely crossed into the mainstream. Louis Armstrong had kicked it into the spotlight with 'Heebie Jeebies' in 1926. From there, jazz greats like Sarah Vaughan and Dizzy Gillespie ran with it, and by the time John started college in 1960, Ella Fitzgerald had become its undisputed queen. Her live album *Ella in Berlin* was rarely off his turntable.

John began to sing and play everywhere he went. 'He could sit down at a piano in your living room and ad-lib for half an hour on one tune,' Gus remembers. If John's voice didn't grab people's attention, the energy he played with certainly did.

'I swear, that piano was coming off the ground,' George Rivera says, remembering when John played the piano in their house. 'He had that thing moving. I couldn't believe how much music he got out of a wooden box.' After John left, George's wife Gloria swore their piano would never be the same again.

John carried a flute around in case a venue lacked a piano. He fiddled with harmonicas, strummed on blues guitar, tapped rhythms on tables, and even played with spoons. Watching this, his friend Bobby mistook it for a tic – until he realized John was conditioning his fingers for speed.

Through the Choir, John met Curt Zastoupil, a talented multi-instrumentalist. They drank together off campus and put together a band with John on piano, Gus Angelo on trumpet, Curt on bass, and John Hall on drums. They named the band 'The Norsemen' but this quickly became a sore point when they kept explaining that no, they weren't Norwegian and no, they didn't play Norwegian music. The name also meant audiences expected folk, so Curt, Gus, and John Hall would walk out for an opening piece and perform music similar to the Limeliters or the Kingston Trio.

'John wouldn't have any part of it,' Gus remembers. 'He was a diehard jazz player. He would laugh at us because he knew I hated it.'

Most venues wanted dance tunes instead of progressive jazz, and John got bored with people-pleasing repetitive rhythm shuffles. The band kept warning him: *don't explode or we'll lose the gig.*

'Every now and again, John would slip in one of his jazz tunes so that he could vent,' Gus said. 'John was so vocal that sometimes he'd scare the audience. He'd get to a peak in the jazz tune and *scream*. Just expressing himself. People would drop their drinks on the table.'

Robin Paul, a Vegas revue singer, noticed The Norsemen and booked them to back him at the Konakai, a club in Riverside County. It paid $75 each a week, plus a cottage on site. Happy with their break, the band moved in. If Paul wasn't headlining, The Norsemen played solo, where John and Gus went back and forth on piano, vibes and horn, playing commercial jazz.

The club was always busy, though it drew a strange mix ('alcoholics and rednecks,' Gus says). Pilots from Flabob Airport, just across the street, would often drift in after landing. One night, one of them – drunk and friendly – approached John after the gig and asked if he wanted to come back to his place for a few drinks.

John said sure, thinking nothing of it. He had no plans anyway – the band was living in the club's on-site cottage. But before he could leave, Gus pulled John aside.

'That guy thinks you're gay,' he said. 'That's why he asked you over.'

Something inside John snapped like a circuit shorting. *Why would this man think that? What have I done or said?*

The Thing, old and unexamined, began to stir in a thick mess of churning confusion and panic. He stamped it down.

After that night, John stayed in Los Angeles and commuted for the gig, keeping his distance from the club. 'My depression was all-pervading in me now,' he said, 'and that pilot was the fuse that triggered it.'

The gig ended shortly afterwards – partly because of John's new reluctance to be there, but also because the band's opinion of the place had soured.

'One time, they were looking for people to play when we weren't there,' Gus says, 'and some very talented Black artists came in to audition and we were blown away. They wouldn't hire any of them. That's when we realized it was restricted.' Soon after, the band took bookings elsewhere and moved on.

At 20, John felt the sanctuary of adolescence disappearing, and he didn't like it. The pilot incident at the Konokai had shaken something loose. The world didn't feel safe anymore.

Stop the train, he felt like screaming. *I want to get off.*

'I realized how screwed up I was and couldn't handle it,' John said. He decided to move back in with his parents. 'My pain was too great,' he said. 'I had to heal.'

Bill and Harriet had relocated to Granada Hills in the San Fernando Valley, where Bill had a new job as an expeditor for Litton Industries in Beverly Hills. Harriet welcomed their youngest son's return. But Bill didn't.

'My dad saw this as weak and didn't like it,' John said. 'He figured I should be out there on my own. He was cold and unsympathetic and acted as if he had prepared me properly. My father was too blind to see that his kid wasn't bad. His kid was wounded.'

Gus Angelo came to visit and found the atmosphere oppressive. 'As soon as John went into that house,' he says, 'he couldn't get out of there fast enough. His whole temperament changed. His stuttering became worse.'

Uncomfortable at home and with his college education hanging by a thread, John cast around for the happiness he'd had with his girlfriends, the fraternity, and the fun playing music. Where had it all gone?

'I was a very troubled young man and didn't know what to do,' he remembered. He hung around the college grounds, sleeping in the parking lot in his car some nights rather than going home. 'The wound of my childhood was now festering,' he said.

Billy, meanwhile, had married Sharon and started a family. John was godfather to their son David, but at the christening, Sharon saw John sitting alone, silent and expressionless. He didn't tell a soul about what was troubling him.

He tried to pull himself together by registering for one more college semester. He signed up for Harmony class, got a room at one of the frat houses, and took a job as a cafeteria cashier.

Then John heard that a popular local band, the Mayo Tiana Septet, needed a piano player. The band specialized in jazz and Latin music. The band leader, Mayo, was using a guitar in place of a piano, but when the guitarist left, John's friend Jimmy Espinoza, the bassist in the band, recommended John.

'Jim introduced us – that was when I realized John stuttered,' Mayo says. 'I remember him being apologetic; I just wanted to hear him play.'

John worried that he didn't read music and wasn't familiar with Latin rhythms either. Since the group didn't rely on notation, the former wasn't a problem. To teach John the basics, Mayo and Jimmy played recordings of artists like Tito Puente and Eddie Palmieri and explained the importance of the clave ('the key to Latin rhythms,' Mayo says).

'John was amazing,' Jimmy remembers. 'He had to hear it, then he felt it, then he got it.' Soon, John and Mayo were scatting to each other and having fun.

Mayo kept John and the band working, with sometimes as many as five gigs over a weekend. John's stuttering didn't bother his bandmates – they even joked about it – but they could see him getting frustrated when he couldn't communicate. When John got really hung up, Mayo would tell him to 'sing it' to him instead.

'He would rhythm his speech as in a monotone rhythmic line,' Mayo recalls. 'It was beautiful to see his frustration subside. He would look shyly downward and say softly, without a stutter, "Mayo Tiana, I love you."'

In Harmony class, John met Tony, a sax player who introduced him to marijuana. Everyone smoked pot and drank alcohol, but Mayo never witnessed anything deeper than what he perceived to be social behaviour. 'I didn't see him during his dark times,' Mayo says, 'but looking back, I can see now that's where he was headed.'

John dropped out of college. The frat house emptied as everyone else graduated, started careers, or got married. John moved in with a friend and his mother in one of East LA's roughest neighborhoods, took a warehouse job filling cases of wine, and was lost.

He empathized with other young men, the ones who went off the rails and ended up killers or thieves. *I'm going out into a cold world with nothing warm inside*, he thought.

'They have penitentiaries for people like me, who were never raised to be able to function in a society that had the same views as my father,' he said. His life reminded him of an essay Billy once had to write in High School: '5000 words on life inside a ping pong ball.'

'I had nothing I could believe in,' he said. 'No one in my family, no God, none of the essentials that make it worthwhile to function and become a self-supporting person in spite of a speech impediment. I couldn't … I just couldn't.'

Inside John, the addict's wiring was complete. Now all it needed was the spark.

6 **THE MISFIT**

John disappeared.

Weeks turned into months. Months blurred into years. Billy, Sharon, and John's parents heard nothing from him. Every so often, snatches of second-hand information filtered down the local grapevine. John wasn't dead or in jail; they knew that much.

'I knew he was on drugs,' Billy says. 'I just backed off. I don't know why. I blame myself for not getting closer to him. But it's a two-way street.'

Billy and Sharon had another baby on the way and wanted nothing to do with the crowd John was hanging around with. Drugs were something to be feared, that their young family wanted no part of.

Had you gone looking for 22-year-old John Larkin in the mid-'60s, you'd wind up in a gritty, low-rent corner of East Los Angeles, the air thick with the tension of a city ready to explode. Barely a dozen miles from where the Watts Riots would erupt a year later, John stood out as one of the few white residents in a vibrant Black, Latino, and Mexican American community. He lived with Clarence, a Black musician who shared his home – and his piano – with him.

John cycled through menial jobs, quitting as soon as he qualified for unemployment benefits. The checks covered his nightly pot habit and his growing taste for speed.

Benzedrine was just one of many over-the-counter amphetamines in a booming, barely regulated market.

'I knew I was coming home,' John said, 'when I felt the effects of my first "Benny."'

Advertised as a wonder drug for mood control and weight loss, the pills were cheap, legal, and handed out like candy by doctors and pharmacists who didn't ask too many questions. John hoarded them.

He tried one last time to clean up his act and enrolled in choir at college again. But he was wolfing down amphetamine pills every day and barely lasted a month. This was it. He had to make a career as a jazz musician work.

He landed a steady gig for his trio at Marty's, a club tucked just off the bustling Whittier Boulevard in East LA. Not to be mistaken for the upscale Marty's On The

Hill over in South Central LA; this and many other after-hours joints weren't for the faint-hearted.

'It could be pretty rough at times,' drummer Chuck Glave remembers. 'Fights would break out.'

During one performance, a drunk grabbed bassist Jimmy Espinoza and punched him through a set of wooden slats near the stage. Without missing a beat, Jimmy spun around and smashed the stand-up bass into his assailant's forehead, knocking him flat.

With John speeding on pills and booze, the nights were long, the music hot, and the audience feral. The club favored 'straight ahead' '50s and '60s jazz – the kind that filled the airwaves on Jazz KNOB – the world's first all-jazz broadcaster out of nearby Long Beach.

Stan Getz, Gerry Mulligan, Thelonious Monk, Miles Davis, and his longtime favourite, Dave Brubeck, were all on John's setlist, and he often learned songs on the fly. The club's singer, Maria, provided vocals and often went home with John in the early hours of the morning.

The police made regular surprise visits, hunting for underage drinkers. Jimmy Espinoza was still under 21, so he wore a big, fake mustache, held precariously in place with spirit glue. One night, John spotted the sheriff at the door.

'Jimmy, they're coming in!' he hissed. As Jimmy turned to look, half his fake mustache peeled off, hanging absurdly from his upper lip. It wouldn't stick back on.

'Turn to your side,' John muttered, 'Like you're really getting into it.'

With a quick nod, he threw Jimmy an extended bass solo, hoping the sheriff wouldn't notice. He didn't. They got away with it.

After the set, John bounded off the stage and heard a strong New York accent cut through the din. A wiry, frantic man introduced himself. John recognized the name immediately: Freddie Gruber.

Freddie was a drummer who'd played with Charlie Parker and other jazz greats on the East Coast, but had recently moved West, trying to outrun a mounting heroin problem after Parker's death. A cantankerous non-conformist who had rejected 'straight living' for years, Freddie was in the middle of a relapse and haunted late-night clubs like Marty's, chasing the old New York City of his mind. Here is a *real* addict, John thought, as their friendship took root.

John's nocturnal existence hadn't bothered his landlord, Clarence, until a new man moved in with them and complained about John's loud playing, long hours, drinking, and bringing Maria back to the house. John responded by threatening to throw his new housemate through the plate glass window.

'Just try it,' the new arrival sneered. John backed off. 'That whole scene shut me up instead of him,' he admitted later.

Not long after, Clarence asked John to leave. Only then did John realize: Clarence and the man were in love. Finally understanding the situation, he left.

'I talked to Clarence some years later at a "Love-In" at Griffith Park,' John remembered. 'They were still together and happy.'

With nowhere to go, John returned to his old frat house. A spare room had opened up, and alumni were welcome. His gig at Marty's was over, and so was the fling with Maria. But Jimmy secured another booking for the trio – this time at the Beverly Bowl in Montebello, in a lively bar called The Masquerade Room.

Chuck Glave couldn't make the gig, so he suggested a strange, brilliant percussionist named Al Surratt, who'd played in Frank Zappa's early band, The Boogie Men.

John visited Al's house and witnessed something bizarre. To take out his frustrations, Al had disassembled his piano, piece by piece, and had thrown it out of the back window. John peered out, fascinated.

'On the driveway sat a pile of rubbish consisting of wood, piano strings, and the rest of what only a few hours before had been a piano,' John remembered. 'It looked so funny to see that heap. I think it touched a part of me that wanted to be destructive.'

With Al on drums, the trio performed regularly to an appreciative audience. During the day, John hung around the frat house, where one afternoon a beautiful woman named Paula walked in. She flirted with everyone, but John put what he called his 'coy mask' on and told her to come and meet him at the Beverly Bowl. This was one of John's favorite things to do. He never mentioned he was a piano player, but said he was 'working' at the venue. Then his prospective date would walk in and see him on stage, playing his heart out. It worked, and they started dating.

Unfortunately, loyalty wasn't Paula's strong point. She left John's gig early one evening with a new male friend, claiming she felt ill. John worried all the way through his next set, then rushed to her apartment to find out what was wrong.

He turned the key in the lock and heard a commotion in the bedroom. When the door swung open, it revealed Paula lying in bed, hand to her forehead. The new friend was shirtless and had dived onto the floor, unable to put himself anywhere else. Somehow, she persuaded John that this man really was just a friend and that she really was ill. John believed her. Looking back, he was pained at how gullible he was. But it didn't stop there.

John sat in with his old Norsemen bandmates for a couple of weeks at The Wonder Palms Hotel out in the Sonoran Desert. He brought Paula along, but watched her attention wander to other men. One weekend, she vanished – word was she'd slept with two of his friends.

'I was devastated,' he remembered, 'I was so naive and trusting.'

A pattern began.

'He would take on strays,' Gus Angelo observed. 'Some women who became his girlfriends were those who needed saving. He would pick up lost souls. He didn't judge.'

After the Paula disaster, John moved into a tiny, noisy apartment beside the freeway. Then Freddie Gruber called. He was newly single, he said, and so was their saxophonist friend Tony. They were looking for a place, and did John want in as the third roommate?

He did. He hauled his piano to San Gabriel, where they dubbed their new pad *Re-Bachelorization Headquarters* because the only female in the house was a black cat named Veronica.

'There we were, three womenless jazzers,' John said. 'And we were all nuts.'

Freddie regaled John with tales of playing alongside Charlie Parker, Zoot Sims, and Joe Springer – Billie Holiday's pianist.

'He was a real impressive guy to a young Californian stuttering piano player,' John said. 'He had been around all the famous jazz cats from New York who had become my idols.'

If John could've been born anywhere, it would've been New York – right in the thick of the jazz revolution of the '40s and '50s, when Charlie 'Bird' Parker, Dizzy Gillespie, and Thelonious Monk broke away from big-band swing into complex, improvised bebop. Then came hard bop and modal jazz – Art Blakey, Bill Evans, Miles Davis. John loved it all, but his heart belonged to Coltrane.

'John Coltrane touched me more than any other human being alive,' he said. 'He wasn't afraid to search and be creative. He was such a spiritual human being, man.'

Freddie was John's bridge to this world. A true East Coaster who had lived and breathed it, including picking up the same occupational hazards. John knew Freddie was using heroin.

'I want to try it,' John told him. Freddie gave him a look. *You don't know what you're getting into*, the look said.

'Cut the shit and get me some,' John insisted. He knew the danger, knew that Parker, Coltrane, Davis, and dozens more had all struggled with heroin addiction. Despite this, or perhaps because of it, John felt an irresistible pull. He *had* to know what it was like.

That night, Freddie and John drove into East LA, located the dealer, scored the heroin, and hurried back to the house. Freddie, meticulous about clean needles, prepped the dose in the kitchen. John watched him boil the syringe on the stove.

'All I needed was a tiny bit, and that's what I got,' John said. 'One little capsule.'

John slid a Bill Evans record onto the turntable and settled into a chair, prepared to relax, get quiet, and see what this 'smack' was all about.

Freddie moved in, needle in hand, and with a quick jab, John was off. A burning sensation quickly dissolved into a warm, liquid rush. John's pain and depression melted away, replaced by an all-consuming wave of euphoric bliss.

After that, they both used. John insisted he wasn't addicted yet – something no one could say about Freddie. Chaos reigned in the Re-Bachelorization Headquarters – not from the three pianos crammed into the place, but from Freddie Gruber screaming and shouting when he was high. Heroin didn't mellow him – it did the opposite.

'He would be in everyone's face,' John said. 'Crazy and loud.'

One night, John shoved his fist against Freddie's forehead and told him if he didn't shut up, he'd bash his head in.

'He'd just look at me with this pathetic look on his face,' John remembered. He wanted to punch Freddie many times, but never did.

One afternoon, Freddie brought a woman named Connie to the house to get high. She was stunning, an addict, and worked as a prostitute. John liked her, but didn't know how to show it. While she sat in the kitchen, he picked up Veronica, the black cat, and handed her to Connie. After that, she clocked his interest, and John started visiting her at home.

Soon, John moved in with her, where they would use heroin, on and off. Connie also had a supply of Dolophine, one of the brand names for methadone, after blackmailing a married doctor who paid her for sex.

John bounced between gigs all over town, returning to play with Mayo Tiana one last time in 1966 in a septet called Groove-Fuss. When he was working, John offered to pay Connie's bills if she promised not to 'turn tricks', but she inevitably did, and got violent when high. When John offered her five bucks to try some of her LSD, she slapped him across the face so hard he left and never went back.

As the mid-'60s edged towards the Summer of Love in 1967, John grew more curious about LSD. He drifted around, crashed on couches, and picked up the odd gig, hearing whispers about acid and the doors it could open.

Since he was near East LA College, he wandered over to the campus, hoping to run into someone he knew. He did: Stanley Crouch, who John called 'a Black rebel with a mohawk haircut.'

Stanley, then a junior, would later become a controversial jazz critic and essayist. At the time, John only knew him from a distance through their mutual interest in jazz and the civil rights movement. But now Stanley seemed different. He had a new intensity about him.

'His eyes were bigger,' John said, 'I could tell something had happened to him.'

When John asked what it was, Stanley told him he wasn't 'ready' to hear it. This drove John nuts. 'What do you mean, I'm not ready?' he kept asking.

Finally, Stanley told him: over the summer, he'd taken LSD and gone on a voyage deep inside himself. John leaned in, listening. At first, what Stanley said scared him, but as Stanley described the LSD trip, John remembered tingling all over.

'There was nothing for me to lose. I was already paralyzed inside and doing a good job of acting like I wasn't,' he said. 'I knew this was for me. I knew I couldn't run.'

Dropping acid was now not just an interest, but a mission. There was no way John was going to be excluded, and he waited for the right time to try it.

When he did, it would tear through his consciousness like a storm, leaving behind a completely transformed man.

7 HAPPY BIRTHDAY

Twenty-year-old Judy McHugh strode down LA's Sunset Boulevard, a box of vinyl records snug under her arm. Her grandfather, songwriter Jimmy McHugh, had given her a mission: get these records into Hollywood's hottest DJ booths.

Half a dozen key radio stations were clustered around Sunset and Vine, and Judy moved between them with the ease of a woman who knew the game well. After her parents divorced when she was three, Judy grew up in the opulent home of her maternal grandfather, actor and comedian Eddie Cantor. Later, she worked for Jimmy as a song plugger.

She thrived on the hustle of pitching songs, charming her way onto DJs' playlists, and keeping her grandfather's music alive in the Great American Songbook. Songs like 'On the Sunny Side of the Street' or 'I Can't Give You Anything But Love, Baby' had been recorded by everyone from Frank Sinatra to Johnny Mathis. The McHugh household was a lively hub of singers, musicians, actors, and even presidents who regularly came to visit.

Even when the Beatles' appearance on *The Ed Sullivan Show* kicked off the 'British Invasion' of the charts in 1964, Judy stayed loyal to the old standards and the smoky allure of straight-ahead jazz. Her idols, Billie Holiday and Judy Garland, embodied everything she admired: they were smart, sexy, and vulnerable, much like Judy herself.

When *Rowan & Martin's Laugh-In* launched in 1968, Judy joined as a production associate, slogging through caffeine-fuelled, chain-smoking hours alongside writers and producers to keep the skits rolling. Cocktails and partying were part of the routine, and Judy began drinking more, both to unwind and to socialize with the cast and crew.

She had no idea that across town, her future husband was lighting another joint, blissfully unaware of the woman whose world would one day collide with his.

A few miles east of where Judy worked at NBC's studio, a TV flickered in a dim apartment, cutting through the haze of lingering weed smoke. John took a long drag, savoring the burn.

Ordained as the Love Generation's newest member, he'd grown his black hair long, letting it spill down to his shoulders in thick waves. His neat beard was gone, replaced by a walrus mustache. He wore beads, a headband, and brightly colored shirts. The counterculture felt as natural as air. *Turn on, tune in, drop out.*

John dove in, adopting every hippie ritual, phrase, and behavior, adding to the jazz vernacular that already peppered his speech and would never leave him. *Be cool, man!* he'd scribble on CDs thirty years later.

John's glazed eyes were fixed on the TV. *Laugh-In* burst in flashes of psychedelic color. Goldie Hawn danced around in body paint one minute, Dan Rowan and Dick Martin made political cracks in tuxedos the next.

Just out of frame was his future wife, working behind the scenes. A few miles away, yet worlds apart.

To John, becoming a Flower Child felt like a chance to put the pieces of his past back together. He re-established distant contact with Billy and his parents, though he only spoke to his mother when he called home. He shared an apartment with a fellow hippie named Mark Papel, a warm and thoughtful soul he'd met through a mutual friend. Mark thrived on deep, meandering conversations – especially when they were both stoned – and John felt safe enough to admit how messed up he really was.

For the first time in years, John's depression lifted. At last, he belonged – to a movement that shared his rage at social and racial injustice, the environment, and the looming specter of war.

When Mark announced he was going on a road trip to San Francisco to visit his sister, John tagged along. Not long after they arrived, her boyfriend casually asked John if he wanted to try LSD. This was it – the right circumstances aligning among the safety of friends.

John said yes.

With a mix of excitement and nervous anticipation, he took the dose.

The acid hit him like a freight train, barrelling through his mind and ripping up the tracks of reality as it went. He was propelled into a new dimension, into ecstasy, into a blistering expansion of his psyche. John Larkin ended. The world began. Then they were one and the same, dissolving into a cosmic whole. He was everyone, and everyone was him; the concept of an ego nothing but a mirage.

This epiphany struck him with a divine energy that left him reeling.

'This was, no doubt, the living nirvana that the Buddhist masters talk about,' John said. 'I had kissed the heart of God, life, the universe, and most of all, I had what is in my opinion the most sought-after and yet most dreaded experience … the awakened state.'

He found himself swaying in the bathroom as waves of life force in every color coursed through him. Minutes or hours later (he couldn't tell, and what did it matter?) John came face to face with the person he truly was.

'I met myself,' he said. 'I descended back into the real authentic person that God had made me. I found out that I was "right", that everything I was told by the church, by my parents, by my peers, by society as a whole, was mostly wrong.'

The wondrous trip blurred night into day, culminating in the strange, almost surreal sight of a piece of newspaper drifting down the street the following morning. John sat and watched it go. It felt like a message, that the world he'd known was gone, scattered to the wind. Something inside John began to loosen, a knot finally coming undone.

Dimensions. Immensities. Ecstasy. John would later attempt to describe the trip, admitting that the restrictions of human language wouldn't, couldn't touch the sides. In the days that followed, he scribbled down lyrics in his characteristic uneven, blocky all-caps:

'At last, you've seen the task / Of taking off each mask / Of all the people you became …' he wrote. 'Try not to keep yourself / Within the limits of the sins / That frightened men have laid on you and me / To stand for …'

He called the song 'Happy Birthday', a tribute to the day he met a higher power and glimpsed a self-acceptance that had evaded him all his life.

But as the memory of the trip began to fade, reality returned, and with it, John's ego and anguish. He was left standing in the ruins of his own mind, struggling to understand why he didn't stay free.

'I couldn't accept that I had come back to the same screwed-up person I was before taking the trip,' John said. 'The only difference was that I was a screwed-up person who'd had a spiritual experience.'

Years later, he would look back and see the truth: that he was still in denial, unwilling or unable to face what was really going on inside him.

'I became a poor version of Timothy Leary, Alan Watts, Aldous Huxley, and John Lennon combined,' he reflected. 'I spent the next twenty-odd years being what I thought was a spiritual person, living on whatever I could experience chemically.'

Whatever John could experience chemically was a long list because of an unexpected side effect: his stutter often disappeared when he was high. Thanks to their effects on the brain, drugs and alcohol can have unpredictable consequences on speech that even fluent people recognize. For some, stuttering worsens, yet the anxiety triggered by some speaking situations is suppressed. For others, like John, the chemical tweaks produced precious moments of fluency, and John clung to them like a lifeline.

After six months of witnessing John do nothing but get high, Mark got sick of John living off him, bought John a Farfisa organ from his father's electronics store and told him to go out and get a job.

John walked into an agency called TAM – Talented Artists Management – and, stuttering heavily, told the booking agent he had an or-or-organ and could suh-suh-sing, too. The agent burst out laughing. Familiar with this ignorant response, John stayed put. *They think I'm a freak*, he thought. *Or a jerk.*

'Can you scream like James Brown?' the agent asked, toying with him.

'Sure,' John said. He jumped in the air and gave the best screech he had. The agent laughed harder, then motioned to the piano and invited John to show them what he'd got.

John sat down and began to play. The atmosphere in the room changed immediately, and John was hired on the spot to join a new group called the De Vons. Rehearsals began, and the band lined up their first gigs in clubs across the San Fernando Valley.

A couple of weeks into the run, John took a break between sets and wandered over to two young women near the front. At first, he noticed the taller Sue, but it was her friend, Nancy, who caught his attention. She was attractive, with a quiet humour that intrigued him, though she clearly lacked confidence. When they started dating, John thought he'd found a good match, but subconsciously knew he was choosing someone unlikely to leave or betray him, or so he thought. Fresh out of college and with no previous serious relationships to guide her, Nancy was soon out of her depth as she orbited John's chaos.

The massive amount of speed John was taking made him paranoid. He was obsessed with the idea that everyone could see right through him; that every 'horrible' sexual act he'd ever done was visible for all to judge. Filled with shame and self-disgust, he found intimacy impossible unless he was high.

'It was only when I was stoned that I could feel any sensuality at all,' John said, 'and then I'd act out in the other extreme to try and make up for all the suppression.' When sober, he withheld affection completely. Nancy, inexperienced and devoted, weathered these storms with a patience that would eventually wear thin.

When the De Vons disbanded after a short run, John lost any inclination to work and instead took all the speed, pot and acid he could lay his hands on. His old school friend Bobby Rivera moved in, but it wasn't long before he moved back out, since John's daily routine consisted of getting loaded and nothing else.

Nancy's modest beautician salary couldn't cover the rent, so they moved into a one-room 'hippie commune' with Sue and her new boyfriend, Robert. Their landlord, Don, was an ex-con 'speed freak' with a sunken, chalk-white face – the result, he claimed, of starting each day with handfuls of Benzedrine (amphetamine). *Nobody can be that loaded and think of being truthful*, John thought. But Don had plenty of pills, and John always bought them.

Outside their one-room hippie haven, the mood across Los Angeles was growing intense and angry. In 1967, ten thousand people had marched in Century

City to protest the Vietnam War. John, a lifelong pacifist, watched as thousands of young men like him were drafted, with hundreds of them killed every week. He had avoided conscription and narrowly missed the 1969 draft lottery cutoff because he was 27 – just over the age limit.

His housemate Robert wasn't so lucky and got called up to fight. Robert told John he planned to flee with Sue to Canada, and John agreed it was a wise move, knowing the system only granted deferments for the rich and well-connected. 'If you've got the dough, you don't have to go,' the saying went, and Robert and Sue wasted no time in heading for the border.

With their friends gone and Nancy out working, John, unemployed and restless, turned to Don for more speed. Knowing John was into everything, Don offered him a taste of Methedrine, a legal, pharmaceutical form of methamphetamine normally prescribed for conditions like obesity and narcolepsy. John loved the two-day buzz it gave him and came back for more, but Don told him he'd have to pay.

Already hooked, John squeezed all the cash he could out of Nancy, then began calling his mother, lying that they were about to be evicted. She wired him rent money several times. John spent it all on meth.

Methamphetamine's ability to keep people unnaturally awake and wired for days was so profound that the German military supplied it to soldiers during World War II. It wouldn't be regulated until 1970, less than a year after John was on the run of his life, taking it day after day after day. By then, medics knew the truth: that prolonged use could trigger paranoia, aggression, and psychosis. John, unaware and unconcerned, lost track of how much he'd taken and how long he'd been awake. Then the money ran out.

Bracing himself for the inevitable comedown, John was up all night, waiting. But nothing happened. The next day dragged on – still awake, still waiting. Then he thought he'd dodged the comedown or somehow missed it.

'I started to get confused … and more confused … and more confused … and that, ladies and gentlemen, was the very *beginning* of the crash,' John said. 'It took two days just to *start* to come down.'

He had taken far more than he'd realized and plunged into a sleepless hell, forced to endure another two nights awake, desperate for sleep that wouldn't come.

John couldn't remember how he got there or who he was with ('when you're that high, there's no one there but you anyway,' he said), but he knew he was sitting inside The International House of Pancakes in Hollywood, trying to eat something, when it hit him.

He convulsed, and his body flailed in the booth. His mind snapped like a twig. Screaming, crying, and yelling, he spiraled into a full-blown psychotic break. After being removed from the restaurant, he staggered into a phone booth and called his friend Mark Papel, begging for some 'reds' – Seconal, a barbiturate sleeping pill.

John found himself on a park bench, staring at a lake. He swallowed four or five pills, yanking his body from hyperdrive to a near-comatose crash, either end of which could have killed him. Later, he tallied that he'd been up for six days straight.

A few days after that, he showed up at his parents' house.

'Oh my *God!*' Harriet gasped, staring at the emaciated figure at her door. Her youngest son was skin and bone. John was filthy, starved, and hollow-eyed. He hadn't eaten, bathed, or slept in days. His mind felt fried. His usually sharp memory remained blank for weeks afterwards.

Not long after John's meth binge, Nancy announced she was going to Scotland for a month and John couldn't come with her. When he was clear-headed enough to notice, John knew a distance was growing between them.

Later, John learned she'd been quietly asking for help, visiting their mutual friends, trying to understand why the man she loved seemed intent on self-destruction. Nobody had an answer. John was so high-functioning onstage that few musicians knew how far gone he was. Hoping things might somehow change, Nancy stuck it out a little longer.

Months after their escape to Canada, their old housemates Robert and Sue called with good news: they'd had a baby. Sue's mother, still in LA, wanted to visit the new grandchild, so John and Nancy offered to drive her to Toronto. In November 1969, they stuffed their belongings into the old Volkswagen and hit the road. John had scored an ounce of hashish and, instead of smoking it, decided to eat it, bit by bit, all the way across the country.

They followed Route 66 in a blur of neon signs, roadside diners, and motels. 'I felt like I was the one who wrote "Route 66" instead of Bobby Troup,' John said. Later, it became one of his favorites to play live.

John was writing again, adding new original songs to his growing catalogue of standards and covers. He was toying with pieces like 'Happy Birthday' and sketching a new track called 'The Misfit'. His notebooks filled with lyrical fragments, many of which he later set to music. At gigs, he slipped some originals into the set, and the audience response was promising.

In Toronto, after reuniting with Robert, Sue, and their newborn, John rented a Yamaha spinet so he could keep composing, jamming, and experimenting. One day, Sue mentioned a production of *Hair* was coming to the Royal Alex Theatre for its Canadian debut. Open auditions were being held. Sue was going to try out for a part, and urged John to join her.

They arrived at the Rock Pile – a converted Masonic Temple and Toronto's main music hall. The room was overflowing with long-haired buskers, singers, actors, and free spirits. The casting team wasn't looking for polished actors, but wanted rebellion and charisma – the real thing.

After waiting for a few hours, Sue auditioned first. Then:

'Next!'

The panel watched John—a 27-year-old blue-eyed, black-haired hippie—stroll onstage with a presence he didn't know he had. He hadn't prepared anything, so winged it with a freestyle version of 'Eleanor Rigby'. He sang it without tempo, milking every line of the song with such intensity it stunned the casting panel. As John came off stage, they broke with protocol and told him there and then that he almost certainly had a part and that they'd call to confirm in a couple of weeks.

While they waited, the group took a trip to Yorkville, the heart of Canada's hippie movement with music, theaters, and coffee shops that had launched the careers of Neil Young, Joni Mitchell, and Gordon Lightfoot. They dropped acid and set off, looking forward to a fun evening. Still chasing the euphoric high of his first trip, John took more than usual.

He was sitting in the car when the LSD tunneled straight into the darkest corners of his mind. The Thing surged to the surface, amplified under the magnifying lens of the acid. Memories bubbled up from places John had never allowed himself to go, with scenes he didn't want to look at. He fought it, panicking, desperate to shove it away, but the acid wouldn't let go.

The old film reel began unspooling.

Now, John was forced to watch.

8 SECRETS TOO HARD TO SEE

John was playing outside, not far from his house on McPherson Avenue, where the lawn was neatly mowed and the car gleamed in the driveway. He walked past his neighbour's place, proudly marveling that he could already count his age on his fingers. *One, two, three, four.*

The older boy who lived there had a family that wasn't like everyone else's. Nobody ever saw the father, and the mother only appeared on her short walks to the liquor store and back.

A year later, maybe two, the boy took an interest in John. They were at the White House, the abandoned building where older boys liked to play. In the fog of John's memory, there was an image: the boy – maybe more than one – putting their hands on him, down his pants. John didn't understand why, but he let them. Maybe it was a game.

The shaky, vague footage rolled in John's head. This time, he was with the boy under his house, in the narrow, dark crawlspace. He was naked. So was the boy. The boy told John to touch him down there.

'Put your mouth on it,' the boy insisted.

John didn't want to. He didn't like it. But he was being held, though, and he enjoyed that. It was warm, comforting.

Soon, the boy was joined by another, older friend. He seemed to want to show John affection, too. So when the older boy led John behind his house, next to the creek, where the neighbours couldn't see, John went willingly. This episode of The Thing would stay with John for life, branding his memory with awful sensory detail. He was naked again. The boy was on top of him.

Years later, John wrote it down. 'I can still feel this sick human being shaking and breathing on me,' he said.

When it was over, there was gooey stuff on his leg.

John included this detail when he finally told his mother about The Thing. He only dared to describe one incident, but in truth, The Thing happened many more times, in many more places, at the hands of those two older boys.

When Harriet did nothing, said nothing, John was condemned to a lifetime of shame, guilt, confusion, and silence. It would take years before he understood that what happened was abuse – that he was a rape survivor, living with trauma so deep and incomprehensible it felt like a shadow following him everywhere, fueling all his pain and fury. On top of that, he stuttered.

Wipe out a kid, why don't we? he raged at the universe.

In the car in Toronto, the memories flooded his conscience. John burst into tears. For years, he feared that because he'd enjoyed physical affection from boys – even if it was abusive and wrong – it meant he might be gay. At a time when society treated homosexuality as a sickness, this thought panicked him. Occasionally, high on acid, he thought some men were beautiful. But he also knew he was attracted to women.

The tears kept coming. He couldn't breathe.

'I finally said it,' John remembered. 'I broke down and said, "I think I'm bisexual".'

As soon as the words left his lips, there was an unexpected sense of release. The panic dissolved. He couldn't remember how anyone in the car reacted – only how he felt.

'That broke the spell,' he said. 'The delusion went away, and the rest of the night was a gas.'

But in his increasingly rare sober moments, the same question kept coming back:

Who am I, really?

9 JAZZ ON THE GIG

A few days later, the casting panel from *Hair* called. John got the part. A prestigious gig. He could stay in Toronto, make a go of it.

But the insidious little voice in his head had other ideas. *Wait until they find out I'm a fraud*, it said. *Then they'll fire me. So I'd better quit now.*

John turned down the role. He returned the rented piano and wanted to go home.

When they got back to LA, Nancy went back to work. John took the civil service test to become a mailman. He cheated, passed, and when the city called him in, he turned that job down, too.

Instead, he kept going to jam sessions in East LA and landed a new gig with God's Children, an eclectic band in the style of Sly and the Family Stone. The group didn't play jazz but thrived on East LA's diverse mix of soul, funk, rock, and Latin influences. John, as always, adapted quickly.

With more money coming in, he and Nancy moved out of their hippie haven into a bigger apartment. But he still felt something was off between them. One day, he overheard Nancy on the phone with her boss, her tone warm and intimate. When John asked what was happening, she refused to answer.

'You're going to leave me,' he said. She didn't deny it.

John was in the middle of a slew of bookings with a Latin band when Nancy finally announced she'd had enough. John took the night off, watching in silence as she went around the room, packing her things.

Alone in their half-empty apartment, crashing off speed, John surveyed the wreckage of the relationship. Nancy had stuck it out for nearly five years.

'All I can say now is, "Hooray for Nancy,"' he later reflected. 'Why she stayed with me so long, I don't know.'

He eventually learned she'd had been having an affair with her boss – likely the catalyst she needed to leave.

'I remember my life falling apart,' John said. 'As if it had been together.'

He buried himself deeper in music, but it was now the early '70s, and rock, soul, funk, and disco were pushing jazz further into the margins. John stayed loyal to it, but also appreciated popular songs that spoke to outsiders, especially John Lennon's 'Working Class Hero'. Its lyrics about rage and toxic conformity would stay with him for years.

At a jam session, he met electric bassist Joe Celia, who moved in with him for a few weeks, along with drummer Gary Seeger. Hurting from his breakup, John funneled all his pain into a new song. Normally, music freed him from his stutter, but when he was troubled, it crept back in.

'We just kept the groove along until he worked through it,' Joe says. 'Music is a conversation, and the three of us talked a lot that way. It was emotional for all of us. We played on that tune all day.'

Joe had a four-night, $20-a-night Latin gig at Virginia's, a club in East LA, through singer-bandleader Sabu. He brought John and drummer Chuck Glave.

The first night started off smoothly enough – the trio kept the Latin rhythm steady with Sabu handling the vocals. But as soon as the instrumental breaks hit, they couldn't resist slipping into jazzier territory, and Sabu freaked out.

'Don't play jazz on the gig!' he shrieked. 'Oh my God, we're gonna lose this gig!'

For John and co., trying not to 'play jazz on the gig' was like trying not to breathe. But they knew the stakes – in certain clubs, letting that instinct take over could get you canned.

The next two nights, John took a better-paying blues gig, and Chuck played with his nineteen-piece jazz orchestra. Joe was left to back Sabu with Julio, a septuagenarian pianist dishing out Latin crowd-pleasers.

When John returned, he was furious. The blues band had cranked up the volume so high it had wrecked the delicate tines of his portable electric Wurlitzer. Joe watched John spend the entire Sunday hunched over the instrument, cursing, soldering and filing to get it back in tune.

Back at Virginia's the following night, the piano was repaired, and John was ready. So was Chuck, fresh from tearing it up with his jazz orchestra. The music kicked off, and they locked in – tight, fast, and intense. By the first break, Chuck was driving straight-ahead jazz at 180 BPM, and John was right there with him.

Joe held on, grateful the charts he'd written somehow fit what John and Chuck were playing. *I'm hanging with this,* he thought. *Just keep breathing, man!*

Sabu was losing his mind. 'Don't play jazz on the gig!' he howled as they tore through the set – only to snap back to the regular tune with mischievous synchronicity whenever Sabu started singing.

'We'd roll right into the next one and do the same thing,' Joe laughs.

The club owner leaned against the bar, the music hitting him like an old speaker ad. 'Oh my God! That was loud,' he said when they'd finished. Joe glanced at his amp, which was only set to one or two, and his guitar was on three. *Geez,* Joe thought. *We were playing that hard?*

'I *told* you,' Sabu hissed. 'I *told* you we're gonna lose this. You played JAZZ!'

But the owner smiled.

'No, man. That was great,' he said. 'Keep doing that.'

John grinned from one end of his mustache to the other, his eyes twinkling. 'Mmm-hmm,' he nodded, as if he knew all along they could take it that far and pull it off. They played like that all night, blending jazz and Latin in a way that shouldn't have worked, but somehow did.

At the end of the night, however, they were told they owed the bar money.

What? Joe thought. He sifted through all the bar receipts and discovered Julio, the fill-in pianist, had knocked back $60 worth of whiskey on a $40 gig. They paid up. If they didn't, they wouldn't be invited back.

John wasn't fazed. He'd had gear, money, and drugs stolen, and had played venues that stiffed him or promised gigs that evaporated. As long as he could play, he kept going.

Joe and others were in awe of John's apparent disregard for material things combined with unwavering generosity. He'd give away anything – his gear, his last dollar, his couch.

'John never had any money,' Gus Angelo says, 'Because the strays he took in would take it from him. He'd get a gig, get paid, and the next day be broke again.'

Joe remembers the day the electricity bill arrived, and they owed $18 each. *Oh man,* they thought. *We gotta have juice or we can't cut loose.* As if on cue, the phone rang. On the other end, a Latin band needed a pianist and a bassist. The fee? $18 each.

'We almost jumped through the phone,' Joe says.

Mimi Smith, who lived next door to John and Joe, remembers jazz constantly pouring from their house, but it was John's kindness that stuck with her. When she needed a car, John loaned her his. When he learned she'd never driven an automatic, he taught her how.

'He was very patient and kind,' Mimi recalls. 'First of all, for lending it to me, and then for teaching me how to use it.'

Drummer Sam Provenzano called him 'a very humble, generous human being who gave more than most people could in three lifetimes.'

Joe and John often played with musicians from more privileged backgrounds – players who talked about childhood lessons, tutors, and recitals. They joked they'd been 'ripped off' as kids, with no fancy lessons or guidance – yet here they were, self-taught, which might explain why John was generous with his encouragement, too.

'He was a very sharing cat, musically,' Joe says. During one gig, Joe had a crisis of confidence on the bandstand.

'I don't even know what I'm doing here,' he muttered.

John leaned over.

'Dude, if you couldn't hang, you wouldn't be here. So just dig it and *play*.'

When John got an offer to join Stax Records West – the LA outpost of the powerhouse Memphis label – he said yes right away. Stax had an impressive roster that included Otis Redding, Sam & Dave and Isaac Hayes. It was 1972, and after the hugely successful Wattstax festival (known as the 'Black Woodstock'), the label opened a West Coast office to promote its artists in TV and film.

Unusual for the era, Stax was racially integrated from the top down. John joined a touring band behind soul singer Luther Ingram, riding high off his hit 'If Loving You Is Wrong (I Don't Want to Be Right)'. They performed in Vegas, New York, and Chicago, and John picked up R&B and soul as easily as he had mastered Latin jazz.

After Stax, he switched gears again, joining Marshall Hooks & Co., a blues-rock band who were playing across the southwest.

Touring meant more gigs. More drugs. More women.

'This period of sex, drugs and rock and roll had me smiling on the outside, but dying on the inside,' John later said. 'It just couldn't last.'

Joe Celia remembers John and his friend Gary Seeger returning to LA from the road.

'He came back a little damaged,' Joe says. 'He got into using harder stuff.'

John's apartment was intact, but the work offers had dried up. His car was totaled. The rent was late. Then he heard Nancy was seeing someone new.

'That screwed me up worse,' he said. He spent most nights either drowning in dark thoughts or pounding a borrowed piano so hard he was smashing it.

Then one evening a strange noise outside punctured his doldrums.

Clunk! Clunk!

Every night, like clockwork, something circled the building. *What the fuck is that weird sound?* John wondered.

Weeks passed, and John bumped into his new neighbour Eric and introduced himself. From the start, he thought Eric was a 'strange bird', but he also recognized a fellow addict. Eric's vice was beer, so they were soon sloshing it together in the afternoons.

Eric helped John get a job delivering pizzas for a place called Pizza Man, after John persuaded his mother to talk his father into buying him a beat-up car for the job. After shifts, he and Eric drank and talked. A few beers in one afternoon, Eric turned to John.

'I've got to tell you something about me,' he said.

Uh-oh, John thought, his stomach tightening. *Something's coming. Brace yourself.*

'Could I have your trust?' Eric asked.

'Sure,' John said despite the tension inside him, 'You've got my trust.'

Eric told John that as a child, he had to wait for his parents to come home after school. To pass the time, he put on his mother's clothes – including her panties, stockings, and shoes. As an adult, this had morphed into a shoe fetish. The *clunk!*

clunk! John heard every night was Eric in stilettos, strolling around the complex in the dark.

Every alarm clanged in John's head.

'I didn't know what to think,' he said. 'At that time, I still had my denial of my own childhood "issues" intact, and that was the first time I had ever heard of a fetish.'

John was already calculating how to distance himself when Eric dropped another bombshell.

'I'm only telling you this because I feel a camaraderie with you,' Eric explained. 'Your stutter is similar to my fetish.'

'What?' John gasped, his mind buckling. He'd encountered all sorts of reactions to his stutter over the years – pity, impatience, mockery – but this was new.

'Hey mmmman,' he said. 'Don't lay your fucking sign on me!' He bolted, horrified at the implications of what he'd just heard.

After that, their interactions dwindled to brittle nods and mumbled greetings of 'Hi, man' whenever they saw each other. A few weeks later, John was amazed to learn that Eric was sleeping with the attractive woman who lived down the street.

'It really blew my image of him away,' John said. 'What gradually got to me was the simple truth … this guy knew who he was! And had the balls to share it and show it, which was more than I could say for myself.'

Years later, John regretted losing Eric's friendship and tried, unsuccessfully, to find him.

'I look back at Eric and realize that he was the first person I met who began to open my mind to accepting the sexual differences in all of us,' John said. 'God bless Eric.'

At the time, however, it shook John more than he cared to admit. His mind flashed back to his admission in Toronto. What if Eric was right? Was it connected? It wasn't a mess he wanted to untangle. Not yet.

John fell two months behind on rent. The scraps of work thrown his way weren't covering the debt, and eviction loomed. *I'm broke on the outside and broken on the inside*, John thought, and considered going home. But he already knew what his parents would say.

'Don't play jazz on the gig' was just another version of what he'd heard his whole life: *Don't play jazz. Don't screw up. Don't stutter. Don't stand out. Get sober. Get a real job. Get a life.*

Thirty years old and out of options, John stepped out of the apartment, leaving behind a scattered mess of belongings and a half-broken piano. With nothing but a handful of clothes, he headed for his parents' house.

When he got there, he knew what he had to say.

'I've quit playing music,' he announced.

10 WORKING-CLASS HERO

'Wise up!'

Bill circled John like a matador. His hair had greyed, but his eyes were still sharp as he sized up his homeless, jobless son.

Harriet looked on as John nodded at everything his father said. Yes, he would 'stop all drug use.' Yes, he was going to turn over a new leaf. Yes, he had made the 'wrong' career choice.

Relief washed over John. He was exhausted. Everything bad that had happened was, he told himself, just the 'occupational hazard' of being a musician. Boy, was he glad those days were over. A straight job was what he needed.

It had to be something that didn't involve too much talking. Employers could legally discriminate against people who stuttered – and did so all the time. It would be years before the Americans with Disabilities Act offered any protection. Until then: no fluency often meant no job, or one you were overqualified for. There was no recourse, either. It wasn't even called discrimination. It was just how things were.

John found work the way he usually did: through a friend. Darryl Jacobs lined up a temp role for John collating tax returns, but tax season was still months away. In the meantime, John took a job driving a laundry truck.

Each morning, he navigated the city streets, dutifully making his pickups and deliveries. The cab smelled of detergent and cigarettes – his last remaining vice – as he clung to his 'new perspective'. Johnny was being a good boy, wasn't he?

But the phone kept ringing. Musicians all over town still wanted him to play. Drummer Sam Provenzano called to ask if he was interested in jamming a bit. John turned him down. He'd just gotten clean, he said, and didn't want to get 'dirty' again. *How diligent,* John congratulated himself as he hung up, ignoring the twinge in his heart.

Weeks went by, and John's relief curdled. The rotten core of emotion that had twisted him up as a child was leeching out.

'The more responsible I was getting, to impress the family, the sicker I was getting,' John said. His role in the family had always been clear to him, even if no one said it out loud. The 'designated loser', the screw-up, the failure, the one who could never get it right. A toxic setup he believed had been running his life long before he ever sat down at a piano.

He felt trapped.

Suffocated by the atmosphere at home, when the laundry job ended John turned to Billy and Sharon. Could he stay with them for a while? They said yes. He slept on their couch while Billy pulled strings to get John a job at Western Electric, the manufacturing arm of AT&T where Billy worked.

Barely two weeks in, they fired John on the spot and sent him home. Billy didn't know what the hell John had done. John wouldn't tell him either, but just kept saying 'I'm sorry'.

After that, John barely moved from their living room. He slept all day on the couch, shirtless and shoeless in a pair of jeans, his long hair a disheveled mess.

'It was kind of exciting, and a bit scary, having someone that looked like that in our house,' remembers his nephew Steve, who brought friends home from school to sneak into the hall and take turns peeking around the corner at the slumbering, wild creature on the couch that was Uncle Johnny.

One afternoon, Steve's older brother David was practicing guitar in his bedroom when John appeared in the doorway.

'Kuh-kuh-keep it as a hhhhobby,' John said. 'It's ruh-rough out th-th-there.'

David remembers that John's stutter was intense. 'Boy, he had a really difficult time,' he remembers. 'Sometimes hard to follow.'

John didn't move from the couch for days, except to smoke, read Timothy Leary books, or play his portable piano out in the garage. There, the old John resurfaced – happy, animated, free, and impressing neighbors who came around to listen. Then, when it was over, he'd go back to sleeping on the couch again, with Sharon bringing him food or whatever else he asked for.

One day, David and Steve were playing too loudly and woke John, who yelled at them. That was the final straw.

'This is not good for us,' Billy told him. 'You're going to have to leave.'

John did.

'I don't know where he went. If I had to do it over again, I think I would have been more patient and understanding,' Billy says. 'I know it wasn't really him.'

Sam Provenzano reached out again, urging John to come and play. John was still off the drugs and booze, and Sam reassured him that the other players didn't drink heavily or get high.

'The more I thought about it, the better the idea sounded,' John said. 'Just good clean fun, playing music.'

He went to Sam's place in Tarzana and started jamming. The energy came back, and bookings followed. The band decided to call themselves *Fred*, with Sam on drums, Duke McVinnie on bass, Bob Bonnafaunt on saxophone, and John on vocals with his Wurlitzer keyboard.

They played all-original music, including some of John's songs, and quickly built a local following. One fan even knitted them a banner.

'What a sweet band that was,' John remembered. 'There was a lot of love in that band. We dug what we were doing.'

One night on the way to a gig, John was scat-singing to himself, as he often liked to do, when his voice produced a strange resonance.   It sounded like more than one note. *What was that?* he thought. *You have to do that again!*

He had stumbled into throat singing – a rare vocal technique used by Tuvan and Mongolian musicians. By manipulating airflow and the resonant chambers in his throat and mouth, John could stack harmonics on top of each other. The result? He had discovered he could sing chords.

At the same time, he'd been sharpening his piano technique, often singing as he practiced, a habit that honed both his control and speed.

John started to sing more at gigs, his confidence building with every performance. At the Bla Bla Café in Studio City, he delivered a playful rendition of 'Happy Birthday' that brought the house to its feet. The same thing happened at the Come Back Inn in Venice Beach. His voice was getting noticed.

By day, he was collating tax returns. By night, he was back onstage. By now, John had been sober for a few months and was still holding it together. He'd taken an interest in Sharla, a woman from the tax office, and invited her to see him play. They finished work late and headed straight to the Bla Bla Café.

'I was tired,' John said. 'My circuitry jammed with visions of tax returns.'

A waiter brought him a glass of wine. John refused it. But the pressure was building.

'The difference between the mental frame it takes to perform music and collate tax returns is an eternity apart,' John said. He needed to perform well, especially in front of Sharla. So when a second glass of wine was offered, John took it and knocked it back.

The old familiar warmth spread through him. The band played and played, and John delivered another sensational performance of 'Happy Birthday'.

'Sharla saw this happen,' he said. 'Collator turns rock star in two hours.'

By the end of the first break, they were all over each other in the backseat of her car.

'I was a hero again,' he remembered. But deep down, he knew the truth. 'The only way I could even feel a piece of myself was to get loaded,' he said. 'I had to have that glass of wine to water down the pain and have the balls to even try to get close to Sharla – or any other woman.'

He ended the night glowing. But the next day, sober again and back in the office, he didn't know how to act. *Sharla could love a rock star but not a measly collator*, he thought. He smoked a little weed to take the edge off, afraid Sharla would see the real him. 'I didn't know how to keep the image up,' he said.

Tax season ramped up, and so did the workload. Returns were flooding in.

'I was rushing on pot and a little speed by now,' John admitted. 'I needed help to work those ten-to-fourteen-hour days.'

When John heard that his old college friend Gus Angelo was getting married, he offered to play at the wedding for free and brought some musician friends along.

The reception was held at a hot springs resort owned by Gus's fiancée's parents. John set up his keyboard, ready to go. At first, he kept it light: commercial jazz standards, with Gus occasionally joining on vibraphone. But John grew restless.

'We're going crazy,' he told Gus. The band was itching to play one of their originals, he said. Gus gave him the nod, unprepared for what followed.

John erupted into free jazz, with explosive crescendos and uninhibited vocals. Midway through the song, he was screaming into the mic.

'People were freaked,' Gus says, remembering that his wedding guests started to leave their tables. His new father-in-law pulled Gus aside.

'Is that guy okay?' he said. 'I'm about to call the police!'

Gus had to tell John to stop with the originals; they were scaring everyone. John grudgingly played another set of standards and gave his bandmates all his pot to smooth things over.

Back in LA, gigs at the Bla Bla Café eventually dried up, and Sharla drifted away.

'I think she sensed I wasn't wrapped together too well,' John said.

At home, John had new neighbors. Newlyweds Gary and Jackie Hewitt remember moving in and hearing tumultuous piano playing through the thin walls.

Is that a stereo? Jackie wondered. Then McCoy Tyner-style crescendos started thundering through. This was no recording.

Gary knocked to see who was playing.

They met John, and a fast friendship bloomed. The couple began going to his shows around town.

'You have to understand who I am – I don't trust people right away,' Jackie remembers. 'It was just the most natural thing in the world to have him just walk into our lives. There was just really a wonderful something about him.'

John had saved a couple of thousand dollars, but was now blowing it on bar tabs. The sax player quit, and Fred became a trio. They picked up a steady weekend slot at the Come Back Inn on Venice Beach, playing straight-ahead jazz.

John had been refining his throat singing and began working it into their sets. Bassist Duke McVinnie remembered how John would raise his hand mid-song, signaling the band to stop so he could chant chords.

'Incredible,' Duke remembers. 'He'd get into harmony with himself.'

Most nights, the audience was stunned into silence by the haunting sound of John's voice – except one night, a table of jocks near the front wouldn't stop talking.

The louder John sang, the louder they got.

John snapped.

He grabbed his Wurlitzer piano – all 56 pounds of it – and hurled it at them.

'It crashed onto the table,' Duke said, 'and everybody went everywhere.'

John leaped off the stage, one of the jocks lunged at him, and chaos broke out. Drummer Sam Provenzano and the chef rushed in to break it up.

'Nobody got seriously hurt,' Duke said. 'It was pretty damn funny. The amazing thing was, they picked up the Wurlitzer, set it back up, and we kept going.'

When that gig ended a few weeks later, John took a solo Sunday afternoon slot at the Winery in the San Fernando Valley.

He fell into a routine of wine, women, and more wine. He was still playing well – 'I became the little star,' he said of his solo performances – but beneath the surface, reality was setting in. He knew it now – he was an alcoholic.

When he tried to recall this period later, it was mostly a blur – fragments of women coming on to him, or him drunkenly grabbing breasts or behinds.

'I really went batso,' John said. 'Most of the outlandishness was done in a blackout, and I only remember a little of it.'

But one moment did stand out. After a set, a petite, attractive brunette got up and smiled at him. John knew from that look that she was his next conquest. She handed him her number and told him to meet her at her new apartment in Hollywood. A few days later, John showed up, large bag of wine in hand.

He knocked on the door, and the next twelve years of his life opened it.

'She stood there, leaning against the door, looking at me like she already knew it,' John said. 'Marcia was the lady's name – and this was the beginning.'

11 THE DANCE OF JOHN AND MARCIA

The soft orange glow of a Hollywood dawn rose behind the hills, flooding the room with diffuse light. Sunbeams crept up walls lined with shelves crammed with records, craft supplies, and books stacked nearly to the ceiling. The air was thick with the scent of stale wine and fresh paint. Wet squares of fabric stampers lay scattered across the floor like confetti from a wild, forgotten party. Only this party was still going.

John and Marcia sat naked in the middle of the floor, their skin sticky with brightly coloured fabric paint. Empty wine bottles and crumpled pill packets lay scattered around them. They had been at it for hours, taking turns stamping each other's bodies with hearts, stars, and who knows what else.

'I was gooey, man,' John remembered. 'Real gooey.'

'The night of the paints,' as John later called it, was one of many hazy nocturnal benders where they'd cut loose and really let go. They had dropped acid, swallowed 'whites' (Benzedrine), and chewed on peyote buttons – small cactus tops loaded with mescaline that sent them on powerful psychedelic trips.

Marcia Gilman was from Seattle, the daughter of a gentle mother and an unpredictable, alcoholic father. When she was fourteen, her brother died, sending her into a nervous breakdown from which she never fully recovered. Shelley, her daughter, would later say that Marcia never really grew past that age; perpetually stuck in the rebellious, unyielding mindset of a teenager.

'She was a terminal fourteen-year-old,' Shelley says, recalling how no one could tell Marcia what to do, her emotional development frozen, her co-dependency assured.

By the time she met John, Marcia had two failed marriages and three children to three different men. One husband went to prison, the second was described as volatile and confrontational. Her new relationship with John was just as turbulent. They fed off each other's psychological wounds, off their shared immaturity that thrived on drama and chaos. The chemistry between John and Marcia was instant and reckless; a match made in heaven.

'She knew I was loaded all the time,' John said, 'but seemed to like it.'

He was still performing at the Winery and had graduated from a few glasses to a few bottles of wine a night. He'd invented a lounge-act alter ego named Johnny Trenard – a Vegas-style performer he used when playing commercial material. He rotated between bands, sometimes giving them ridiculous, temporary names like Two Dollar Turkey.

John was so popular that he took over the Saturday evening slot as well as his regular Sunday gig. When he started dating Marcia, she wanted him to give up the many conquests that popularity brought him. But John wasn't ready – the attention fed his self-esteem.

'I didn't want her to think I was that easy,' he said. 'I was the king of charisma, a legend in my own mind.'

One night, they went to a party in the Hollywood Hills. John, drunk, came on to nearly every woman there. He pawed, flirted, and ignored Marcia's growing fury. By the time they got home, her rage boiled over, and she lit into him.

Unlike their usual arguments about other women, this one trended darker and sharper. John would later remember this as the moment when their dynamic began to change. They'd been dating for a couple of years, and he always felt in control, even when drunkenly pushing things too far. But that night, Marcia would tilt things to the extreme.

John couldn't remember how it happened, but they were screaming at each other, and then the next thing he knew, blood was pouring down Marcia's arms. She had grabbed a knife and slashed her wrists.

'It was like a horror movie, even as drunk as I was,' he said. 'She had me totally unglued.'

Before he could react, Marcia disappeared into the kitchen.

John followed and found her with her head in the oven, the gas turned on, a low hiss filling the air. For a moment, he froze. Then something inside him flipped.

'My drunk kicked in,' he said.

In a move he'd later reflect on with disbelief, John looked at her, calmly said 'bye-bye' and staggered out. He wasn't going to play that game. *No more*, he told himself. He was done. That night, he stayed with a female friend, and as the booze wore off, he trembled in her arms, unable to stop crying.

Less than a week later, the phone rang. It was Marcia. They talked, and in the end, John couldn't stay away. He told her if she ever pulled something like that again, he was gone for good. But they both knew that wasn't true.

The fights, jealous rages and drug-addled shouting matches continued.

'I was hung up on Marcia,' John said, 'I thought if I stopped fooling around, she would probably cool out.' The solution? He proposed.

On a cool, drizzly 24 June 1979, John and Marcia were married in Marcia's parents' backyard in Los Alamitos. It was a modest, private ceremony inviting only close family and friends, including Billy and Sharon. Their mixed feelings reflected what many people thought of the union: This would either be a good, settling influence, or things were going to get very bad indeed.

Marcia's three children, Damien, Sheri, and Shelley, visited them but hadn't lived with her since they were small. To them, John was 'Mom's new husband' rather than a new stepfather. Damien lived with his father, the jazz bassist Hersh Hamel, but visited John and Marcia almost every weekend, where they would watch movies or Saturday Night Live.

John took Damien to the park, out hiking, or to music rehearsals.

'It was positive, and I treasure it,' Damien says. 'We had some great times.' Once, they went to the mall, and John wandered into a piano store and began playing.

'All mouths would drop when he hit that keyboard,' Damien remembers, 'And next thing you know, people in the mall would come and crowd around the piano store. Because he was so insanely gifted as a jazz pianist.'

But outside family time, a slew of chemicals, both prescribed and illegal, were coming in the door. Marcia's psychiatrist had prescribed Mellaril (thioridazine) – an antipsychotic drug often used in the 1970s for schizophrenia and agitation. It helped manage these symptoms by dampening dopamine activity in the brain.

At first, it seemed to take the edge off, cooling the boiling-point arguments that pockmarked the relationship. But as the weeks wore on, Marcia became 'insensitive and gone'. John watched her spark disappear, replaced by an unnerving emptiness that was almost worse than their fights.

John tried the Mellaril himself, to see what was going on. He hated the disconnected, uncaring state it put him into. When it wore off, he begged Marcia to quit taking it. Marcia refused. After several weeks, John lost it.

'I went into an insanity act,' he said, 'and was screaming and panting and screaming, and I didn't care who heard me.' It frightened Marcia enough that she agreed to stop taking it.

Without the stabilizing effects of her meds and instead of seeking help, Marcia self-medicated alongside John, diving into a chaotic mix of drugs, matching him pill for pill, line for line.

At a home gathering with friends, Marcia and John smoked huge amounts of Angel Dust (phencyclidine or PCP), a dissociative anesthetic notorious for triggering paranoia, confusion, and violent outbursts. Standing in the kitchen, John thought he heard Marcia in the living room saying awful things about him.

'I went charging in there,' he said. He lunged at Marcia and slapped her. A male friend grabbed John, pinned him down, and started punching his lights out.

John was left bleeding and bruised on the floor as Marcia and friends slammed the door on their way out. He lay there, seething, the drugs amplifying every ounce of rage he'd tried to contain. That night, he lurched from room to room, tearing down every plant in the house.

As he came down, the reality of John's actions left him shaken and disgusted.

'For years I'd said I abhorred physical violence, and now I was becoming the very thing I hated,' he said. 'I was hating myself now more than ever.'

He realized he was on a dangerous path. *I am a sick person*, he thought, *and a violent one. If I am to have any life at all, I have to keep that foremost in my mind.* The fear of what he might be capable of was what finally pushed him to take control.

'That fact had to be etched in my psyche,' he said. 'I had long since destroyed the "Flower Child" image I cherished so much. The Dance of John and Marcia had taught me that maybe I wasn't so spiritual, after all.'

In that moment, he decided he had to leave Marcia or find a way to control himself. He extinguished the violence that day, but it was the only fire he ever truly put out. Almost everything else in his life was about to go up in flames.

John reconnected with singer Sabu and got a gig at a club called Atkins, where he kept playing – and drinking – hard. After finishing one evening, John packed his gear into his car and set off. Marcia was at her mother's house. Liquored up and suddenly feeling amorous, John decided that he'd drive to Los Alamitos to see Marcia instead of going home.

He U-turned the car and smashed it straight into the center divider. John sat still for a moment, the metalwork creaking. Had he wrecked the car? He eased it in reverse. It seemed all right. He joined the on-ramp to the freeway and was hit in the eyes by red and white flashing lights.

I'm fucked, John thought as he pulled over. He tried to tally up what he'd had. At least a pint of vodka. God knows what else. As the cop approached, John rolled down the window.

'You got me,' he said. 'I'm drunk. No need for a drunk test. Just take me in.' And that's exactly what they did.

John was arrested and carted off to county jail. Mat and blanket in hand, he walked through the central holding block. The building was the size of a penitentiary, about three stories high.

'Full of the worst thugs and madmen,' John said. 'And it was loud, man.'

Adrenaline sobered John up, and he was scared. A guard held open a gate, and John entered the belly of the beast. The metallic clang echoed down the corridor, swallowed by shouting and laughter from inside. Before he could get his bearings, a huge, ugly guy stepped into John's path, blocking the way forward like a human wall.

'How's your tongue?' the man snarled.

'What?' John said.

'How's your tongue?' the man repeated, eyes narrowing as he took a step closer.

John's mind raced. *There's no way to answer that question without giving him something to jump on*, he thought. He had to fight, or he was in for it.

'Get the fuck away from me, man!' John bristled, and pushed past, trying to look as 'bad' as he could until he got to his cell. He threw his mat and blanket on the steel bunk and turned around, fists up. Just then, the speaker crackled into life.

'John Larkin! Roll up!'

'What does that mean?' he asked another inmate.

'Get your stuff,' someone told him. 'You're getting out.'

The relief was dizzying. John remembered leaving the building, but the rest of the night was a blank.

It didn't take long for John to rationalize what had happened, especially because he considered himself a wonderful driver. *Anyone could have missed that center divider*, he concluded. *The street was poorly lit.*

He also made a noble choice: to stop drinking and driving. But a few weeks later he was back behind the wheel after 'only' drinking a couple of quarts of beer. Thinking one more couldn't hurt, he drove to the liquor store, bought two more, and headed home, right past a squad car.

When he saw them turn around in his rearview mirror, he stomped on the gas. His house was only a block away. He made it, but the cops followed and caught John sitting in his driveway, beer on his breath.

'Get in the car,' they said.

John slurred that he was home and could he please just go upstairs.

'*Get in the car,*' they repeated.

John climbed in, bracing for another trip to county jail and a reunion with Mr. How'sYourTongue. But his breathalyzer result was in the grey zone – not legally drunk, and not quite sober. They had to let him go.

'The jig was up,' John said. 'I couldn't rationalize it anymore.' The rage, the violence, the car accidents, being thrown in jail … maybe the universe was trying to tell him something? *I'm a walking time bomb*, he concluded, and the truth of it scared him.

Then the 'other' thought popped up; the one that had been lurking for a while. The one he'd been avoiding. But it was time.

The chemicals and booze had to stop.

12 **SPEEDBALL**

Oh God, no.
Drugs are my life.
I will do anything not to stutter.
Without chemicals, life would be impossible.

So went John's 'Junkie's Credo.' Yet he knew he was losing control, so he cut a deal with himself: no more hard drugs, no more booze. From now on, weed only.

He and Marcia moved to a cramped, shadowy apartment in Southeast LA. With the new 'pot only' rule in place, things felt calmer as the 1970s ended.

Jazz fusion was rising, and John's versatility kept him working. He played six nights a week at the Akasaka, a Downtown LA club, smoking pot until it came out of his ears. He justified it with stoner logic: John thought Hindus in India used it as a sacred herb. If it was good enough for their ceremonies, it was good enough for him.

'Of course, I ignored the fact that most Indians weren't addicts,' he admitted. 'I *was* an addict, and had to be stoned all the time.'

John found his rhythm at thirty joints a day. To fund his habit, he started selling on the side – buying a quarter pound, selling three ounces to break even, and keeping one for himself.

After three months of sticking to cigarettes and marijuana, John felt better. He was working constantly and managed to save money.

Even his marriage felt steadier. He couldn't stop replaying the night he'd lost his temper, and talked it through with Marcia again and again.

'When are you going to forgive yourself?' she asked. He never quite made peace with it, and never forgot it.

When the Akasaka gig ended, John had saved over $2,500, so he and Marcia decided to visit her extended family in Seattle. John had crashed his car again – no one remembered how – so he talked his parents into buying him another, this time an old Toyota Station Wagon.

John tossed a half-pound of grass into the luggage, then they hit the road. A few miles in, Marcia pulled out a bottle of codeine. *Screw it*, John thought. He was on vacation and could afford to have a little fun. He popped two pills. The effects slammed into him. He was flying, in love with everything in sight.

Marcia had scored the codeine from a crooked doctor eager to cozy up to the 'hip' jazz scene, and who was known for handing out scripts to musicians like party favors.

'We were fucked up all the way to Seattle,' John said. They burned through the entire bottle of 100 pills during the three-day drive.

In Seattle, they first stayed with Marcia's aunt and uncle across the bay, who introduced John to their homemade blackberry wine. John was drunk for a week, despite swearing off alcohol. Afterwards, he and Marcia booked a month at a hotel perched on a hillside.

One crisp morning, snow fell. John, thin and fragile, stood at the window, staring out with wide, six-year-old's eyes at a transformed world, soft and brilliant. *Beautiful*, was all he could think. For a moment, something stirred in him, like his younger self was trying to speak. But he wasn't ready to listen. Not yet.

John re-established his 'pot only' policy when they got back to LA. He wanted to keep working, which meant drinking was out. To stay grounded, he returned to his job at the tax office. Marcia, meanwhile, found a new hustle: dealing cocaine.

It was now 1980, and the fading psychedelic LSD and pot haze of the '60s and '70s had given way to the razor-sharp buzz of a new high. Nearly forgotten since the 1950s, cocaine had come roaring back.

Los Angeles was blanketed in it, driven by Colombian cartels like Pablo Escobar's as they expanded their reach into the United States. It was the party drug of choice in Hollywood circles, ubiquitous at clubs and gatherings, easy to find, and easy to sell.

'Marcia had no problem handling coke,' John said. 'She dug the money.'

Hoping a day job routine would keep him clean, John returned to being 'Captain Collator', smoking weed and working tax returns. But two weeks in, he got a call: a gig playing on a cruise ship.

A cruise ship! John couldn't believe it. He didn't even have to audition – the band already had the job. All John had to do was show up.

'Take it, man!' his boss Darryl urged him.

The band – Kim, Steve, and Mike – started rehearsing straight away.

'We were cookin', man, we got tight pretty quick,' John said. They set sail from LA Harbor, with John's Fender Rhodes piano packed to the tines with smuggled pot.

The cruise stopped in Acapulco, the Panama Canal, and Caribbean ports like Aruba and the Virgin Islands. Their home was the *Island Princess*, famously known as *The Love Boat* from the TV series. And it was paradise.

With only three hours of music to play each night, the band had the run of the ship. Most evenings, John would stand on the top deck, passing joints, watching the glow of the coastline fade into the distance. *Is this really happening?* He wondered. The Panama Canal was one of the most gorgeous sights he'd ever seen, stoned or not.

Halfway through the gig, the ship reversed course and headed back the way it came. John had stuck to his 'pot only' rule until temptation got the better of him in Puerto Rico when someone handed him a large plastic cup of local rum.

It didn't seem like much until he finished it, and suddenly the floor wasn't where it used to be. He realized he'd just chugged an amount of rum the size of a medium soda. His tolerance in tatters, John staggered back to his cabin, propped up by Steve and Kim. He barely made it to his bunk.

A few hours later, groggy and desperate to pee, John flopped out of bed. He fumbled for the light switch, missed, and stumbled into what he thought was the bathroom. Relieved, he listened to the steady stream of urine hitting what he assumed was the toilet bowl. Job done, he collapsed back into bed.

Morning came with a pounding hangover. Breakfast barely helped, so John returned to his cabin but found the door blocked by Mike, crouched on the floor.

'What are you doing?' John asked.

Mike didn't answer. He was on his hands and knees, scrubbing breathlessly. Clothes were strewn everywhere.

'What's going on?' John demanded. Then the smell hit him.

John hadn't opened the bathroom door in the night. He'd closed it. The 'toilet' was the wall, now dripping. *I've pissed all over the wall and floor of my cabin*, John realized.

Mortified, he offered to clean up, but Mike waved him off.

Red-faced, John went next door and told Steve and Kim, who laughed so hard they nearly cried.

See? John thought. *I knew I couldn't drink.*

John got Marcia a job collating tax returns alongside him, but working together all day drove them up the wall. To escape, John joined marathon jam sessions with his friends. Among them was Puerto Rican jazz and rock pianist Carli Muñoz, who had toured with the Beach Boys.

'He fought through his stuttering to express himself,' Carli says. 'And he was passionate, passionate as anyone could be. Crazy passionate.'

Another was Sam 'Sluggo' Phipps, a multi-instrumentalist with the LA New Wave band *Oingo Boingo*. John and Sam had already shared the stage for a few gigs around the city.

'I had this concept of doing a solo album,' Sam says, 'And I wanted John to be the piano player.'

On 14 June 1980, Sam turned his mother's living room into a makeshift studio to lay down tracks for *Animal Sounds*. The quartet featured Sam on sax, Noah Young on bass, Steve Larrance on drums, and John on piano.

'John's playing was the perfect combination of McCoy Tyner, who was John Coltrane's piano player, and Cecil Taylor, who was the most avant-garde piano player,' Sam says. 'He could go either way, and that's the kind of music I liked.'

The six-track album was released in 1981 on Sam's Dream Records label, becoming one of the first known commercial recordings of John's playing.

Around the same time, John landed a lucrative gig at a club called The Lotus. The shows were electric, pulling in big crowds, but after months of six-night-a-week sets, John cracked and started knocking back Screwdrivers.

'That started a slow progression back to madness,' John said. Then he started scoring coke off the club's singer. Within three months, any money he earned was going straight up his nose. He was burning out so fast he often sent in fellow pianist Jon Hartmann to fill in for him.

Cash dwindling, John asked around to see if anyone could supply coke in bulk, thinking he'd do what he did with weed and sell on the side.

Cocaine was often diluted with lidocaine, mannitol, caffeine, or even baking powder to stretch the product and the profits. Not long after Marcia scored a quarter of an ounce (7 grams), they learned how to cut it themselves. Their first sale – to their upstairs neighbour – netted them over a thousand dollars in a single night. *Hey*, John thought. *There's real money in this*, not knowing he was setting an irreversible trap.

They kept buying, selling, and reselling, making over five thousand dollars in profit. They were real drug dealers now, edging into the lower ranks of the big leagues. John also got a running prescription for No. 4 codeine pills – the strongest made – from the corrupt, jazz-obsessed doctor. Intended for severe pain like cancer or complex injuries, John popped twenty of them a day on top of coke, yet was somehow still able to play.

In 1982 Sam Phipps invited John, now 40, to perform live on KPFK radio out of North Hollywood. It would be just the two of them, with John on piano and Sam on sax. The recording for *Animal Sounds* had gone well, and there was no reason to think this would be any different.

The performance got off to a good start, but Sam noticed John's stutter was 'extreme'. By now, drugs had long stopped working on suppressing John's dysfluencies, and many noticed he was struggling to speak more than ever.

'He had a lot of frustration, obviously, that would come out when he was speaking. But he would channel that energy into his playing,' Sam says. 'I loved his playing so much. I heard the beauty, but I also heard the frustration. That night, he was almost smashing the piano.'

In the break, Sam took John aside. 'You're too good of a piano player to pound that nice piano into the ground', he told him.

John didn't take it well and disappeared into the night, leaving Sam to finish solo. Sam ended the broadcast with an improvised, spontaneous piece: 'A Lark in The Wind' as a tribute to John, hoping he'd hear it in his car on the way home.

'I'll never know,' Sam says, 'since I never heard from him again.'

It would be years until John's voice reached Sam once more. When it did, Sam wouldn't believe what he was hearing.

The atmosphere at John and Marcia's home was changing. 'The people who had started to come around were getting shadier and shadier as word got out that we were dealers,' John said. 'Our insides were toughening up.'

Concerned about safety, they moved to a nicer neighborhood, into a second-floor apartment with a clear vantage point to see and hear anyone approaching. Years later, John could still hear the loud groan of their heavy iron gate creaking shut.

John and Marcia knew the cops rarely bothered with small-time pot users, even though it was still illegal under state and federal law. White dealers had it easier, too – drug enforcement was brutally racist. But coke carried serious penalties.

John often thought about what would happen if they got 'poped' (caught) with the grams, half grams, and quarter grams neatly packaged for sale. Jail time was certain. The War on Drugs had escalated after Reagan took office with a hardline stance. If you were a dealer, you weren't just a criminal – you were considered a threat to the very fabric of society. By 1982, federal funding for drug enforcement had doubled.

Marcia's three kids – Sheri, Damien, and Shelley – didn't live with them and were spared most of the details. It was John and Marcia's operation, bringing in more money than they'd ever had in their lives, so they swallowed the fear and kept going.

'We rationalized that we would only do it for a short time and "invest" the money,' John said. 'Well, we invested alright, we started investing all the coke right up our noses.'

The coke dulled their anxiety and supercharged their social life. They hosted parties with a mix of drugs, drink, music, and laughter that kept paranoia at arm's length.

'Everyone's noses were packed, and we were having a splendid time,' John remembered.

John and Marcia dipped into the stash more and more. Sex and coke marathons became a ritual, and just like it had with Nancy, what started as a rush became a tether, with John only able to engage in any kind of intimacy if he was high.

One night, Marcia was out and John was bored. He had a gig the next day at Merlin McFly's, a bar with a magical theme where he'd been playing on and off since 1981. He told himself he'd just do a 'little' coke. *I have to take it easy*, he thought. *I have a gig tomorrow.*

One line turned into ten. Then twenty. Thirty lines in, the high twisted, and his euphoria collapsed into a nightmare of rage, lust, and buried trauma. The memories of abuse resurfaced again. He spiraled helplessly, dragged deeper into a haze of chaos and self-loathing. By the time John stopped, he'd blown through forty lines of coke, and he'd been up all night and well into the following day.

He looked at the clock. His gig was in two hours.

'I was in such a pitifully demoralized state that I couldn't let anyone see me,' John said. 'I was gone, man.'

He called Bill, the drummer who had hired him, and spun him a story about not being able to play. When Bill asked why, John admitted he was an addict.

'So what?' Bill shot back. 'That's no excuse; a lot of us are addicts.'

'I know' John wailed, 'but I'm too fucked up to make it.'

Bill slammed the phone down.

I've done the unspeakable, John thought. *I've hung up a gig.*

'I thought I had really plummeted down to the depths,' John said later. 'But this was just the beginning of the discovery of how far into demoralization a human being can go.'

John kept dipping into the stash. Marcia noticed. The fights reignited, spilling out into the communal hallway of their apartment building.

John had taken a half ounce for himself and was on the floor, screaming and screaming as dollar notes and powder cascaded out of his pockets.

Jon Hartmann, who had been subbing for him at gigs, walked in, took one look at the unraveling madness in front of him and quietly backed out, becoming one of many friends John would never see again.

John tried to distract himself with a change of scenery. He had to get away from home, get away from temptation. When Tenor sax player Rusty Crutcher offered him another cruise ship job on *The Rotterdam*, he took it. Rusty had never met John before, and when he saw him at the airport, he was aghast. 'There was John – with no front tooth,' Rusty remembers. "He was raggedy looking. You could tell he'd been drugging it up and drinking the night before. I'm thinking, oh my God, what have I done?"

But that first night on the bandstand, 'He blew me away' Rusty remembers. 'But that was before he started having the DTs.'

John's Delirium Tremens (DTs) – a potentially life-threatening form of alcohol withdrawal – totally consumed him on the second night. Suddenly John couldn't even read music. 'He was lost' Rusty says. 'I didn't know what I was dealing with.' On night three, the bass player complained that John was keeping him awake by screaming and cursing in his sleep for hours.

Rusty tried to hold it all together and even had the ship's dentist replace John's missing tooth, but John tossed his 'no drinking' rule overboard as he downed White Russians and Vodka Gimlets every night. His playing improved but his grip on reality didn't. When a group of tipsy passengers heckled him with a request for 'Tie a Yellow Ribbon Round the Ole Oak Tree' ('the biggest insult' Rusty adds),

John kicked his drink across the room at them. The glass shattered, passengers fled in terror, and Rusty was left trying to stop the whole gig from sinking.

One afternoon, John spotted a banner: *Friends of Bill W*. He asked what it meant. A passenger explained it referred to Bill Wilson, co-founder of Alcoholics Anonymous. Meetings were held on board, he told John. Maybe he should join one.

John attended one AA meeting – his first – but it didn't stick. His blood alcohol level barely dropped before he was drinking again.

After the cruise, desperate to dry out, John joined his friend Gary Seeger on a cycling trip. Even as self-described 'druggies', they still pushed themselves to cycle 40 miles a day. John's physical endurance defied logic. But his breaking point was closer than he realized.

John's cruise pay and Marcia's coke profit meant the couple were rolling in money. Marcia picked John up from the harbour in a limo. Once back home, they wasted no time in getting down to sex, coke, and more sex. What started as a biweekly binge became weekly, and then the gaps between binges got even shorter. One stretch lasted four days.

'We were burning up,' John said, 'and desperately needed to come down.'

They got in the car and headed for the Dragon Man's house in the San Fernando Valley, named for 'Dragon', the purest heroin around. They'd used it to come down before, but never after a binge this long. *We're fried*, they told the Dragon Man and his girlfriend. *We need relief.*

Heroin and cocaine pull in opposite directions – depressant and stimulant – which feeds the myth that they cancel each other out. But this combination – known as a speedball – is far more dangerous than either drug alone.

John and Marcia handed over the cash. The Dragon Man prepped both needles and shot them up together.

Aaah, John thought. It felt so good to finally relax.

He drifted into the front room, sat on the floor, and propped himself up against a chair, savoring the sweet relief of letting go.

Moments later, his body went limp.

The Dragon Man rushed to him.

John wasn't breathing.

13 BREATH OF LIGHT

Whump. Whump. Whump.

The Dragon Man dove down, forcing air into John's lungs with a ragged exhale. *Huuuuuuffff.*

The air escaped quickly. Too quickly. He straightened up and pressed his hands on John's sternum.

Whump. Whump. Whump.

Nearby, his girlfriend worked on Marcia, her compressions mirroring his. Seconds after John collapsed, Marcia had stopped breathing too.

The Dragon Man pushed harder, feeling the resistance of a chest that no longer rose on its own. No way were these two junkies dying on his floor. Not today.

He forced another breath into John's lungs.

Press. Breathe. Press. Breathe.

A few miles away and years before, Judy McHugh's life had also teetered on a threshold – this one facing a Coldwater Canyon cliff. Years of a delicate dance between survival and self-destruction had led her, ultimately, to this moment. The pressure to 'be someone' was both her inheritance and her undoing. She was going too fast. The afternoon sun glinted off her car as she lost control and the jagged edge rushed to meet her.

The car skidded, yawed over the precipice, and crashed onto the rocky ground below. The impact was almost anticlimactic. Dazed, bruised but miraculously conscious, Judy blinked, but then let her eyes flutter shut, feigning unconsciousness when firefighters arrived and swarmed around her.

The car and the cliff were the wake-up call. Her son, Lee, the product of her first, less tumultuous marriage to Eddie Kafafian, saw what was happening. Empty bottles hidden under bathroom sinks, her sudden disappearances during meals, the fainting, the falls. After her time on *Laugh-In*, she worked at Universal Studios and later as a talent agent. She was brilliant when she chose to work, but loathed being forced to. Confrontation led to anger, tears, or collapse, as if gravity was heavier on her frail shoulders than anyone else's.

In the middle of her failing second marriage to composer Joe Harnell, she felt she was never enough, never allowed to be 'just Judy'. He wanted to change her. Couples therapy was a futile parade of accusations and finger-pointing.

'Structure,' the therapist suggested. 'Get a job,' he said. She lit a cigarette in defiance and was promptly thrown out.

As the firefighters lifted her from the wreckage, her knees buckled. Sirens blared, radios crackled. Inside, it was all muffled, the only sound the pounding of her own blood. It was times like these when she wanted to scream, to make herself heard above the noise, but nothing would come out.

Back in the Valley, the Dragon Man fought for John's life. The seconds dragged. He pushed again, and again.

Whump. Whump. Whump. A relentless mechanical drumbeat.

Finally, a ragged gasp tore from John's throat. His eyes shot open. Air gushed through him in a wheezing burst.

He lay there, awake but unfocused, lungs burning.

Coldwater Canyon had seen John's future spouse dragged back from the edge and wheeled away. Now he turned to face his present wife – alive, and awake.

He sat up. Marcia was talking to herself, rambling about being connected to a 'string of life'.

A miracle we were both still alive, John thought later. He couldn't remember if they even thanked their rescuers. What he did remember was that the moment they got home, they felt so good, they snorted more coke.

'Insanity was not a word to adequately describe Marcia and me,' John said. 'We were so loaded that we were indifferent to the fact that our lives had just been saved. Such is the desensitizing nature of heavy-duty drugs.'

John's overdose didn't slow him down. He kept a furious schedule of jam sessions and jazz workshops, playing at friends' houses hidden up the winding roads of the Los Angeles hills. Frustrated neighbors would call the cops, but the free, whipsawing jazz bounced around the canyons, and the police couldn't always tell where it was coming from.

Like the jazz legends he idolized, John was about to hit new creative heights, just as his personal life frayed to its last thread.

It was time, he decided, to record his own album.

Michael Totten was sleeping in a makeshift bungalow above Central Sound Recorders in downtown Hollywood when a burst of loud jazz piano from the studio downstairs jolted him awake.

He crept downstairs. A skinny, short-haired, moustachioed man in a white shirt and black slacks was attacking their Kawai Concert Grand Piano, mumbling and scat-singing to himself.

Michael lingered, listening. The man acknowledged him with a brief glance, but kept playing. Eventually, the final note rang out.

'Wow,' Michael whispered.

'I *love* your piano,' John said.

John had met Central Sound's original owner, Marlin Jones, in rehab during one of his fleeting attempts to get clean. Marlin had invited John to check out his Hollywood recording studio, run by Philip Cacayorin, who would later take over the business.

Philip and his business partner didn't just hear but felt the vibrations of John playing the 9-foot grand.

'The piano was actually shaking,' Philip recalled. 'I turned to my partner and said, "Have you ever heard anything like this before?" It had never been that loud.'

Pleased with the instrument, John booked a weekend session. He had the money – Marcia's coke profits took care of that – and he had a big-name collaborator: Joe Farrell.

A founding member of Chick Corea's *Return to Forever*, Joe was a soulful yet dynamic jazz saxophonist and flutist. He'd played with a ton of jazz legends in the '70s but had moved to Los Angeles at the turn of the '80s, where he and John used together and played together.

In late 1983, Joe introduced John to bassist Bob Harrison and drummer Clark Woodard. If Joe vouched for someone, Bob says, you didn't question it, so he immediately went to meet John.

'The fact he stuttered made him endearing,' Bob says. 'I had no problem with how he spoke. I thought about what he said – how he said it was irrelevant.'

Together, they formed 1984's John Larkin Quartet. On a Saturday morning in August of that year, Bob and Clark arrived at the studio, followed by John.

'I realized this is not your everyday guy,' Philip says. 'This brilliant, brilliant man, a range of creativity ... but there's no ego. That's the first thing I noticed.'

John threw on his headphones and scat-sang during the sound check, a pleasant shock to Michael.

'He was introverted but energetic,' Michael says. 'Later, I wondered if that was partly a compensation for his stutter.'

An hour passed, then two. No Joe. The group smoked, lingered, and grabbed lunch at Martoni's across the street. Joe finally appeared and set up, resisting any and all attempts to have his sound toned down, insisting on a Neumann U87 mic and nothing else.

Was he ready? Not quite.

'I gotta go somewhere first. I need a hundred and twenty dollars,' Joe told Philip. Philip relayed Joe's demand to John.

'He wants it right now?' John said.

'Yeah. What do I do?'

'Give it to him,' John said. 'You'll hear something you've never heard in your life.'

Joe took the cash and vanished for another hour. By now, it was the middle of the afternoon, the clock was still running, but nobody seemed to care. Suddenly, the back door flew open, and Joe stumbled in, sweating.

'I'm ready,' he announced.

Philip glanced around. Now John had disappeared. *I've never had a session like this*, he remembered thinking. *I'm losing all the musicians.* They found John meditating under the piano.

With John acting as both producer and bandleader, the quartet was primed, John's handwritten charts in hand. 'The Misfit' erupted like a firecracker – an exhilarating explosion of free jazz that John had been perfecting since the '70s. Captured in a single take, it became the album's opener, grabbing future listeners from the moment the needle hit the wax.

The 2-inch, 24-track tape rolled, catching John stabbing the keys with frenzied precision, his punchy scat-singing weaving through Joe Farrell's tenor sax lines. The semi-autobiographical lyrics spoke of the pain and defiance of a social outcast, 'caged' for being weird and different. Unknown to John, a handful of lines from 'The Misfit' would later propel a very different song that would reach millions.

Next, the mood shifted to a sombre, introspective piece.

'"Last Night I Dreamed" is the best ballad I have ever recorded,' Bob Harrison says. 'Lyrically, harmoniously, that sax solo … I've played many ballads with many people, but that fucking ballad … ' He trails off, overcome.

'Love Cry' followed; another John had worked on for years. It kicked off with a solo piano performance so precise and expressive that, decades later, a mastering engineer would call it 'so perfectly executed that it's hard to believe it's real.'

The quartet was a tightly wound machine, yet whenever John was forced to stop after messing up a note or a line, he'd bang random piano keys and mumble something about 'Misfit, misfits.' There were other interruptions, too.

'The shitty part for John was when Joe had to take a fix every couple of hours,' Michael Totten recalls. 'We'd all have to stop what we're doing and clear out of the studio, standing around outside jabbering and having cigarettes while John would be sadly pacing in the office and worrying about his tight friend Joe.'

The final tracks recorded that weekend were 'Charley's Samba' – later renamed 'Charley's Place', which didn't make the cut – and the only cover: an instrumental version of 'Softly, as in a Morning Sunrise' from the 1928 operetta *The New Moon*; a favorite of modern jazz musicians with a dialed-up tempo.

John wanted to sing everything live at the piano, but bleed-through on the mics forced him to overdub some vocals a few weeks later.

When he walked out of Central Sound clutching his first set of masters, the project wasn't finished, but already left a lasting impression.

'It was the most incredible sound I've ever had out of that studio,' Philip says. Michael agrees. 'I've never worked with such exquisite artists in one session as with these guys,' he says. 'The sessions were a breath of light. The songs, tracks, and mixes were beautiful.'

Nearly a year passed before John returned to the studio. In June 1985, the quartet reconvened at Blue Dolphin Studios in LA, with engineer Morgan Cavett at the board; a connection John likely made through Shelby Flint, who sang vocals on John's unreleased cover of Coltrane's 'Naima.'

Despite the ten-month hiatus, the high-energy chemistry was intact. They tore through covers like Chick Corea's '500 Miles High' and Rodgers and Hart's 'My Funny Valentine'. But it was another of John's originals – 'Angel's Flight' – that earned its place on the album: a ten-minute odyssey of fearless, avant-garde jazz.

Whether his fellow musicians realized it or not, they were playing with a man nearing physical, spiritual, and psychological collapse. John's unraveling found its purest expression on the album's most devastating track: 'John Coltrane'.

The song begins quietly – the quartet absent, John exposed. Ten words: *I sing a song of love for you, John Coltrane*. Not a declaration, but a prayer.

John begins scatting, throat-chanting harmonics for almost a minute. Pushing the limits of human vocal expression, his smoke-burnished voice rises as the piano builds with weight, momentum, and fury.

Then John hammers the keys in a deafening, tumultuous wall of sound; a controlled demolition climbing to a shattering crescendo. By the end, he's screaming himself hoarse, the piano almost buckling beneath the emotional weight of his expression.

Then, just as abruptly, the storm subsides. From the wreckage, John's voice rises again – fragile, spent – while the piano's final notes dissolve into the hiss of the tape machine.

Raw, fractured , and brutal, 'John Coltrane' was an exorcism and a testimony so intense that it unsettled those close to John and never appeared on any other album. Deemed too angry for reissue, it became a fiery outlier buried in the archives, consigned to obscurity.

John now had all the raw material he needed for a debut album, but the tapes sat untouched. He was tapped out.

He and Marcia decided to get away from the cocaine for a while and went to Yosemite on vacation. John couldn't understand why he was in so much physical pain, not realizing his body was detoxing from all the coke and heroin. To combat this, he got drunk.

One day he found Marcia in tears. *Everything is coming to an end*, she said. John didn't think much of it, and reassured her that he loved her.

But she was right.

14 **GOING OUT**

The house was still. Peaceful.

Marcia was at her mother's, and her daughter Sheri – now in her 20s – was staying with them for a while in the spare room.

John had been out most of the evening. Bed called, but first, he needed to pee. He was enjoying the quiet, clear-headed and nearly seven months sober. The whole house was pristine; maybe Sheri had cleaned while he was gone.

When he went to wash his hands, he noticed something odd. A lone razor blade on the otherwise spotless sink.

Why is that there?

Leaning closer, he saw a thin line of blood on the blade.

A chill ran through him.

He walked to the spare bedroom and hesitated at the door. Sheri had been struggling with her mental health, and Marcia had once accused John of being attracted to her. What would it look like if he knocked? What if he didn't?

He tapped on the door. No answer.

He knocked again, louder. Still nothing.

'Sheri?' he called, cracking the door open. Silence, then a low groan. He stepped inside the room. Sheri was slumped across the bed in her bathrobe.

'Are you all right?' he asked, though he already knew the answer. She groaned again and mumbled something incoherent. *She's loaded on something*, John thought.

'You don't look all right to me,' he said, leaning in to shake her. Her body was heavy and limp.

John carried her into the hallway. That's when he saw it. Deep slashes scored both arms. The red robe had masked the blood in the dim bedroom, but now it was everywhere. His mind scrambled for sense.

She murmured something about taking pills.

'How many?' he yelled. 'HOW MANY?'

Sheri slurred a number. John struggled to keep her upright and fumbled for the phone on its cradle. As he adjusted her weight, his finger slipped into one of her wounds. It was an eerie sensation he never forgot.

For someone who stutters, calling 911 can be a special kind of nightmare; the pressure to speak compounded by the fear of being misunderstood or, worse, for the operator to dismiss the call as a prank and hang up. But John got through it, his words tripping and catching as he held Sheri up, trying to keep her conscious.

Paramedics arrived in a blur of lights. They worked on Sheri in the hallway, but when she didn't respond, they strapped her onto a stretcher and raced her to the emergency room.

John stayed behind, frozen, her blood still tacky on his hands as he listened to the wail of the siren fading into the night. It took him half an hour to pull himself together enough to drive.

In the hospital waiting room, he sat while doctors worked to pump dozens of pills from Sheri's stomach. A TV flickered in the corner with muted programming – usually news, but also a newer channel called MTV, playing a rotation of mid-'80s music videos.

The way the fluorescent lights hummed overhead, the sound of shoes scuffing against linoleum, the tang of disinfectant – it was all familiar. Eight months ago, it had been John waking up on a gurney, wondering – yet again – how he'd ended up there.

Not long after the album recording sessions, he and Marcia were evicted. They'd agreed to split up and get clean. Marcia did, but John didn't.

Marcia was right, he thought. Something was ending, because he just didn't care anymore. Holed up in a hotel, he unraveled and was shooting heroin daily. None of his friends heard from him, and the days morphed together, punctuated only by ER visits and the strange familiarity of the hospital ceiling.

One day John dragged himself to see Marcia. He never forgot the heartbroken way she looked at him.

'Oh, John,' she said as he stood there, gaunt and hollow-eyed. He told her he was strung out, worse than he'd ever been, but he'd try to get on the methadone program.

John had messed with methadone before, buying it off the street, but now he was going to get the full dosage, tapered down over twenty-one days under medical supervision.

'Blowtorches to fight fire,' John called it as he entered a month-long living hell; a sleepless twilight racked with vicious agony that burrowed deep into the marrow of the bones.

'No other pain is like the pain of withdrawing from heroin,' he said, 'and when withdrawing from methadone, you can amplify that by ten.'

John had agreed to separate from Marcia and attend AA meetings. He moved in with Buddy Arnold, a jazz saxophonist who was clean after decades of addiction and now helped other musicians do the same.

John's roommate at Buddy's was Joe Farrell, also clean but physically deteriorating. A hospital visit confirmed the worst: myelodysplastic syndrome –

a type of blood cancer. Joe was admitted, and John moved into his room, not expecting him to return.

But Joe did come back – thin, weak, and exhausted – and asked for his room again. At first, John didn't want to give it up.

'Here I am, not willing to give a dying man his room,' he admitted later. He did give it back and apologized to Joe.

'It was starting to show,' John reflected. 'Getting sober does not mean that the sick behaviour suddenly stops.'

In January 1986, John was at a meditation retreat when the news came that Joe had died. John took 'time off' to go to his wake.

'How noble of me,' John said. 'Joe Farrell had done everything he could to put me on the map. This guy had done more for my career than anyone, and I "found time" to go to his wake! Boy, was I a selfish little shit. I was getting sober all right. I was finding out parts of myself I didn't want to look at.'

Buddy and John found a new roommate: Paul Butterfield, of the Butterfield Blues Band. Another musician, another addict. He would die of an overdose the following year.

Eventually, the house filled with music again. Buddy's grand piano became the heart of nightly jam sessions. John played often, finding it healing. But loneliness gnawed at him. He missed Marcia.

Despite the warnings – *returning to your old life is a relapse waiting to happen* – months of sobriety gave John enough misplaced confidence to move back in with her. The decision, reckless as it would turn out to be, put him in the right place at the right time.

At the hospital, the doctors came out of the room. Sheri was stable, they said. They had pumped enough undissolved pills out of her stomach to kill someone three times over. If John had called for the ambulance even ten minutes later, Sheri wouldn't have made it. He had saved her life.

'Most of us try the waters again,' John's new AA friends told him. 'But you can be sure: your drinking and using has been ruined.'

In AA, relapse had a name: *Going Out*. Forty to sixty percent of people in recovery fall back into old habits at least once. For John, saving a life wasn't enough to steady his own. The gaps between his meeting attendance widened. A day here, a week there. Then it became months.

The warnings from the group buzzed in his head: *Stay close to the fellowship. Your old life will pull you back in.* Like countless addicts before him, John wasn't entirely convinced.

Instead of going to a meeting one day, he visited an old musician buddy who lived nearby; a heavy pot user who was self-medicating to cope with health issues caused by Agent Orange, a toxic herbicide used during the Vietnam War. One afternoon was all it took for John to end his longest sober streak yet.

He remembered the first, heady puff of marijuana after months of abstinence.

'I was off, man,' he remembered, 'off to the races, the race back downhill to skin and bones because it wasn't too much longer when I decided to have a couple of half quart cans of beer.'

Ashamed, John tried to hide the relapse from Marcia, but she was slipping too. Sheri had left, and Marcia was back selling coke. One of her friends came over constantly, and Marcia claimed she was just letting her friend try coke, but it was obvious she was dipping in herself. She also started popping the pills she'd stockpiled during sobriety.

Soon they were both swept up into the same toxic cycle of cocaine, sex, pills, and booze.

'I got hold of myself for a while, which is all one can do without help,' John said. He eased off the hard stuff, stuck to smoking pot again, and poured what energy he had left into something tangible.

In mid-1986, John learned that Marcia's friend Beverley owned an old jazz label called Transition. He bought it from her for a dollar, dug out his quartet recordings, and had his album pressed to vinyl. He titled the LP *John Larkin*.

Marcia, still creatively sharp, designed the cover, while John added a poem on the back. It spoke of the nature of time, of endings and beginnings, of cycles that endlessly fold back into themselves. *Part of the longing of what was, is as sureness of what must and will return*, he wrote, as though trying to convince himself as much as anyone else that there was still a way to end up where he belonged.

He was so close. Closer than he'd ever been.

Closer with every line of coke packed into his nose, closer with every morning drunk, closer as 1986 began to dissolve into an endless, suffocating blur.

Closer as he smashed piano keys night after night, almost breaking his fingers as blood blisters bloomed beneath every fingernail.

Closer as club patrons talked over him, the clatter of drinks and laughter drowning him out. *Listen to me*, he wanted to scream. *See? I'm somebody. Stop talking. Somebody listen to me.*

Closer as the truth deafened him: *They're not listening to you. Because you're not enough.*

Closer still, as he drove down the freeway and his lung collapsed, his breath stolen, the world tilting for a man drowning above the surface.

Then on the grey, drizzly afternoon of 14 November 1986, John woke after drinking all morning. He sat up. Looked around. Then spoke aloud to the empty room:

'I can't live like this anymore.'

And just like that – he was there.

15 UNCOVERY

By John Larkin

That was it. I was finished and I knew it.

The next day, 15 November 1986, was my first full day of sobriety. Twenty-four hours. In AA your sobriety date is determined on the day of your first twenty-four hours.

Recovery isn't the word to describe what I needed by now. I didn't need to 'recover' anything. To recover is to add another layer on an already existing surface ... and that description spells out the negative pattern of my life until 1986. Layers and layers of neuroses that set in motion a pattern of death and destruction.

No, 'recovery' was not for me. 'Uncovery' was.

That word 'uncovery' better paints the process that I needed to undergo, because I desperately needed to peel off the old ideas and concepts that drove me into oblivion. But before I could even begin that, I had to get sober, and that took time.

Defeated would be an understatement, if that word were used to describe my condition. The word has a subtle implication that I might have 'just' gone down for the count and still had some fight 'til the moment of knockdown. Well, I hadn't 'just' gone down for the count. I had been down for years. I hadn't had any fight for years.

I knew I couldn't play professionally any more, though I couldn't admit it. Admitting that would have meant I was destroyed because, you see, my total self-image was hooked on to the fact that I was a jazz player.

I stopped using dope and got sober enough to discover just how far years of 'acting out' behind the cocaine and heroin had driven my body into deterioration and my mind and soul into such a state of pitiful demoralization.

I knew now that if I were to live, it had to be without Marcia. I loved Marcia, but what does love have to do with a hopeless disease? We were both co-addicts, we fed off each other and created enough havoc in each other to keep us both either using or in enough pain to wish we were.

It was my choice and mine alone.

I had decided to live instead of die.

16 SURRENDER MEANS WIN

All eyes turned to the man seated on a plastic chair near the back. Head bowed, eyes shut, locked in battle with eight simple words.

'M-m-my n-n-name is J-J-J ...'

Spittle flecked his lips.

'... is Juh-Juh-Juh ...'

Glances flicked around the room, but no one interrupted. To the uninitiated, stuttering can be awkward, even unsettling. *What's wrong with him? Is he slow? Drunk? Mentally ill?*

'J-J-John, and I'm an aaaaaaaal ...'

John's neural pathways misfired, derailing the words he knew he wanted to say.

'... alc-c-coholic.'

John opened his eyes. Even when people understand what's going on, there's still *the look*. Pity. Sympathy. Whether wanted or not.

But this room fostered listening without judgment.

'Hi, John,' several people said back.

When he'd first stepped into the Musicians' AA Meeting in the San Fernando Valley, the place struck him like a Fats Waller song: 'The Joint is Jumpin'. There were nearly 200 people there.

'The place was rumbling with a sense of vitality that I had always hoped I would find at jazz gigs or parties,' John said.

Only a few months earlier, he'd been slumped in his living room, riding out a brutal codeine crash, longing for a place he could go where people understood him. *Well*, he thought now, *ask and you shall receive*.

'He was shy in the beginning,' remembered those who were there. 'Didn't want to raise his hand, didn't want to communicate.'

It was Walter Urban Jr. – a jazz bassist, fellow addict, and occasional bandmate at the Winery – who'd sent him. Walter had spent his life around music. He also happened to be the stepfather of a kid nicknamed Flea, bassist for an up-and-coming local band called the Red Hot Chili Peppers.

Walter knew exactly what John needed. If John had stumbled into a 'quiet subdued meeting of old, crotchety hard-nosed old timers' he might've had a different impression of AA. But these people?

'These people were like me,' John said, 'and they were sober! It was the right place and I was in love. I had indeed come home.'

As John detoxed, his mind burned up. He could barely think straight, and lived to go to meetings – morning, noon, and night. *Surrender*, he said. That's all he could manage as he clung to anything he could conceive of as God.

To ease his symptoms, he started taking Catapres, a brand name for clonidine that eased the unpleasant side effects of alcohol and opiate withdrawal. He took more than he should; his relationship with pills still tangled up in habits waiting to be kicked.

There were hugs and hand-holding in the meetings; everything John had longed for on the outside but never found.

'I would stand there and hold and be held, by some beautiful women I might add,' he said. 'But at that time I would have surrendered to a horse's ass because that would have looked beautiful too.'

He stayed a while with his close friend, bass player John Lasonio, also in recovery. After a few weeks, he felt steady enough to leave the couch-hopping behind and moved into a room once rented by Sheri, Marcia's daughter. He and Marcia were still speaking, cautiously navigating their separate recoveries, but they kept their distance.

The new room in Studio City was Zen-like, filled with orchids and quiet spaces. *Perfect for healing*, John thought.

John made friends with a couple of women in the program, but there was an unspoken rule: no dating in the first year. Substance abuse, he was told, distorts perception – both of yourself, and others. Relationships forged too soon often collapsed. At first, John was disappointed by the platonic boundaries. Then he saw the value in it.

'A lot of the stuff you don't want people to see comes out, which is very healthy,' he said. 'It's very difficult to save face and save your ass at the same time.'

By 1987, he hadn't played in months. He listened back to his *John Larkin* LP and was so horrified by his performance that he shoved all the records into his closet. They stayed there – unreleased and unheard – except for a few copies given to friends and family.

But he missed performing.

So when his friend Jim Miller called with a cruise ship booking on the MS *Stardancer*, John said yes immediately. But the moment he hung up the phone, he started fretting. It would be his first sober gig. A return to old, dangerous ground. He already knew how easily that ground could give way.

He shared his fears at a meeting. *Trust God, and go ahead*, they told him. Someone showed him a passage in the 'Big Book' – AA's foundational text – explaining that recovering addicts could work in places where alcohol was served, if they were on strong spiritual ground.

But was he? John thought so, but his anxiety mounted. To prepare, he mapped out every AA meeting in the Mexican towns where the ship would dock. With hope and apprehension, he left the sanctuary of his familiar routine and stepped aboard.

The first week went well. The quartet was solid, and the crowds were receptive. But performing sober felt off. His playing was 'tight', and he was using the same musical expressions and phrases every night – anathema to a jazz player. Then, just as he began to adjust, Prince Robinson, the newly sober guitarist, relapsed.

John knew Prince from way back, though their memories of each other were hazy. Now, Prince was drunk and running wild through the ship like a one-man storm. John was furious. *He's a threat to my sobriety*, he told the band.

One evening, Prince staggered into John's cabin with his copy of the AA Big Book and started spouting drunken passages from it. John didn't kick him out. He let him stay. Night after night, Prince would ramble drunken monologues from the book, and John would sit there, staying sober by holding fast to the quotes Prince was mangling.

A few weeks in, John's playing loosened up a little.

'I knew how to surrender,' John remembered, 'and would practice meditation between breaks and come back on stage hypnotized by my own mental energy.'

Jim Miller, the bandleader and drummer, became suspicious after John ducked behind the curtain one night to blow his nose, followed by a sudden explosion of his old energy onstage.

'You're snorting coke, aren't you?' Jim said.

'No,' John replied.

It didn't matter how many times he explained. Jim wouldn't believe him. John had relapsed so often, he realized his denials had lost their currency. Friends, family, bandmates – everyone assumed it was only a matter of time before the madness started again. John remembered it took another six months before Jim even began to believe him, and even longer for his family to do the same.

By the fifth week of the gig, John's stamina was shot, and the strain of staying clean was too much.

'I have to get off this ship,' he told Jim. 'My sobriety is at stake.'

Jim didn't argue. John took two weeks off and then returned to finish the gig, his sobriety intact. He had passed the test, and gave himself a rare pat on the back.

'I did marvelously for where I was at the time,' he said.

John, now 45, had been sober for nearly a year. His sister-in-law Sharon planned a fiftieth anniversary party for his parents. John turned up and performed, entertaining the crowd with a band as his family got used to the new, sober Johnny.

Maybe this time it'll stick, Billy thought.

For John, this only underscored how far he still had to go. He was managing the physical addiction. Now he needed to move forward in his recovery, and he knew what that meant. The 'why'. The past. The stuttering. The Thing.

Walter Urban had a way of spotting the invisible fractures in John and began pointing them out, much to John's discomfort. It was time, Walter said, to join another twelve-step program called ACA (Adult Children of Alcoholics), a program that had expanded to include people whose lives had been warped by their childhoods and the environment they'd grown up in.

John argued and resisted. But Walter didn't back down.

'He worked with me day and night,' John remembered. 'It was as if he used a spiritual chisel to chip away the denial and minimization I had developed throughout my life.'

At his first ACA meeting, John listened. *Neglect. Unhealthy behavior. Abuse.*

Stories of homes where it wasn't okay to feel, where childhood survival meant dragging unspoken pain inside you until it destroyed you. It felt like the truth. *His* truth.

Then he heard the line from the ACA preamble: 'You will recover the child within you, learning to love and accept yourself.'

Love and accept myself? For a man who had spent years trying to slowly kill himself, it seemed impossible. But as John listened to strangers share their stories, he felt a flicker of recognition. These people weren't just telling their stories. They were telling his. He wasn't alone.

It was the next miracle. John stood up.

The Thing was waiting, as it always was; the emotional landmine he never dared touch. Standing before the table, his armor stripped, his coping mechanisms dismantled, John knew he had to detonate it here and now or he would never heal – or stay sober.

The anger came slowly, simmering.

'Why didn't my mother do anything? Where was God when that was happening?' His voice cracked.

'How the *fuck* could anybody do that to an innocent child?'

He slammed his fist on the table, the sound carrying across the silent room.

His breathing quickened as he began to cry.

'Why was I taught that what created me was out to get me? Why did my father make me feel inadequate?'

The questions ripped through him, unstoppable.

'Where in the fuck were Mommy and Daddy? *Why didn't they come to my rescue?*'

He sobbed, his body trembling as he banged his fist on the table again and again. 'Why was I destroyed before I even had a crack at life?'

It was out. John sat down, his face wet, the grief of his lost childhood pouring out of him in waves. He had done it. He had said it. He had shared it.

He had told a room full of people, and every one of them understood.

Afterwards, John embraced the phrase: *We're only as sick as our secrets.* He learned he could exorcize the pain by exposing it.

ACA introduced John to the concept of the inner child. It had been gaining traction in the late '80s; an idea that we all carry the child we once were, a time capsule shaping how we think, feel, and act as adults.

Hearing all this, John wondered: *Whatever became of the whole, perfect child I once was, before everything that had happened to me? Before overwhelming toxic shame drove me into full flight from myself?*

'I discovered that the precious child inside me was still there,' John said, 'the child that no one ever recognized or championed.'

He named that child Paul – his middle name.

But when he first reached for him, Paul barely stirred, silent and neglected.

'I set out to regain, love, heal, and nourish that child back to health and happiness by no longer denying its voice and feelings,' he said. 'I was slowly becoming the whole person I never was.'

He knew the road ahead would be long. The outside world barely talked about these things, especially in the 1980s, and especially if you were a man.

'Society's very existence depends on the denial of its dysfunction,' he later said. He likened this journey to another spiritual awakening – one more profound and authentic than the one sparked by his LSD trip in San Francisco.

'In San Francisco, I discovered the nature of life,' he said. 'But now, I was discovering the nature of myself. I was coming alive, from the inside out.'

Toward the end of 1987, John was still attending the Musicians' Meeting and ACA when a sax player mentioned an agent friend looking to book a hotel pianist. John put together a package, remembering being uncharacteristically assertive chasing the gig because he wanted to work.

He insisted on meeting the agent in person, to show he was clean, presentable – and sober. He got the job: a long-term booking, three nights a week at the Commerce Hyatt in Southeast LA, playing jazz standards as the mellow backdrop to the afternoon cocktail hour.

With his other evenings free, John's recovery circle kept his social calendar full. One night, a friend invited him to a birthday party in Sherman Oaks for someone in the program.

When they arrived, John paused at the door, taking it all in. The condo was stylish, with soft lighting, modern furniture, and the faint smell of delicious food wafting from the kitchen.

He loved AA parties; the unspoken bond made conversation easier, stuttering or not. Jazz played in the background, voices rose and fell, and laughter spilled from the living room where musicians swapped war stories.

He mingled politely, scanning faces, making small talk.

Then, as he was standing in the hallway, he saw her – a petite blonde walking toward him with an elegance so unassuming it felt magnetic.

'John,' someone said, snapping him back to the moment. 'This is Judy McHugh.'

17 OIL AND WATER

John introduced himself, struck by Judy's presence despite the puffiness in her face from detoxing. She was coming off 'a drunk to end all drunks', she said – a year of round-the-clock drinking. Yet tonight, she had generously opened her home to celebrate her friend's birthday. *Poised but stressed*, John thought.

Even though she was still in the early stages of recovery, Judy radiated something John couldn't name.

'She was attractive, alright,' he admitted, 'but she had something else in her that was not familiar to me. It was a kind of style that wasn't "of the streets."'

What came across in her voice, her presence, was something deeper.

'Even in her depression from all the booze, there was a solidness, innocence, and dignity in the way she spoke and presented herself,' John said. '"Class" is an insufficient word, because she was more than that. Whatever it was, was webbed into her very nature. She had the regalness of royalty, and it was inimitable.'

Meeting Judy was like encountering two people at once: one solid, unshakable, and dignified; the other raw, broken, and still navigating her way out of a devastating year. It was a contrast that intimidated yet intrigued John. *What is it with this woman?* he thought. *I have to find out.*

Judy had a piano in the house. As the guests filtered out, John walked toward it. Judy watched, curious as he slid onto the bench. He'd been quiet most of the evening, a man skimming the edges of the room.

'He was shy and frightened and didn't socialize much,' she said. But now, as his fingers found the keys, he fascinated her.

'Put me in a room of 200 people,' Judy later said, 'and I'll find the piano player.'

John played a slow bass line with his left hand, his voice rising softly to meet it.

Judy stood still, transfixed. The room, now empty, seemed to disappear.

Oh my God, she thought. 'I knew in an instant I was hearing someone extraordinary.'

John felt it too.

'She dug me, and I dug her,' he said.

They began spending time together, lingering after meetings, and talking late into the night. But there was a snag: the one-year no-dating recommendation.

Judy was only weeks sober, and her footing was still shaky despite years of trying to quit drinking.

Her friends noticed what was happening and pulled her aside.

'This'll never work,' one said. 'Oil and water,' said another. Or, simply, 'Are you *crazy?*'

Judy ignored them. She kept inviting John over. They would talk for hours about addiction, shame, and what had brought them here. John learned about her first husband, Eddie Kafafian, with whom she'd had a son, Lee, who was studying in New York. She had divorced her second husband, Joe Harnell, in 1984; the trigger for her most recent drinking binge.

She told John about her famous family, but unlike most, he wasn't drawn to her because of it. He saw Judy, not her lineage. He understood the flight from self, the depression, the failed rehab, and those terrifying moments waking up facing hospital ceilings.

In those first few months, he shared his own story – his childhood, his marriage to Marcia, every awful detail. Judy didn't flinch. She intuitively understood the shame wrapped around his stutter.

'Stuttering can do to the soul what cancer does to the body,' she would later say. She *got it*.

By 1988, the question arose of whether John should move in. Judy's roommate had left. John agreed on one condition – he'd take the spare room.

'I had to have *my* room to live *my* life,' John said. 'After all, I was the vicar of codependent recovery, and I wasn't about to let anyone step on my boundaries. The truth is … I was afraid of losing myself again.'

Judy accepted it. She was patient with John, who had memorized the twelve steps but had barely begun to live them.

'I was literally a baby in the program, and Judy, though she struggled with sobriety, was the veteran,' John said.

But soon, John tried to lay all his ACA discoveries on Judy.

'I had an answer for every problem, action, behaviour and gesture that went on in my life and hers,' he said. 'I would like to say I meant well, and my intentions were good, but in retrospect I see that my intentions were to control, to "present her to herself,"' he remembered. 'I had barely begun to learn the meaning of minding my own business.'

Judy wasn't having it. She stood firm. *You have your path*, she told him. *I have mine*.

Unsettled, John joined CODA, another twelve-step program, this time for codependency. He needed to understand why a functional relationship felt so hard.

'I had become addicted to the program,' he reflected, 'and the very nature of any addictive process is to keep a person from their own pain. I was using the information as a safeguard against what the information was saying.'

As John wrestled with all this, his father's health declined. In early 1989, doctors diagnosed Bill with bowel cancer. They had to operate, but Bill didn't survive the surgery. He died on 29 March 1989.

'It was better that he did,' John said. 'He had suffered long enough.'

After the funeral, his grief tangled and unresolved, John and Judy kept trying to get along, but they were fighting constantly.

'Of course, I didn't know that what I was doing was just another fucking victim of survival mechanisms that weren't working anymore,' John said. 'They were working against us.'

John packed up and moved out, convinced it was better that he and Judy temporarily split. With a small inheritance from his father, he moved into his own place near his mother and stayed in solitude, with no dating and no distractions.

But Judy wasn't giving up. The silver lining of her childhood was a razor-sharp instinct for star quality. She'd grown up hearing the best – Frank Sinatra, Johnny Mathis – playing in her grandfather's living room.

'I don't think John had a clue as to how talented he really was,' she said. 'I knew instinctively how to "handle" John and very gently began to guide and direct him.'

Unable to stay apart, John and Judy had reunited by 1990, and John promised to stop letting his faulty belief systems sabotage them. Judy, meanwhile, was determined to revive his stalled career.

'She started gearing me,' he said. 'She was the one who got me to pay attention and start owning my music again.'

John was playing intermittent gigs around LA, including North Hollywood's Iguana Café, a beloved anti-trend sanctuary described by the *Los Angeles Times* as 'The land of the unemployed misfit' where John kept afloat by passing a can for tips.

Judy's modest income from her family's trust filled the gaps, but it wasn't sustainable, and something had to change.

The answer came unexpectedly from Jim Miller, John's old drummer friend, who was also playing at the Iguana Café. He'd just returned from Germany and was raving about it. There was a lively jazz scene there, he told John. A real one.

That night, John walked through the door, looked at Judy, and said:

'We're going to Berlin.'

18 ON THE SUNNY SIDE OF THE STREET

The sharp clang of chisels on concrete rang through the air as the taxi inched along Berlin's crowded streets. John and Judy pressed their faces to the windows. There it was – The Wall – a jagged scar of concrete and wire, tattooed with bursts of graffiti.

Clusters of *Mauerspechte* ('Wall Peckers') chipped away at it with hammers and chisels, sending chunks crashing to the ground; the city's history crumbling as fast as it was being written.

They crawled past newly opened checkpoints, where East German Trabants sputtered beside sleek Western Audis. East Berliners streamed through on foot, clutching 'welcome money', eyes wide at supermarket aisles overflowing with goods they'd only seen on illicit TV broadcasts. West Berliners crossed in the other direction, curious to explore the grey streets of the East that had been forbidden for so long.

The taxi turned onto a narrow street lined with dilapidated buildings and dark windows.

'Kreuzberg', the driver announced as they rolled to a stop. John and Judy staggered out, dragging four oversized suitcases onto the sidewalk.

A month earlier, they'd rented out their condo, thrown their belongings into storage, and booked flights to Germany in a giddy rush of momentum and faith. The idea felt exhilarating. Spontaneous. Romantic.

At the airport, exhausted but elated, they smiled at strangers and chirped, 'So nice to be in your country!' The stares didn't faze them; they were too thrilled to care.

Judy confessed she'd always had a fantasy of being a 'bag lady', free of possessions, living day to day. As they shuffled through the terminal with their cases, John nudged her.

'Feel like your secret wish has come true?' he laughed.

Their only contact in Berlin was through AA – a friend's sister, Gretchen, who'd offered them a spare room. It seemed ideal – a soft landing in an unfamiliar city. They had no idea that Kreuzberg, once pinned against the Wall on three sides, was one of the poorest districts in West Berlin.

Now they'd arrived at Gretchen's door, their confidence wavered. A haze of coal smoke hung in the air, laced with fried onions and damp. Punks and squatters clustered in doorways of gutted buildings. Somewhere nearby, a techno bassline thumped – music that would soon define not just Berlin's rebirth, but John's, too.

They rang the doorbell, and down came Gretchen, muttering something about not having time to clean. She led them to the spare room. Inside was a small, filthy mattress shoved into the corner with a heap of mismatched sofa pillows tossed on top. Everything smelled of stale alcohol.

The door clicked shut.

John stared at Judy, dread pooling in his stomach. *What have we done?*

Too exhausted to think, they decided to sleep on it. John gave Judy the mattress and curled up beside her on the sofa pillows.

'We snuggled as best we could,' he remembered. 'All we had was each other.'

Neither of them slept much in a haze of jet lag and culture shock, so a few hours later they ventured out to explore. Judy tied a bandana around her head, declaring it made her look German. John chuckled at his ballsy Beverly Hills girlfriend, throwing herself into Kreuzberg without a second thought.

They soon discovered they'd arrived in a city not just in upheaval, but where English wasn't widely spoken either. Life slowed to a crawl as even simple errands like buying bread or milk felt like an obstacle course. After a few days adjusting, they heard about an American-style mall in the city called the Europa Center. Curious and restless, they caught a bus into Berlin and wandered through the streets until they saw it: a three-story hub of shops and cafés resembling the kind of malls they were used to.

Outside, John stared at the Kaiser Wilhelm Memorial Church, its shattered spire jutting into the sky. 'The Hollow Tooth', as Berliners called it, was left as a reminder of World War II. It unsettled John, as he thought of the conflict that was raging when he was born. Judy, who had Jewish ancestry on the Cantor side of her family, was rattled too.

'I could feel something immediately,' John remembered. 'A strain, if you will, in the spirit of the people that was etched from the after-effects.'

After a few hours of walking around, they were ready to head back. But they hadn't written down or remembered the bus number or the stop where they'd got off. They had no idea how to get back to Kreuzberg.

They got on what seemed like the right bus, but as the blocks rolled past, they saw nothing familiar outside the window. John stood and approached the driver.

'W-Will th-th-this bbbbus,' he began.

The driver frowned at John. *He's looking at me like I'm crazy*, John thought. A common reaction to his stutter. He tried again.

'Wuh-wuh-will this bbbbus t-t-take us to K-K-K-K …'

John held the handrail, leaning over to the driver. Judy stayed seated. She knew better than to speak for him. But the driver cut him off.

'*Sit down!*' he barked.

John returned to his seat, heat rising in his face. He could see Judy was getting anxious. *Where were they going?*

John stood up once more, only for a passenger to shout: 'Sit down!'

John and Judy tumbled off the bus at the next stop.

'We were frozen in fear,' John said. A man walked by and saw them stranded, gibbering on the sidewalk. He shook his head and hailed a cab.

'That was all we had to do,' John said. 'Flag down a cab. Sounds simple, doesn't it? But it's a remote idea when you're panicked to that degree.'

In the back seat, John silently handed the driver a slip of paper with Gretchen's address on it.

A couple of days later, they decided to try again. If they got lost, they reassured themselves, they could always hail a cab.

They went back to the Europa Center. It was a Sunday, and the building was buzzing with shoppers. Over the crowd noise, swinging band music floated through the air. John and Judy stopped, not believing what they were hearing. It was one of Judy's grandfather's songs, transformed into a Dixieland arrangement.

They followed the sound to the second floor, where a seven-piece band was playing to an enthusiastic crowd.

When the song ended, John walked over and introduced himself to the trumpet player, a man in a black cowboy vest. Jimmy Wallat spoke good English and listened as John and Judy explained they were visiting from the US – and that Judy's grandfather had written the song they'd just played.

John asked if he could sit in and play another McHugh tune, and Jimmy agreed.

'The next thing I know,' John remembered, 'I was singing "On the Sunny Side of the Street".'

Shoppers gathered around, and when John finished, they yelled and applauded.

'The audience went nuts,' John said. 'I'd established my first musical communication in Europe – and it was a smash.'

Jimmy Wallat and his wife, Ingrid, quickly became their friends. Jimmy got John some work with his Magnolia Jazz Band, and promised to line up hotel bookings too. They bonded over their love of Louis Armstrong. Jimmy, to John's delight, could nail a spot-on Satchmo impression in both voice and trumpet.

There was more than enough work to go around – Berlin's reunification had created a golden moment for musicians of all stripes, and venues were popping up everywhere.

Techno, born in Detroit's Black clubs from funk and electro roots, had landed in Berlin like a match on dry grass. With the Wall down, a generation took over and partied in the ruins of abandoned factories, East German power stations, or even old air-raid bunkers with no ventilation and wild acoustics. There were no rules, no curfews, and no permits – just sound systems, strobe lights, and the 'four on the floor' 4/4 beat. The dancefloor was a place to disappear and be reborn, where nobody cared who you were.

Meanwhile, jazz and soul were also sweeping across East Berlin. Audiences long starved of Western music were eager to hear it, and for a performer like John, whose baritone carried the warmth of old-school American jazz, the timing couldn't have been better.

In February 1990, he was booked at Café Moskau, an iconic relic of East Berlin's socialist heyday, its sleek modernist exterior crowned with a life-sized replica Sputnik above the entrance.

Inside, the café still had retro, mid-century elegance: polished wood, geometric light fixtures, and clean, minimalist lines. Slightly worn but sonically rich, the intimate space was ideal for John's swinging versions of standards like 'Have You Met Miss Jones' or 'Makin' Whoopee', a song popularized decades earlier by Judy's other grandfather, Eddie Cantor.

At the end of the set, John swept his fingers across the piano keys in a final flourish.

The 400-strong crowd rose to their feet, applauding.

'I began to own that I really could sing, that I was good,' he later said. 'The German people were of great help. They loved me. That changed my whole attitude.'

John's confidence was up, and gigs were coming in, but John and Judy couldn't escape the alcoholic vibes of Gretchen's apartment. West Germany's housing market was overwhelmed. As people poured in from the East, rentals were impossible to find, hotels were booked solid, and apartment waiting lists stretched over a year. They were stuck.

John had adapted quickly. He considered himself 'of the streets' and was fine with chaos and unpredictability. But Judy struggled. She hustled alongside him for gigs, but her evenings were often spent alone while John performed. They found some English-speaking AA meetings, but her loneliness deepened. Making friends felt impossible, since she didn't speak German.

Her Jewish ancestry meant she was uncomfortable in Germany, even though nobody had said anything unpleasant to her. At every turn, she was reminded – consciously or not – of where she was. She grew restless and disorientated, then hot flashes and mood swings added to the stress. She began opening up at meetings, admitting how isolated she felt.

She had just turned 50, and on a drive with Jimmy and Ingrid to one of John's gigs in northern Germany, Judy handed John an article about menopause and its link to depression.

For John, this was a wake-up call. Until now, he believed working the Twelve Steps could fix anything.

'It was true for me,' he said, 'but Judy had some other problems that were physical and I refused to see them. My not being any help probably only served to escalate her depression, and it got worse.'

They booked flights home, but just as they were preparing to leave, Judy said she was feeling better. This was the first of several pairs of plane tickets they'd buy and never use.

In the spring of 1990, they got a break: a gig at a high-end club called Chez Alex. Best of all, the job came with an apartment.

Singer and musician Rashidii Graffiti was at the club when John arrived and introduced himself, stuttering heavily. Then he sat down at the piano, and Rashidii listened as John suddenly sang totally fluently.

'He's singing his butt off,' Rashidii remembers. 'I said, well, this guy just fooled me, right? I didn't realize he stuttered.'

John got the gig, and at one of the first performances, he asked for a Coke. But the bartender, used to serving rum and Coke for Rashidii, mistakenly served John the same.

Rashidii remembers John took a sip, froze, then spat it violently onto the floor. Chez Alex's lush carpets be damned – getting the alcohol out of his mouth was all that mattered.

The gig was steady and the apartment was theirs if they wanted it. It should have been the turning point. But it was too late.

'Judy's depression was at full blossom,' John said.

She had begun self-soothing by talking aloud to herself. Sometimes she rambled. Sometimes she didn't make any sense.

We have to leave, John thought. He didn't give any notice. They went to Gretchen's, packed their things, and were on the next flight out. As Berlin disappeared beneath the clouds, John exhaled.

Once back in the US, however, the emotional hangover set in quickly. Their condo was still rented, so John and Judy moved into a hotel – and fought nonstop. Each had their version of what had happened, of why the trip had failed.

In Berlin, their new friends and fellow musicians were confused, wondering why they'd disappeared without a word. John resented the way he'd left – unprofessional and unfinished.

Judy felt John had never truly understood how alien and overwhelming Berlin was for her. The city's appreciation for jazz didn't matter, she said, when everything else felt so cold and unfamiliar. John thought she hadn't given herself time to adjust.

Judy, in turn, said he'd minimized her struggle and refused to see how unprepared she was.

There was no resolution. The fights intensified.

'The arrival of separation number two had approached,' John said. 'It seemed worse when we were together than apart.'

After a particularly vicious argument, John had enough. Through a mutual friend, he found a vacant studio apartment and, without ceremony, gathered his belongings, packed up his keyboard, and left.

19 U-TURN

Pass by John Larkin's cramped studio apartment on most summer days in 1990, and you'd catch the sound of clattering keys – what kind depended on the hour.

Mornings and afternoons, it was the tapping of a computer keyboard as John hunted and pecked his way through WordPerfect; word processing software installed by a friend who'd convinced John to buy his first computer.

At night, the room filled with cascading jazz riffs from John's electronic keyboard, his fingers flowing with skill that belied the lack of confidence that still crept into his live performances.

Typing became a new obsession, and John tried to master it the same way he had the piano. When he reached a decent speed, the prospect of a steady paycheck in a non-verbal office job was enough to tempt him into applying for one. But when the typing test came, nerves took over and he flunked it. The familiar sting of rejection reminded him why he rarely ventured into the 'day world'. He returned instead to the unforgiving grind of LA's jazz scene, where steady gigs were scarce, competition was fierce, and clubs were struggling with rising costs.

He and Judy were still circling each other, unable to stay apart.

'I didn't realize it then,' John said, 'we really loved each other. We just didn't know how to live with each other.'

Returning to Europe felt impossible after Berlin, so with Judy's encouragement, John pushed harder for work in LA. He needed a demo tape, so he called his drummer friend Jim Miller and bassist Nils Johnson, and booked a session with engineer Richard Rosen.

Over a few intense hours, John led the trio through forty takes of jazz standards, all covers ranging from Fats Waller's 'Ain't Misbehavin'' and Miles Davis's 'So What' to a rendition of Thelonious Monk's 'Well You Needn't', the latter complete with ninety seconds of improvisational scat-singing.

John's stutter never stopped him from directing his band, demanding retakes, or reminding them to loosen up. 'Don't have it all that exact. Take it easy; it isn't Carnegie Hall, man. It's cool,' he told them. Then, he joked: 'We all get some heroin after this!'

As usual, his biggest critic was himself. 'I'm overdoing it,' he muttered between takes, or tutted or scolded himself for 'trying to get fancy.'

He picked nine tracks. *John Larkin Sings* was dubbed onto cassette. Judy put her old agent hat on and took charge of promoting it. Each tape was printed with 'Judy McHugh Management' and her phone and fax numbers.

The two were slowly reconciling their differences, and John began to see that he might have been the problem.

'I was still selfish,' he admitted, 'as I needed to be at that time. I had to protect my sobriety at all costs.'

Though John and Marcia were now divorced, Judy felt insecure, and Berlin had left her wondering if he'd vanish again when things got difficult.

'Judy needed to know I wasn't going to run anymore when the temperature got hot,' he said. 'I made the decision that I was going to be with her for good, and let her know it.'

John's commitment brought an end to the volatile, ping-pong nature of their four years together.

'That was what the relationship really needed,' he said, 'because the fighting stopped.'

In late 1990, John and Judy went to a jazz concert at the Biltmore Hotel's Grand Avenue Bar, hosted by Diane Varga, a well-known jazz performer and promoter in Los Angeles. They went for the music, but Judy had an ulterior motive to get John's tape into the right hands.

After the show, Judy handed Diane a copy of *John Larkin Sings*. Less than 24 hours later, Diane called. 'She was raving about the tape,' John said. Diane told Judy she'd get John bookings – starting with Lunaria's, a prestigious jazz supper club on Santa Monica Boulevard known for showcasing major jazz talent.

My introduction into the big leagues, John thought. But there was a catch. Clubs at that level expected the full package. You couldn't just play – you had to chat to the crowd between songs.

'I was scared to death and hadn't yet developed any real confidence,' John admitted. 'We were talking spotlights and all, and – the horror of horrors – I would be talking to my audiences. Me, the stutterer.'

He had always hidden behind the piano. Looking cool, shades on, never having to utter a word.

'My speaking off stage would never let me forget that awful thorn in my side,' John said. 'I would pretend that I didn't stutter. It was as if I was going through life trying to conceal the fact that an elephant was following me everywhere I went.'

Now, just the thought of speaking onstage turned John into an anxious mess. Judy saw what he couldn't: that downplaying or hiding his stutter was the real problem – it made people uncomfortable because *he* was. She told him to incorporate it into his act.

'Go out there as you are,' she told him. 'You're *enough*, John.'

Judy's advice wasn't just practical; it was rooted in a principle long advocated by the stuttering community: disclosure. By openly acknowledging his stutter, John could remove tension and avoid misunderstandings. Many stutterers know horror stories of listeners mistaking dysfluent speech for medical emergencies like seizures or strokes, or worse, of law enforcement arresting people for appearing nervous or evasive, misreading stuttering as a sign of lying or guilt.

Judy's point was clear: if John owned it, his stutter could become a tool for connection. Reluctantly, he agreed. He took the Lunaria gig and tried a little disclosure.

'It was a struggle at first,' he admitted. 'I wasn't able to do it very much.'

Still, his playing and scat-singing did most of the talking, as always. The crowd loved him so much that Lunaria booked him three nights a week, though they did scold him for playing too loud.

'I was still trying to assault my audiences with my lingering insecurity about my playing and singing,' he said. He wasn't used to performing for discerning clientele. But slowly, he realized he wasn't just there to fill space. He was there because he was good.

The buzz grew. His name started popping up in jazz listings for both the *LA Times* and *LA Weekly*.

'His scat – worth hearing,' noted the *Times*, and *LA Weekly* called him 'Scatman John Larkin.' In December 1990, he was interviewed by Zan Stewart for the *Los Angeles Times*.

'John Larkin can hardly get through a sentence without coming upon a word that takes six or seven attempts to get out,' the article began. It explored how his stutter shaped his scat-singing, his reception in Germany, and how he was looking forward to the future. 'I'm just trying to say, Hello World,' he told Stewart.

John cut out the article and kept it. Yet, despite the praise, the shame around his speech still gnawed at him. It was holding him back, and he knew it.

It was time, he decided, to finally face the elephant.

'I'm here to talk about my stuttering,' John said, all eyes on him.

Gail Wilson Lew, a speech-language therapist who also stutters, remembers it clearly. 'He walks in, and he sits down and says, "I've had alcohol, drugs, and now I'm sober. And now I want to figure out my stuttering."' John had just shown up at her Los Angeles chapter of the National Stuttering Project (NSP).

He was nearly 50. He'd faced his addictions. Now it was time to face what he'd spent a lifetime avoiding.

'A stutterer's problem is no more stuttering than an alcoholic's problem is liquor,' he later wrote. He wasn't chasing fluency – he was looking for freedom: from shame, silence, and denial.

At the time, most speech therapy still focused on fixing the stutter itself, not the emotions underneath. But the NSP – now the National Stuttering Association – offered space for choice and connection through self-help groups. Some members wanted tools to speak more easily. Others, like John, sought acceptance. There was – and still is – no single path.

'I always thought John was very comfortable talking anywhere,' Gail said. 'But maybe he was more comfortable because he knew I stuttered, too.'

John became a regular at the LA meetings.

'I was growing,' he said later, 'and the world was shrinking into its proper perspective.'

As John began to confront the shame he'd carried for so long, he moved back in with Judy. But he made one thing clear: no more talk about Europe. Judy agreed, but as the weeks went on, his three-night-a-week gig and her modest trust fund still weren't enough to pay the bills.

'She was pretty good about it outwardly,' John said. 'But inwardly, she had other ideas.'

Judy, gently but persistently, urged John to reconsider. By the end of 1991, he relented. They packed up their lives once more, threw everything back into storage, rented out their condo, and boarded a plane – this time to Amsterdam. Fifteen hours later, they arrived, ready to give Europe another shot.

John noticed that Judy was different this time. She was more grounded and more prepared to rough it. He admired her for that. Through an AA contact, they secured an apartment before they got there, avoiding the missteps they'd made in Berlin. They anchored themselves with English-speaking AA meetings, too, giving their new life a quick shot of stability.

In the kitchen of one such meeting was Stacey Heaver, who was there more for the free coffee and cookies than sobriety. She'd been born in Germany but came to Amsterdam to make a career with a dance company, building and painting sets. But her ambitions had derailed.

'I was too busy drinking and having a good time,' she says. The work dried up, leaving her destitute and alone, squatting in abandoned buildings and scraping by.

That night, she was rifling through the meeting's kitchen for leftovers when John and Judy walked in.

The meetings usually had a heavy, despairing vibe, Stacey thought, as people 'shared' – AA's term for speaking openly about struggles or victories. Then Judy stood up. *What the hell?* Stacey thought as she listened to Judy share. *My God, she's a shining light.*

After the meeting, afraid Judy might vanish like a dream, Stacey introduced herself. She was dishevelled, thin, had uncombed hair, bad teeth, and wore a dirty leather jacket – the only clothes she owned. She asked Judy to be her sponsor.

In AA, a sponsor is a more experienced member who provides guidance, support, and accountability to someone new. Judy said yes.

'Judy saved many lives, including my own,' Stacey says. 'She was the first friend in my life who told me that everything was going to be OK. She let me be me.'

The three of them would tramp through Amsterdam's streets late at night, often starting at 11 p.m., searching for jazz clubs where John could make introductions. Without cell phones or directories, they wandered on foot, hoping to stumble across a venue.

Stacey remembers John walking in, asking: 'Uh, is it p-p-p-p-possible to juh-juh-join in with the b-b-b-band?' Owners and patrons eyed him skeptically, puzzled by this 49-year-old man who struggled to speak, roaming the city with two women. John had also just had his ear pierced after Judy said it would look good. Some of the clubs ignored him. Others laughed. Some shut the door.

But those who gave him a chance were often surprised. John would sit down at the house piano and unleash a whirlwind, stretching tunes to twenty minutes of improvisational solo before skillfully reeling it back to the original melody.

'It was fantastic,' Stacey said.

Word spread. A trumpet player named Yoost befriended John and introduced him to musicians on the local scene. One of them was Mike Del Ferro, a young jazz pianist whose trio recorded another demo with John.

'Scat-singing at that level requires a lot of different skills,' he says. 'You cannot just go *shooby-dooby-do* and then it's going to sound great. You really need to know about the chord structure, the harmonies. It's another level of singing.'

Clare Foster, a British jazz vocalist, ran vocal sessions at Heeren van Amstel in Thorbeckeplein, and John occasionally performed with her.

'He had the energy of a lion,' she recalls. 'He just went onto the bandstand with this unbelievable energy.' Clare sometimes rehearsed with John and Judy at their apartment, but admits, 'I was quite intimidated by his talent.'

Work was still hard to come by, but eventually, an agent named Hans offered John a six-week run over the Christmas season at The Boeddha, a Chinese-themed restaurant. They hyped him in their ads as 'the fantastic international pianist/singer John Larkin,' promising ballads, blues, evergreens, and soft jazz. But John mostly knew jazz.

Complaints trickled in. Customers expected pop songs and weren't hearing them. Word got back to Hans, who came in to see for himself.

John spotted Hans in the audience as he played.

'I still remember his face,' John said. 'I felt like I was on trial.'

Hans sat frowning through John's jazz-heavy set. *He thinks I've deceived him*, John thought.

That night, the phone rang. Judy answered. It was Hans, and his message was short and clear. Not only was John's Christmas gig cancelled, but every other booking Hans had arranged was gone, too.

Just like that, John was fired.

FIGURE 1 John (left) aged around 9 months, with his older brother Billy (right) 1942 © Larkin Family Archive

FIGURE 2 John the cowboy, aged around 5 © Larkin Family Archive

FIGURE 3 John with his parents, Harriet and Bill, at his 8th grade graduation © Larkin Family Archive

FIGURE 4 John aged 18, about to start college © Larkin Family Archive

FIGURE 5 John (second from left) as the organist in septet Groove-Fuss in 1966 © Larkin Family Archive

FIGURE 6 John (left) with his bandmate Sam Provenzano in the early 1970s Photo © Mimi Smith

FIGURE 7 Marcia, John and Harriet in the late 1970s © Larkin Family Archive

FIGURE 8 John with Marcia's grandson Jonathan in 1981. Photo used with kind permission of Shelley Gilman

FIGURE 9 The John Larkin Quartet in 1985: Joe Farrell, John Larkin, Bob Harrison, Clark Woodard © John and Judy Larkin Archive, courtesy of Lee Newman

FIGURE 10 John performing jazz in Amsterdam, circa 1993 © John and Judy Larkin Archive, courtesy of Lee Newman

FIGURE 11 Judy and John's wedding reception, 1994 © John and Judy Larkin Archive, courtesy of Lee Newman

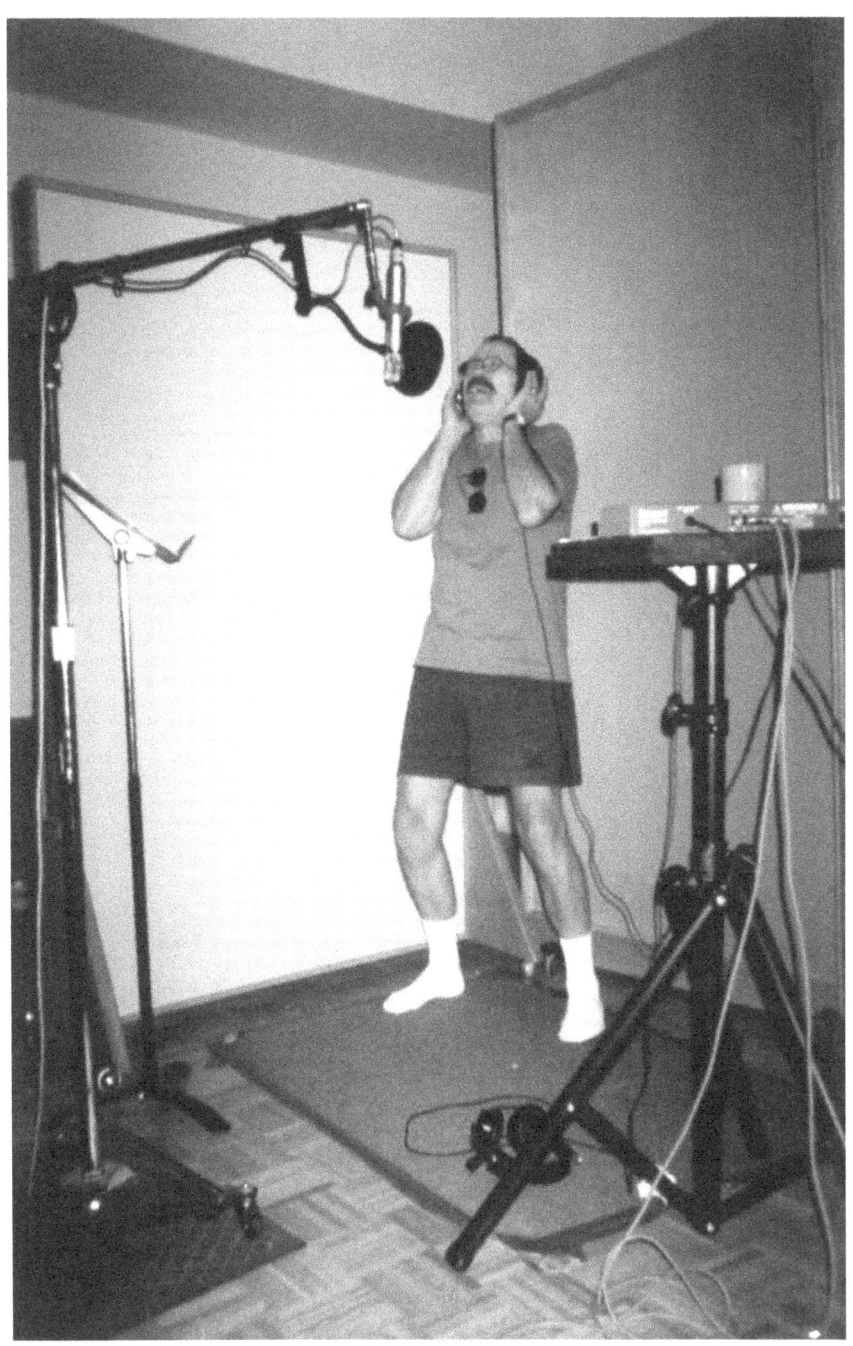

FIGURE 12 John singing and chewing nicotine gum at the same time at Enterprise Studios, 1995 Unknown photographer / RCA-BMG session, courtesy of Iceberg Records

FIGURE 13 John and the 'architects of Scatman', Tony Catania (left) and Ingo Kays (right) Photo: H. Choi in *Fachblatt Magazine*, 1995

FIGURE 14 The Scatman John craze spreads across Europe, 1995 © John and Judy Larkin Archive, courtesy of Lee Newman

FIGURE 15 Manfred and Mette Zahringer presenting John with his first Gold awards, 1995 © Iceberg Records

FIGURE 16 John accepts flowers from children at a press conference for Ultraman's cover of Scatman, Japan, 1995 © Iceberg Records

FIGURE 17 John shows the crowd his shoeless feet, Hungary, 1996 © photo by morpho

FIGURE 18 John entertaining Japanese fans, 1996 © John and Judy Larkin Archive, courtesy of Lee Newman

FIGURE 19 John performing in Kaunas, Lithuania in October 1997. His last public performances. Used with kind permission of Vaidas Stackevičius

FIGURE 20 John, Judy and her son, John's stepson Lee Newman with their beloved animals, circa 1997 © John and Judy Larkin Archive, courtesy of Lee Newman

20 DON'T KILL ME, BUT I HAVE AN IDEA

The autobahn stretched ahead like a steel blade as Manfred Zähringer sped out of Frankfurt. Small towns blew by at 220 kilometers per hour, the headlights of his BMW slicing through the darkness. To his right, trucks lumbered along the slow lane, while the left belonged to sleek sedans, roaring sports cars, and the occasional reckless idiot pushing a clunky Opel past its limits.

Manfred slid the cassette tape into the car's deck and leaned back against the leather seat, one hand on the wheel, the other cradling a glowing Monte Cristo cigar. Smoke curled from his lips as the tape spun to life. He cracked the window slightly, letting the cold air rush in, nipping his face and stirring his ponytail against the seatback. Ahead, the faint glow of Hanover smudged the horizon, but it wasn't the city that held his attention now.

It was the tape.

John's voice soared and tumbled through Thelonious Monk's 'Well You Needn't'. A torrent of scat-singing – unrestrained yet precise – burst through the car speaker. It was manic, audacious, electrifying. John's lungs seemed bottomless, firing syllables with machine-like force. This wasn't just skill. It was audacity. The kind of audacity Manfred admired.

A slow car wandered into the left lane ahead, breaking the spell. Manfred cursed softly and flicked his high beams – once, twice – a silent but firm command, forcing the car to slink back into the right lane like a chastised dog.

He exhaled a plume of cigar smoke, listening again as John began Fats Waller's 'Ain't Misbehavin'; a seamless combination of scatting and swing that transported Manfred to the smoky, riotous jazz clubs of the 1920s.

Years ago, Manfred had been the one on stage, guitar in hand. But that was a different life, back in Konstanz, Germany, before he swapped the limelight for spreadsheets and studios in Denmark. Now, Iceberg Records was his baby, and if he wasn't the one playing, at least he was the one deciding who did.

His cigar glowed in the rearview mirror as John belted out 'The Song Is You', the piano crescendos and sharp, staccato stabs raising Manfred's eyebrows as he flicked the stub towards the BMW's ashtray.

His decision made, Manfred pulled into a gas station, strode to a payphone, and dialed the Intercontinental Hotel in Frankfurt where John was staying. Speaking carefully in German, he instructed the receptionist to leave a message for John's room in English. The receptionist laughed, scribbled it down, and hung up.

The Intercontinental was one of a string of high-end hotels where John had been working in recent months. After John was fired in Amsterdam for not knowing enough pop, Judy, devastated but undeterred, kept pushing John's demo tape around the city. The results were disheartening. They took the train to Germany to give the country a second chance, and John landed gigs in a few bars and at the newly opened Treudelberg Hotel outside Hamburg. But when that ended, they were back to square one. They detoured to Spain, for both a vacation and to expand their options.

They met a pianist there who introduced them to Martin Skibb, a German agent running a Danish agency called Pan with his friend Manfred Zähringer. Pan specialized in booking residential artists – in-house musicians who delivered polished, crowd-pleasing sets for cruise ships and luxury hotels.

Anticipating the expectations of this new world, John reshaped his sets. He'd recorded a new demo of what he jokingly referred to as 'watered-down' standards – no scat-singing, no creative piano improvisations, just straight-ahead, reliable entertainment. He also expanded his repertoire, adding evergreens and pop hits by Sinatra, Elton John, and the Beatles to avoid another embarrassment like the one at The Boeddha.

The compromise paid off. Martin Skibb secured John a job aboard the *Dana Anglia*, a cruise ship shuttling between Esbjerg, Denmark, and Harwich, England, followed by a string of bookings playing in luxury hotels.

Judy, however, remained frustrated. While John didn't complain, she sensed his unhappiness. 'He wasn't too fond of these engagements,' she said. 'A lot of drunks, nobody listened.'

John had once compared his life to the 1989 movie *The Fabulous Baker Boys*, a has-been pianist playing while people drank, talked over him, and treated him like wallpaper.

Another musician, John Morrell, remembered venting to John about the loud, intoxicated patrons at his own gig. Curious, he came to see John play at what was supposed to be a more upscale venue. Partway through, a tipsy woman stumbled and flung her drink all over the piano.

'Same gig. Different clothes,' John quipped.

Still, he was grateful. *How many jazz piano players like me can say they make a living playing piano?* he thought. *This is as good as it gets for a jazzer like me.*

But Judy wasn't satisfied. She was convinced that hotels and restaurants were 'hardly the venue for John's talent' and knew Manfred owned Iceberg Records alongside running Pan. So when Manfred mentioned he was coming to visit John at the Intercontinental, Judy slipped a copy of the *John Larkin Sings* cassette into her jacket pocket and went downstairs to the piano lounge to meet him.

John had never met Manfred before, but as soon as he saw him, he began a dramatic, show-stopping rendition of 'As Time Goes By', with every note calculated to draw greater-than-usual applause from the crowd. Manfred looked impressed, so Judy pounced and asked him about the possibility of getting John on a record.

'He made it very clear he was not interested in jazz,' Judy remembered, 'and would not be at all interested in the tape I had concealed in my pocket.'

Manfred explained that, while he truly loved jazz – it was the music of his youth – it wasn't a commercially viable path. Iceberg Records had learned the hard way when, early on, he and his wife Mette had chosen artists they loved rather than ones who could sell. It was a mistake they couldn't afford to repeat. Jazz, no matter how good, wasn't part of the equation.

The conversation wound down, and Manfred was heading out the door. Judy made her move.

'I wasn't about to let him leave without the tape,' she said. She knew John's 'watered-down' repertoire didn't capture what he was capable of. What Manfred needed to hear was the scat-singing on *John Larkin Sings*. Somehow, she persuaded Manfred to take the tape and listen to it on his drive back home.

Later that night, Judy and John returned to their hotel room at the Intercontinental. The TV blinked with a new message from Manfred. John loaded it up.

'IT'S FUCKING GREAT,' it read.

In 1992, John shuttled between Los Angeles and Europe, working as a grand-a-week hotel pianist while Manfred pitched him to jazz labels. Iceberg Records had never released a jazz album, but that didn't deter Manfred. The label itself had been born out of necessity – when no one would record a demo for a band he'd discovered called The Flyers, Manfred decided to do it himself.

John's steady stream of gigs took him all over Europe, though Judy and John kept the Amsterdam apartment as a base. Occasionally, they heard from Manfred about how the album pitches were going. The response was worse than rejection: it was silence.

Meanwhile, John's stable income gave Judy some breathing room away from Europe. Sometimes, she traveled with John, but often, she returned to California, where the familiarity helped her manage her sobriety and mental health. Back in Los Angeles, speech therapist Gail Wilson Lew made sure John received the National Stuttering Project newsletter, *Letting Go*, no matter where he was in the world.

In March 1992, a piece on the front page caught John's attention. Written by 19-year-old Nora O'Connor, who was staying at a California drug and alcohol treatment center, it began: 'Who says stuttering is not a disability? It single-handedly destroyed my life.'

Nora candidly described how stuttering had driven her to self-harm, failed grades, and suicide attempts.

'I'm a lesbian,' she wrote, 'and it would torture me that I couldn't talk to the girls I liked.' She explained how she turned to drugs and alcohol to cope, but ended on a hopeful note, crediting anti-anxiety and antidepressant medication for her newfound fluency.

That final detail raised a red flag to John. He didn't know Nora, but he understood her pain. Sitting in the Amsterdam apartment, he wrote her a letter.

'It worried me when I read that you were taking medication,' he began. 'I must be honest with you and tell you with love: I believe that you are trying to stop the symptom instead of dealing with the cause. Don't shut yourself off from yourself any more. We've both done enough of that. You are whole and precious at this very moment. It will take time for you to realize it.'

John was starting to live the Twelfth Step of AA: helping others. Though he wasn't ready to sponsor anyone, he wanted to pass on what he'd learned. *Go out and try to help people*, he'd been told at meetings. *If you try that, the desire to drink and use drugs will never come back*. It had stuck with him.

'I'll do whatever you want,' he'd said.

Nora remembers receiving a handful of responses to her article, but John's letter stood out because he'd written with depth and care. Their correspondence grew, and John openly shared his story. He described his 'slow, painful flight into a hell' where he was 'literally robbed of a childhood, adolescence, and adulthood. Throughout that entire time, I felt *I didn't matter*, he said, and therefore totally abandoned myself.'

Though sober for nearly six years, John admitted he still struggled, especially when isolated, especially on cruise ships without access to AA meetings.

'I may have left you with a false impression of my progress,' he wrote to her later in 1992. 'Several times during my engagement out here, I have been brought to my knees by this disease, with nowhere to run except to the heart of God via the 12 Steps.'

In his downtime, John called Judy, jotted fragments of his memoir, composed jazz pieces, and meditated. He tore out sections of AA literature and taped them to his wall, including his favorite passage from page 449 of the Big Book: 'When I stopped living in the problem and began living in the answer, the problem went away. Acceptance is the answer to all my problems today.'

He faxed notes to his brother Billy and sister-in-law Sharon, asking them to pass messages to their mother, gradually rebuilding relationships that had long been strained. His family began believing what once seemed impossible: John's sobriety was holding. He was also trying to quit smoking – an addiction he said was harder to beat than heroin.

Despite a few wobbles, John stayed sober, and continued to work in hotels. In early 1994, Manfred visited John at the Montreux Palace Hotel in Switzerland with an announcement.

'I have good news and bad news,' Manfred said.

John asked for the bad news first.

After two years of pitching John to multiple US and European jazz labels, Manfred admitted he'd only had a couple of lukewarm responses that had gone nowhere. It was time to give up, he said. Nobody wanted John on a jazz label.

Although disappointed, John accepted this and asked for the good news.

'John, don't kill me,' Manfred began. 'But I have an idea.'

Manfred explained he wanted to try putting John's scatting into contemporary dance music.

'Doof, doof, doof,' he said, imitating the relentless 4/4 techno beats dominating the charts. Because of John's age – he was now 52 – Manfred proposed that he could play the role of a professor or uncle figure, teaching kids how to scat-sing.

'You could be John Scatman,' Manfred suggested, watching John closely for a reaction. *He's almost certainly going to say no*, he remembered thinking.

'No way, Manfred ...' John began.

I was right, Manfred thought, heart sinking. *A jazz cat would never go for this.*

John turned to look at Manfred with a sly grin.

'I'm not John Scatman,' he declared. 'I'm Scatman John!'

PART TWO

21 THE STUTTER AND THE SCAT IS THE SAME THING

'Scat-rap,' Manfred said, even though he had no idea what such a thing might sound like.

'Scat-rap?' John laughed. 'Oh yeah, sure. Right on, man.'

The idea had struck Manfred the way all his best ones did – while driving. The charts were in flux; dance acts fresh out of nowhere could elbow past big-name stars if they had a catchy or novelty tune. It was a market ripe for a moonshot gamble. If it failed, Manfred reassured John, nobody would need to know.

John didn't follow chart trends, but he remembered sitting in a hotel bar talking to Manfred when 'No Limit' by 2 Unlimited and 'Pump Up The Jam' by Technotronic came through the speakers. Eurodance – with its drum-machine beats, heavy synths, and rapped verses – had been a fixture on European charts since the early '90s.

'Glamorized electronic imitation,' John had once called it, bemoaning the lack of musicians. It was alien territory. But his instincts, sharpened over decades of artistic reinvention, twitched. Pop and jazz were unlikely bedfellows, but at 52, what did he have to lose? The clincher, though, had nothing to do with the music. It was the idea of reaching children.

A few years earlier, John was jogging laps in a Los Angeles park when a little boy ran up to him, talking a mile a minute. Something about the boy's frantic energy and lack of boundaries made John uneasy. He sensed trauma, and backed away from him, recognizing with terrible clarity the learned behaviors of an abused child.

'That kid was me,' John said later. 'I had spent all my childhood willing to be sexual with any man who would give me the unconditional love and acceptance I had been looking for.'

The encounter disturbed John profoundly, and shook loose his own childhood memories. When the boy's father appeared and dragged him away, John couldn't forget what he'd witnessed. Later, he wrote a note: *This world is not a safe place for children.*

'In God's world, there are no coincidences,' he would later say. 'I believe to the fabric of my bones that kid was a Godsend to show me that.'

John had always played for audiences of adults, but now he was considering impressionable young ears. If recording a pop song was the only way to reach them, he reasoned, then so be it.

On 17 January 1994, the 6.7 magnitude Northridge Earthquake struck Los Angeles in the early morning hours.

'I've never seen him so frightened,' remembers Mette Zähringer as John frantically called friends and family back home. He and Judy were thousands of miles away, playing a gig at Reid's Palace Hotel in Funchal, Madeira.

Judy's LA apartment had partially collapsed, and John's portable piano had crashed through the floors below. They had to find somewhere else to live. The disaster jolted them back to LA – and to a decision.

On 24 March 1994, John and Judy quietly married in Laughlin, Nevada. Nobody who knew them was surprised.

'I thought that was terrific,' their friend Gregg Pincus says. 'They were a perfect couple.'

Although FEMA (the Federal Emergency Management Agency) covered some of the damage, 'we still had very little money,' Judy said. Their wedding reception, held at a Mexican restaurant in Los Angeles, had fewer than a dozen guests including Gregg, actor Dick Van Dyke, John's brother Billy, sister-in-law Sharon, and nephew David. John performed as the entertainment, toasting his future with apple juice.

Meanwhile, in Hamburg, Germany, Manfred was sitting in the office of his friend Axel Alexander, head of Artists & Repertoire at BMG Ariola Hamburg. Manfred played him a few bars of John's scat from *John Larkin Sings*. Axel listened. Then he got up, shut the door, and turned back to Manfred.

'Have you signed him yet?'

'Not yet,' Manfred admitted.

'Better sign him,' Axel said. 'Or we will.'

Axel had heard thousands of demos. But this one – John's virtuosic scatting coupled with Manfred's 'Scat-rap' pitch – clicked with the seasoned executive. 'I knew it was something special,' he said. They struck a deal: John would sign with Iceberg Records, and BMG/RCA would handle all territories outside the Nordic countries.

Deal done, Axel and his colleague Janine Ramond (then Becker) searched for dance producers capable of blending John's scat-singing with contemporary sounds. Germany, the cradle of Eurodance, had no shortage of candidates. BMG sent John's scat samples to several producers, but the first demos were underwhelming.

After the 1994 Popkomm music trade show, Janine got a tip from a friend about a young production duo. *They're new*, the friend said, *but they're making very special music*.

Tony Catania and Ingo Kays weren't yet household names, but word was spreading. They'd met by chance on vacation in Spain – a coincidence considering they both lived in Gelsenkirchen, Germany.

Tony, originally from Italy, had been in several bands and played guitar in London's punk and New Wave era before moving to Germany. Ingo, a local, was a skilled producer and keyboardist.

'We were on the same wavelength straight away – we simply had the same ideas about music,' Tony said in a 1995 interview. 'We complemented each other well because I came from more of a live department. Ingo was more technically oriented and worked with keyboards.'

Known for club remixes of acts like DJ Hooligan, Haddaway, Maxx, and Marusha, they'd even worked with Frank Farian of Boney M and Milli Vanilli fame. By 1994, they'd reinvested their earnings into a studio in an attic apartment on Sterkrader Street in Bottrop – a city better known for coal mines than club hits.

Given a copy of *John Larkin Sings*, Ingo and Tony crafted a jazz-tinged dance demo. Manfred and Axel heard it and knew right away: this was the team.

It was time to get John into the studio.

John was still shuttling between California and Europe, working as the resident pianist at the Alexandra Hotel, a luxurious property sandwiched between mountains and fjords in the rural town of Loen, Norway.

'There really isn't a heck of a lot to do here,' John wrote in a letter to his mother, 'kinda like being in the Norwegian Ozarks.'

Everyone knew everybody else's business in a town the size of Loen. Word spread about the hotel's eccentric jazz pianist after John saw the Northern Lights for the first time and reacted with childlike glee.

'It was a spectacle!' John said, 'The whole sky lit up, and the lights did a dance. I was excited and carrying on like a kid. The other people were all laughing.'

When not enjoying the scenery or performing in the dining room every evening, John spent hours in his cabin, endlessly chewing nicotine gum and writing his memoir. He figured his life had been so eventful so far that it was worth documenting. On 15 August 1994, he had no idea just how eventful it was about to get.

Unexpectedly, the phone rang. It was Manfred.

The Scatman idea, he said, was a 'go'.

A couple of months later, Ingo Kays watched their newest musical project step off the train at Essen station, wearing a fedora and looking tired, contrite, and lost.

'He was friendly, but he was a bit suspicious,' Ingo says.

John approached, dragging his small suitcase behind him. Ingo imagined what might be running through John's mind: *What the fuck am I doing here? These dance producers probably only know two or three chords.*

'Are you Iiiiiingo?' John asked, sizing him up.

They went straight to a local Italian restaurant to meet Tony. Over dinner, John realized there was more to these guys than he thought. Tony played saxophone, guitar, and came from a classical background. Ingo played keyboards and could handle electronic instruments, samplers, and computers. They'd been in a band together but had pivoted to dance music and remixing because that's where the opportunities were.

'As producers, we have to focus on what millions want to hear,' Tony told a journalist a few months later. 'We are flexible.'

'Chameleon-like,' Ingo agreed.

John quickly warmed to them. Ingo spoke more English and did most of the talking, since John's stutter sometimes made it hard for Tony to follow. But the next day, it wouldn't matter when John switched to his first language of music.

After a night's rest at the Ramada Hotel in Bottrop, John slung off his shoes and climbed the forty-two steps to the attic studio. He stood in the doorway, catching his breath. The place was modest but serious: 120 compact, functional square meters with a gear-laden recording room, an editing suite, and a small kitchen with a constantly bubbling espresso machine.

To make John comfortable, Tony and Ingo rented the best keyboard they could find – a large Korg with weighted keys. It allowed John to play naturally while the output fed into their MIDI setup for maximum flexibility.

Fueled by his first espresso of the day, John was ready.

'We had zero songs,' Tony says. 'We had nothing.'

The pair told John to improvise over a bass line.

'They gave me an F minor beat,' John remembered, 'and that's all I had.'

For hours, John throat-chanted, growled, yelled, and scat-sang every imaginable syllable his voice box could produce, pausing only for more espresso as every nuance was captured by a Tascam DA-88, one of the latest digital multitrack recorders.

Ingo noticed how calm and focused John was, and Tony admired his professionalism. Despite the quirky circumstances, John approached the process like a seasoned musician. The scatting was done. Now came the part John wasn't so sure about: the rap.

Before boarding the train to Germany, John had a crisis of confidence. The ever-present saboteur was back. Stuttering support groups had helped him address his feelings of shame, but he'd barely begun to work through them. The fact that a single release might become a reality terrified him.

'Any normal artist would have been happy about that kind of news. But not me,' he admitted later. 'My thinking was, Oh my God, *what if the world finds out that I stutter?*'

If it succeeded, John knew there'd be interviews. 'I might have to encounter the horror of horrors – radio,' John said. 'And maybe even, oh no … television.'

John worked himself up into a panic. 'How can I put myself out there with how I talk?' he asked Judy.

Calm as ever, Judy said what she'd always said: Disclosure. *Take off the veil*, she told him. *Start getting into the habit of telling people you stutter*. They both decided that the best way to do this would be through the song itself.

Before the recording, Manfred had told John to bring some lyrics. Dance music usually followed a formula: two verses, sixteen bars each, a chorus, and a bridge. The lyrics were usually simple, lightweight afterthoughts designed to be repeated on dance floors. But John had other ideas.

'He was a very good writer when it came to lyrics,' Tony says. 'They were very well thought out. The text had a message for all the kids.'

John pulled some lines from his jazz tune 'The Misfit' and combined them with his intended message. *Everybody stutters one way or the other*, it began.

'We all have problems,' John would later explain. 'It's what we do with those problems that counts.'

'*As a matter of fact, don't let nothing hold you back. If the Scatman can do it, so can you.*'

John was adamant: the song would be positive and encouraging. But could he really do it? Standing in the studio, doubt crept in. *I can't rap*, he confessed to Judy. *I'm not a rapper.*

'He had to bend himself to get it done,' Ingo Kays says, though he remembers John was open to trying anything. Facing the mic, John held onto Judy's encouragement. *Just try*, she told him. *Just give it a go.*

The beat was slowed to a more forgiving 100 BPM – slower than most dance tracks – to give John a chance at fitting in all the rapped words. Like singing, rapping to a rhythm can bypass stuttering. Even so, John's lyrics had to be simplified.

'Too complicated,' Tony said, and Ingo remembers John's original lines 'didn't really fit into the scheme of contemporary pop music.'

I hear you all ask about the meaning of scat, he rapped, reading from his laptop. *Well, I'm the professor*, he declared, embracing his role as a teacher. *The things you call dead haven't yet had the chance to be born.*

Scat, he believed, was an endangered art form. This was a chance to resurrect it for a new generation. To cap it off, he couldn't resist a sly dig at politicians (*heathens who would try to change the seasons if they could*); a nod to his anti-establishment hippie roots.

That night, after a long day in the studio, the trio shared a final dinner. John's return flight was in the morning.

'He couldn't understand that that was it, for him,' Ingo says. To a musician like John, Ingo thought, the process of singing and playing over a loop without any sense of the song's final shape must have felt strange and unsatisfying.

In just six hours of scat-singing, a couple more of rapping, and, according to Tony, no fewer than twenty espressos, John had delivered the raw material for *Scatman*.

Next was the painstaking process of turning an old jazz form into a modern dance track.

'He came here and had no idea what it would be,' Ingo said. 'We had no idea either.' Tony and Ingo set about mixing the single that would carry John's voice – and his message – into uncharted territory.

They began by slicing John's scat-singing into smaller phrases and loading them into an Akai Sampler – a digital device that let them trigger, tweak, and rearrange sound clips with precision.

'A laborious but very flexible process,' Tony said. Sampling was second nature to Ingo and Tony, but it was new to John – and it fascinated him. First popularized in early hip-hop and inspired by the looping tricks of turntablists like Grandmaster Flash, sampling had exploded by the late '80s and '90s. Producers could now build entirely new songs from fragments of old ones – funk, soul, gospel, or in John's case, jazz.

They sifted through hours of scatting to pull out phrases with the most 'commercial' or 'recognition value,' as Ingo put it. They adjusted pitch, tone, and speed to fit the high-energy tempo of Eurodance, pushing John's vocals to between 127 and 136 BPM. But editing John's voice while preserving its natural sound was difficult.

'At that time, it wasn't so easy to do it without generating artifacts,' Ingo recalls. 'Sometimes it doesn't sound natural anymore. So it was a lot of hard work.'

Some parts didn't need touching at all. John's explosive opening scat riff was left completely intact. Elsewhere his voice had been broken down, rearranged, and reimagined, including one phrase destined to become iconic: *ski-ba-bop-ba-dop-bop*; the essential hook that soon, millions of people wouldn't be able to get out of their heads.

'We developed a new melody with new harmonies that he had never sung in this form,' Tony said.

The first results leaned too far into techno for Manfred's liking.

'Melody, guys, melody,' he insisted. Janine Ramond, listening to an early mix, also suggested adding another scat phrase. Slowly, the song evolved.

Manfred visited the Bottrop studio often, including during the final mixing sessions. A month in, with the deadline looming, he settled into his chair at the back of the studio, cigar smoke trailing behind him.

'Out, out, out,' Manfred would say, cutting sound effects and clutter. He was measured but quietly confident, his excitement restrained.

On the final night, Manfred, Ingo, and Tony worked until 3 a.m., running on pizza and adrenaline to finish the track. The next morning, Manfred replayed the song with fresh ears. *Maybe*, he thought. *Just maybe.*

That afternoon, he held a conference call. Janine, Axel, and Eckhart Gundel – Managing Director of BMG Ariola Hamburg – were listening.

'They had it,' Janine said. 'It was unbelievable. I was so happy.'

'This was, for me, a sure number one,' Axel said.

Manfred felt the urgency rising.

'We had to be fast,' he said. 'And maybe no one would steal the idea.'

The race to release *Scatman (Ski-Ba-Bop-Ba-Dop-Bop)* had begun.

Oblivious to the promotional machine roaring to life in Germany on his behalf, John returned to California at the end of October 1994. His new record deal with a respectable label earned him an evening performance at the Jazz Bakery, a prestigious venue where many of California's finest jazz musicians had played.

Ruth Price, the venue's founder, told the crowd she'd heard John at a tribute to Judy's grandfather, Jimmy McHugh.

'He just knocked me out,' she said, 'he was wonderful.' Price also hinted at John's new project. 'It's not exactly a jazz album,' she admitted, 'but it's going to be good if it's him.'

John stepped up and did what he'd promised Judy he'd do more often.

'I've got to tell you something,' he began. 'I have a g-gift. If you hear something funny coming over the m-m-microphone, do not adjust your headsets. I happen to be a person that stutters.'

During his set, John ad-libbed verses from *Scatman* and joked about his recent venture into sampled music.

'They'll ruin a jazz artist,' he quipped, drawing laughter. He speculated about the music video, still unshot, imagining himself as a superhero – a 'super-scat' character he believed would be great for kids.

John nailed the performance, as always, but a well-trained eye might have noticed John's subtle unease when the piano fell silent. His hands gave him away, wringing or clasping whenever he lifted them from the keys to speak.

Gail Wilson Lew was in the audience with her husband, along with Annie Bradberry, Executive Director of the National Stuttering Project.

'We have to get this guy as our keynote speaker,' Annie whispered.

By the end of the night, she'd invited John to speak at the NSP conference the following summer – a commitment he would eventually fulfill, albeit as an international star.

For now, he stood under the Jazz Bakery's soft lights, a man at the cusp of something extraordinary, unaware that his audience that night would be the last to see him before the world discovered Scatman John.

22 **POPSTAR**

Manfred Zähringer paced the German booth at MIDEM, the sprawling music industry market in Cannes, a bag of Iceberg's sample CDs slung over his shoulder. The January 1995 charts were inching out of the fax machine, line by excruciating line.

Then there was the 'tip sheet' – a coveted list compiled by DJs, music journalists, and tastemakers; considered a bellwether for new singles. Land on it, and you had momentum. Miss it for two weeks in a row, and your track was as good as dead. The week before, 'Scatman' had been a no-show.

Finally, the machine spat out the last page. Manfred snatched it up and scanned the columns.

'Woohoo!'

He hurled the bag of CDs into the air, startling the booths around him. Heads turned, people smiled. Everyone knew what that meant: 'Scatman' had landed. Not only had it made the tip sheet – it had entered the official German charts at number 44.

A couple of months earlier, a padded airmail envelope from Bottrop had arrived at John and Judy's apartment in California. John tore it open, fished out the cassette, and slid it into the player.

He heard himself scat-sing. Then – bam! Three and a half minutes of him rapping and scatting at 136 BPM, layered over synths and an electronic drumbeat.

'Where's the Scatman? I'm the Scatman!'

It was him, all right. But not like any version of himself he'd ever heard.

This is what's happening in the pop scene?

He rewound it. Played it again. And again.

'It blew my mind,' he remembered. 'I had no idea of what was possible in today's studios. Of course, I started to judge it. But I had learned early on in sobriety – don't judge anything, man. You're not the judge. Somebody else is the judge.'

He sat with it, listening over and over, marveling at what they'd done to his voice. Then he grabbed the phone and dialed Ingo Kays.

'II-I-Iiiingoooo,' John grinned down the phone. 'Did I really sing that?'

The song's official title was now 'Scatman (Ski-Ba-Bop-Ba-Dop-Bop)', a deliberate mouthful to emphasize the scat-singing hook. During production, Janine Ramond called John to confirm the exact syllables.

'S-s-s-suh-ski-buh-buh … ' John began, but Janine got confused.

'He tried and tried and tried,' she remembered, but she couldn't tell where the stutter ended and the scat began – an irony not lost on either of them. They both burst out laughing.

'Fuh-fuh-forget it Janini,' John said. 'I'll fax it to you.'

The label rushed the single out on 30 November 1994 – smack in the middle of the holiday market.

'You never do that just before Christmas,' Manfred says. 'All artists, living and dead, have their music out. It's very crowded.' But they couldn't risk waiting in case someone else jumped on the idea of mixing scat-singing with dance. The single hit shelves before the music video was even shot.

In the middle of December 1994, BMG flew John to London to shoot the video, but worried about how audiences would react to a balding, 52-year-old man in the youth-driven dance music scene. They'd already kept John's face off the single cover, replacing it with a young, anonymous, clean-shaven open mouth with zig-zagged lines inside it to symbolize scat-singing.

They debated disguising him in the video, too. Someone floated the idea of using morphing effects like Michael Jackson had in 1991's 'Black or White'. But the final concept, pitched by Chopstick Productions, was simpler: a split-screen video celebrating diversity and joy, aligned with John's ethos.

German director Gregor Schnitzler signed on. 'The budget was pretty low,' he remembers. Around a dozen extras from all walks of life were asked to dance and lip-sync to the song, so everyone in the video looked like they might be singing it – a holdover from the same obfuscation strategy.

'We were very sure that if just John had been in this video, they wouldn't have played it,' Janine Ramond says. 'We wanted him in the background.'

Gregor, meanwhile, was charmed from the start. The song was catchy – he couldn't get it out of his head. But when he saw photos of John, he did a double-take. *This was the guy?* On the morning of 15 December 1994, he went to collect John from his London hotel.

'He was so polite, kind, and thankful,' Gregor remembers. During the cab ride, John impressed him by demonstrating his multi-chord throat singing.

On set, Gregor likened John to a little boy, curious about everything, politely asking if he could move a certain way or try something new.

'He was the kind of artist who gives other artists room to do their thing, to create synergy,' Gregor recalls. 'He wasn't a control freak. He had a great respect for filmmaking.'

The camera transformed John. He laughed, delivered his lines with playful energy, and nailed both singing and miming the song at its new turbocharged BPM.

'He was fast,' Tony Catania said. 'He learned that really quickly after we recorded. He was a genius guy.'

Gregor directed with a light touch, letting John's natural charisma take over.

'A day full of fun,' he concluded.

The video was rushed into post-production. The song had been out for a couple of weeks, but hardly anyone had paid attention to it. Stacks of promos landed on DJs' and journalists' desks between Christmas and New Year, each with a feedback form. DJs spun the track, checked reactions, and jotted notes.

'The evaluation from these feedback sheets was terrible,' Ingo recalls. 'Nobody played it.' Even Tony Catania's DJ friends didn't hold back. 'This is the worst thing you've ever done,' they told him.

Radio wasn't much kinder. The first airplay came from a station in Munich – but they cut the wild opening scat, afraid it would scare listeners off. Only later did they admit it to Manfred, who would never have allowed it, had he known.

Then, a flicker of hope. On 7 January 1995, *Music & Media* magazine tipped the track:

> Try to say that title in one go without choking on your words. Impossible! But Scatman has no problems scatting his nonsensical rhyme, a serious candidate for a novelty dance hit.

There was no time left to color-grade the music video. It went out in black and white – an unplanned decision that would accidentally become a defining aesthetic. Until now, the song had been largely ignored. But when the music video aired that same month, it changed everything.

'First shock – the song itself,' Ingo Kays says. 'Second shock – he's a white guy. And he looks like *that*.'

'Now it's even worse, but back in the day, they were looking for young, good-looking guys,' Tony Catania says, 'the way John looked was so original, nobody was expecting it. The entire package was different.'

John took the small advance from the single and spent it all on one key investment – a set of dentures. Years of smoking and drugs had wrecked his teeth.

'I'll be smiling a lot,' he joked to his sister-in-law Sharon.

He'd worn a rented suit for the music video. Now it was time to define what Scatman John should look like as a public figure. To work that out, BMG brought in a stylist.

'It was easy to work with what he already was,' Axel Alexander says, referencing John's jazz background.

'I think the hat was his idea,' Janine said, and remembered John had strong opinions about his image, unlike younger stars willing to be remade. They went for a 1950s jazz cat look: suit, tie and fedora, even though John had spent much of his life in jeans and T-shirts, often barefoot or in socks, with hair that hadn't seen a comb for days. Many of his friends had never seen him in a suit.

The first photoshoot was in Germany, including shots where John held – but didn't smoke – a cigar. Those were nixed – he'd just quit smoking for good.

'I don't want kids to see me with a cigarette in my hand,' he said.

The Scatman image was complete. Now, it was time to test it.

'I was very afraid when he had his first performance,' Janine Ramond says. The venue was a small discotheque in Nordhorn, Germany – a trial by fire in front of a test crowd of DJs and teenagers they presumed would either be indifferent or downright hostile to a man old enough to be their grandfather singing a dance record.

'I was so nervous,' Janine admitted. 'Afraid they'd throw eggs at the stage.' John, exhibiting nothing but calm, saw the worry on her face and pulled her into a hug.

'It'll work out, Janini,' he said. Then he walked onstage – and the place exploded.

'It was brilliant,' Janine remembers. 'They went crazy when they saw him, at his age, rocking the stage.'

The real breakthrough came soon after. Germany's VIVA music channel picked up the Scatman video and put it in heavy rotation. MTV Europe followed. The black-and-white visuals stood out amid the glossy, hyper-saturated music videos of the '90s. It was everywhere – on screen dozens of times a day.

As the song spread, so did the story behind it. Suddenly, 'Scatman' wasn't just an earworm; it was a challenge to every assumption about who could be a star.

The single was still climbing in Germany and had entered the Norwegian and Danish charts. Manfred called to tell John.

'Is this real?' John said. 'You mean I'm on a chart? As a *popstar?*'

After that, if Manfred didn't call or fax the latest chart updates, John was on the phone chasing him. It kept climbing.

'I flipped out,' John remembered. 'I said, oh man, it's not going to get any better than this.'

Everything seemed to be falling into place – the video was out, the song was selling, his first live performance was a success, and his image was taking shape. But there was still one thing left that John dreaded the most: interviews.

The first major request came from NRK, a Norwegian radio station, for a live on-air conversation. John was still in California but agreed to do the interview via long-distance call with DJ Hans Christian Andersen.

John listened to his single – his new identity – playing in the background. He sat with the phone, his heart hammering. The studio patched him through, and the DJ's bright and energetic voice introduced him.

What happened next was something John never saw coming.

23 **LET IT GO**

John leaned into the receiver, gripping it tightly. Judy hovered nearby in silent support.

'Pleaaaaaaasure to be speaking t-t-t ....' He stopped, backtracked, tried again. 'Pleasure to be speaking to you.'

Across the line in Norway, NRK's Hans Christian Andersen introduced John as someone with 'terrible small speech problems and an incredibly quick tongue.' Andersen was already betting big on the song, predicting it would be a hit – so much so that he later joked that if it wasn't, he'd jump off the roof of Denmark's Marienlyst Castle.

John sounded hesitant. He explained scat-singing, his jazz background, and how his stutter had shaped his music. He flipped between a stutter and a scat, demonstrating how one influenced the other. Then the old instinct kicked in – the inner voice telling him: *don't stutter!* His internalized shame reared up, and John did what so many stutterers learn to do: he strained for smoother speech. He over-enunciated. He changed his voice to sound more fluent.

Then came the shock: skepticism.

Andersen, a popular DJ with a large audience, was used to being bombarded with press kits and gimmicks – acts where image mattered more than substance. He assumed this was more of the same.

'I initially made the mistake of suspecting that Scatman might be someone using stuttering as a tool to gain attention,' Andersen admitted. 'I felt it was my job as a journalist to address this.'

It wasn't an unreasonable conclusion to jump to. By 1995, the charts were flooded with gimmicks, manufactured personas, and marketing stunts. If you could throw a beat under it, you could sell it. Doop had recycled the Charleston into dance in 1994. Swedish group Rednex parodied American hillbilly culture and scored a massive hit with a dance version of country song 'Cotton Eye Joe'. You didn't even have to be a real person. Even The Smurfs had a techno album out.

Labels knew that image alone could move records, and some were happy to fake it. In 1990, Milli Vanilli became the biggest scandal of them all when their Grammy was revoked for lip-syncing songs they hadn't sung. It should have been a cautionary tale, but the industry kept churning out attractive or just plain bizarre acts that often had little connection to the music they were selling. So when a middle-aged jazz pianist in a fedora showed up singing a Eurodance track, saying his stutter helped shape it, suspicion wasn't far behind.

'The fact that the "front figure" had a speech challenge was something completely new,' Andersen says. It reeked of an industry publicity stunt.

What didn't help was that John was now forcing fluency on the phone, and his rapping voice on the Scatman single showed no hint of struggle either. Andersen, like many more to come, questioned this contradiction: 'How is it possible to say that many words in that short time when you stutter?'

John had heard it before. He explained, just as the song itself did – *everyone's saying that the Scatman stutters but doesn't ever stutter when he sings*. But even as he answered, John was already running up against the same tired stigmas stutterers had faced for decades. If you can sing or rap so fluently, why is it so hard for you to talk?

As the call wrapped, Andersen told his audience, in Norwegian, that he was still skeptical, that he doubted John's stuttering was as bad as he said it was. He asked John if he was worried people would doubt his authenticity.

'No,' John said straight away. 'I would like to tell the audience out there that I'm a genuine, bona fide stutterer. It is ... ' he paused, corrected himself. 'It *was* a negative for a long time. And now it's turned into a positive.'

The call ended, but the doubt didn't.

Later, Andersen would meet John in person and become not just a friend but one of his greatest media advocates, but not before he would press John again about whether he was genuine.

He wasn't the only one.

'There were some – quite a lot, in fact – who believed the whole thing was a promotion trick,' Manfred says. 'What could I do? Call them all and say, he's a stutterer, you idiots?'

John hadn't expected this. It hadn't even crossed his mind. His stutter had nearly destroyed him – his greatest emotional callus, the thing he spent decades trying to hide. And now, just as he was finally owning it ... people thought he was *faking*?

For those who stutter – especially covert stutterers – it happens all the time. The world doesn't see the word switching, the avoidance, the constant mental contortions it takes to pass for fluent in a society that demands it.

Andersen had unknowingly opened the floodgates. John realized it wasn't enough to talk about stuttering. *He had to go ahead and stutter*. If he held back, if he used tricks to smooth it out, people wouldn't believe him. Worse, speech differences wouldn't be normalized, and kids who stuttered wouldn't hear themselves in him. 'That was the first shame I'd ever felt over NOT stuttering,' John said.

He had spent a lifetime running from it. Now, he had to do the one thing he feared most. He had to stop fighting it. He had to let it go.

By late January 1995, 'Scatman' was refusing to slow down.

'I'll never forget,' Tony Catania says. 'The song went into the charts on my birthday.' After years of remixing other people's hits, one of Tony and Ingo's own had finally broken through.

In Silkeborg, Denmark, Iceberg Records had gone all-in. The Zähringers and their team dropped everything to focus on pushing the song worldwide, urging other territories to take their option before it was too late. They tried something unorthodox: pressure by countdown.

'Five weeks to go,' their faxes warned. 'Have you taken your option?'

It worked. Canada signed on to release the single. Then Spain, Hong Kong, Singapore, the Netherlands, Switzerland, Austria, and South Africa. More countries jumped in by the day.

But one major territory still refused to bite: Japan.

Manfred had a gut feeling 'Scatman' could do well there, but BMG Tokyo wasn't convinced. English-language singles were a tough sell in a market that favoured domestic acts, and they didn't want to take the risk.

While on business in Hong Kong, Manfred decided to gamble. He bought a ticket to Tokyo and asked for a meeting, figuring the worst-case scenario would be another no and a wasted plane ticket.

Inside the boardroom, BMG Japan's executives sat in perfect formation – smiling, polite, formal. They listened patiently as Manfred-san made his case. The song, they explained, wasn't easy to understand. It was very fast. It was in English. Japanese audiences preferred songs they could follow. Manfred leaned forward.

'Gentlemen,' he said. 'Repeat after me.'

And then, to their surprise, Manfred sang the hook: *Ski-ba-bop-ba-dop-bop.*

Silence. Then a few hesitant voices echoed it back. Manfred grinned.

'Louder, gentlemen!' he insisted, as if hyping up a concert crowd.

This time, the room joined in, more confident: *Ski-ba-bop-ba-dop-bop!*

'There!' Manfred said, triumphant. 'You see? It's not English. It's *Scatish*. Everyone can understand it.'

Manfred walked out, unsure if his eccentric pitch had landed. A few days later, the answer came: Japan was in.

No one in that boardroom could have predicted that Scatman John would go on to sell more records in Japan than anywhere else in the world, and would become one of the country's best-selling foreign artists of all time.

Back in Scandinavia, the single was catching fire. After John's Norwegian radio interview, the track shot up the charts in Norway, Denmark, and Finland. In Germany, it had moved 10,000 copies in its first week.

By February, Manfred had already asked Ingo and Tony to prepare the next single and an album. Mette Zähringer flooded newsrooms with press releases ahead of John's first promo tour.

John and Judy landed in Copenhagen in the early hours, jet-lagged but buzzing. With only one wobbly phone interview under his belt, nobody knew how John would handle the spotlight. Mette, wanting to ensure a considerate reception, added a footnote on her faxes to journalists: 'PS: REMEMBER HE STUTTERS.'

John and Judy checked into their hotel room. John's 'Scat Suit' was laid out, waiting. He changed and stepped into the crisp Danish morning for his first face-to-face interview as a pop star, his song now sitting at #4 on the Danish charts.

Some artists, Manfred and Mette knew, needed hand-holding in these situations. Some froze, others rambled. Nobody was sure which camp John belonged to, so Manfred or Mette sat in for the first few interviews, just in case.

Philip Thomsen from Danish tabloid *BT* arrived at the café where they'd agreed to meet and found John sitting by the window, smiling at snowflakes drifting down outside.

'Scatman John does not look like a dance or hip-hop star,' he wrote. 'Rather, a professor.'

But John was at ease, especially when it came to stuttering. He wanted to talk about it. How it shaped his music. How it shaped him. He admitted his past musical snobbery, too.

'I had a biased attitude towards so-called modern music,' he confessed. 'But now I've discovered that there's an incredible amount of talent in the modern music genres, and talent is always worth listening to.'

For the first and only time, John didn't want to reveal his real name. 'Scatman John' was all he wanted the world to know. But the impulse to hide was old circuitry. As the days passed, he realized openness and vulnerability were no longer something to fear. They were the key.

The media blitz had begun. Twelve radio interviews in two hours. Four in-studio radio sessions. Half a dozen newspapers and magazines. John laughed, chatted, stuttered away. 'I've never had so much fun,' he told Norwegian paper *Dagbladet*, arms thrown wide, grinning.

Every article mentioned his age. Fifty-two. Old enough to be his fans' grandfather, and, supposedly, old enough to know better. But that was the point. John loved it.

'Isn't it wonderful?' he told Danish journalist Annette Heick. 'I'm proud to have become a youth idol. Just imagine what kind of messages I can bring to them with my age and experience behind me.'

The first TV invitations arrived – first from *Eleva2oren* in Denmark, then *Rondo*, a new Norwegian talk show.

This was great news, but they wanted a live performance.

Most Eurodance artists – and most pop stars, for that matter – mimed to a backing track. It was standard practice for studio-built hits, designed more for machines than musicians. But John wasn't most pop stars. It drove him crazy. How could he perform this thing live?

'I have tried singing only the words, and I have tried singing only the scat … both are impossible to do without making a fool of myself and defeating our own purpose,' he wrote in a desperate fax to Manfred Zähringer. 'I will be laughed off the stage.'

Even at his lowest point when he'd been strung out, John had never faced a performance he couldn't pull off, and he wasn't about to start now.

'I am not going to make an ass out of myself because of the way this song was engineered,' he continued. 'You must believe me when I tell you – *Scatman cannot be performed live!*'

And yet – fast forward a few weeks to Oslo, Norway, in February 1995, and there was John, on the *Rondo* stage, backed by a full band.

About to prove himself wrong.

24 THE OLD NEWCOMER

'The most famous stutterer in the world!' *Rondo* host Petter Nome declared as he joined John onstage. First topic of conversation, as always, was John's age. John smiled over his spectacles, stuttering as he explained that this 52-year-old rapper was having a ball.

'Oh yeah!' John interrupted himself. 'I'm a person that stutters. I have to tell everyone that, so t-t-t-they don't think I'm crazy up here,' he said – a jab at the tired assumption that stuttering had anything to do with mental illness.

He explained how stuttering had influenced his scat-singing and then stepped behind the keyboard.

'Here's a v-v-version of my current hit,' he told the audience. 'Everybody's heard "Scatman" now. We're gonna do it *our* way'. He gestured for them to applaud the band and then threw himself into 'Scatman' – live.

Immediately, things threatened to go sideways. He started in the wrong key. He clasped and wrung his hands together. He wasn't used to this – performing stiff behind a keyboard under hot TV lights.

But about a minute in, something clicked. John's old and new selves stopped battling for control and finally fused into one. He locked in. He took off. His hands found the keys, his voice found its rhythm. He encouraged the crowd to clap along.

The song broke free from its neat little radio edit, blooming into a six-minute, electro-swing jazz-fusion jam. John scatted, soloed, zipped up and down the keyboard. The band kept up. The audience roared.

When it ended, John stepped back, breathless and beaming. He had done it.

It would go down, even decades later, as one of the most iconic performances of the song. But he wouldn't be able to repeat it often. TV slots were tight, radio schedules even tighter, and there was no room for improvisation. So John complied – for now. But he wouldn't stay in the box forever.

The *Rondo* performance lit a fuse. Headlines poured in: 'The Old Newcomer', 'The Man Who Sings Faster Than His Shadow', 'The Tongue Acrobat', 'Machine Lips.'

Everything that had made the press dubious – John's age, his looks, his unfiltered sincerity – became exactly what won them over. In an era where disability was often invisible or wrapped in pity, John wasn't talking about 'overcoming' anything. He accepted himself as he was. The press ate it up with a spoon.

Early on, Manfred and Mette stopped tagging along to interviews.

'Why should somebody like me correct him or help him out?' Manfred says. 'There was no need. He had them eating out of his hand. He was the master of interviews. We never had another artist who could do the same.'

Dozens of journalists who met John during those whirlwind first weeks of 1995 were caught off guard. Deadlines evaporated as they sat across from John, their carefully planned questions unraveling in real time. Not because he stuttered overtly and frequently (which he did, and it was usually the first thing they mentioned) but because he was on a roll: fast, funny, holding people's attention in a situation where he was *expected* to stutter.

'He has to start three times per word before he can express his joy at his chart attack,' one magazine wrote.

'You have to be equipped with a certain amount of patience when talking to Scatman John,' said another.

Whether they knew it back then or not, the press wasn't helping with the negative language they used. John's way of speaking was referred to as 'a severe speech impediment', 'a nagging stammer', or something he was 'suffering' from. John was not suffering from anything, nor was he impeded, since the journalists all understood him just fine. He was communicating – clearly and authentically. He just needed a bit more time. And once he got going, he couldn't be stopped.

The 'Scat Suit' was a stage costume, one he sometimes failed to bring and had to be pestered not to forget. Offstage, he lived in T-shirts, jeans, and sneakers.

'The suitcase is packed with sensible clothes,' one interviewer noted, watching John pop his dentures back in between laughs about maintaining a smart image.

Another reporter showed up to find him still in bed. John told them to take a seat on the edge of the mattress, where they talked like old friends. 'In bed with Scatman,' the article read.

He made them coffee. Let them poke around his hotel room. His laptop was usually plugged into the wall, lyric scraps littering the desk. When he moved between hotels, there were no blacked-out cars or entourage. He took the train. He never checked in under his stage name. Journalists would arrive at the front desk, asking for Scatman John, only to be met with blank stares.

Many came expecting fluff – an easy profile on the novelty act with the funny hat and the scat syllables. Vi Unge magazine later made him drop for push-ups to prove he could keep up with the "young," and a TV show threatened to shave off his mustache. Some tried cheap laughs at his expense, but instead they got discussions about astronomy, philosophy, and kids' self-esteem. During a 1996 interview in Finland, John's opening gambit was a critique of famine and global inequity. Journalist Pasi Kostiainen was floored.

'This was supposed to be a harmless guy who babbles the same swinging nonsense as his records,' he said.

As the stories piled up, the headlines softened.

Gentleman John. Likeable Scatman.

If they couldn't get to him in person, they called, and John always answered. During one phone interview, the reporter dared to suggest that scat-singing couldn't be performed alongside the piano. John didn't argue. Instead, he reached across his hotel room desk, grabbed his portable keyboard, and launched into an off-kilter harmonic sequence of piano and scat syllables, sending them tumbling down the phone.

On the other end of the line, the journalist's open-plan office came to a standstill. Heads turned toward the rhythmic chaos pouring through the receiver.

They had called expecting a novelty act. They hung up knowing they had just met someone else entirely.

In the US, Steve Larkin – John's youngest nephew – was deep in grad school when his parents, Billy and Sharon, called with news too ridiculous to believe. 'Scatman' hadn't yet been released in the US, but its arrival was imminent.

'Uncle Johnny is going to be famous,' they insisted.

The same Uncle Johnny who did drugs, slept all day on their couch, barefoot, shirtless, shoeless, with hair past his shoulders? Impossible.

'The first time I began to believe,' Steve said, 'was when I heard "Scatman" follow a Michael Jackson song on the radio.'

The BVSS (Bundesvereinigung Stotterer-Selbsthilfe) – the German Stuttering Association – was among the first organizations to reach out to the most famous stutterer in Europe. Board member Konrad Schaefers sat down with John for an interview and found not the cartoonish figure in the fedora, but a thoughtful, vulnerable man.

'The point I'm at', John told him, 'is not to try to overcome the stuttering itself, but to get rid of the shame.'

He was trying not to let it sabotage his life anymore, he said, but still felt uncomfortable and embarrassed about his stuttering. But he took a spiritual perspective, that life's challenges – stuttering included – had a deeper meaning, and were an opportunity for growth.

Then Konrad asked: Would it have helped you if there had been a stuttering star when you were a kid? A stuttering Elvis?

John thought for a moment.

'He would have been God, now that I think about it,' he answered, before quickly shrugging off any delusions of grandeur. 'I'm selfish, I have an ego, and I'm definitely not a saint.' He smiled. 'I'm just trying to help.'

A few hundred miles away, in northern England, 14-year-old Eloise Pitchford sat slumped in the front seat of the car, silently watching the Yorkshire countryside drift by in dull shades of green and grey.

As they made a turn towards the town, her father leaned over and switched on the radio. Take That were crooning about wanting someone Back for Good. Oasis drawled about sunshine following thunder.

Then, suddenly, a bunch of hyper-speed syllables exploded out of the radio. A catchy dance beat kicked in, and a weird voice began singing:

'Everybody stutters one way or the other, so check out my message to you,
As a matter of fact, don't let nothin' hold you back,
If the Scatman can do it, so can you...'

Followed by more vocal acrobatics.

Did this guy just mention stuttering? She shifted in her seat, staring at the speaker grille as if it had just revealed a secret.

'Dad,' she said, 'turn this up.' He did, happy that Eloise appeared to be enjoying something for a change. That day would have been her mother's 40th birthday if cancer hadn't taken her four years earlier. Her father had put music on, as he usually did, in an unsuccessful attempt to lift the heavy feeling in the car as he drove Eloise and her sister to her grandmother's.

The track ended, leaving a powerful emotional residue. *That song was about stuttering.* She had never heard anyone talk about stuttering on the radio before. Not on TV. Not anywhere.

She knew she stuttered, but not in the way people noticed. Hers could be hidden and masked. It had started when her mom got sick, and then it had stayed. No one had ever acknowledged it. No one had told her what to do about it. No one had even spoken the word. But this man had. Who was the Scatman? *A young Black rapper*, she thought. *Maybe American.*

At their grandmother's, Eloise and her sister flopped onto the couch to watch *The Chart Show*, the UK's weekly music video countdown. The top ten rolled out the usual suspects: Ballads from Boyzone and Celine Dion, and even that weird Latin track from the Guinness advert. Manchester United had jumped on the novelty train, singing about *Doin' It Again* with all the enthusiasm of a team more comfortable on a pitch than in a recording booth.

Then, there he was.

No young Black rapper. Eloise stared at this balding guy in his fifties, in a suit, jumping around all over the place, singing those unmistakable lines through a bushy mustache. *Scatman John?*

'Eloise, love, eat your sandwich,' her grandma said. Eloise barely heard her.

A text box popped up over the video, saying something about Scatman being a lifelong stutterer who had reinvented himself through this fusion of jazz, pop, and techno music that Eloise had instantly fallen in love with.

She listened carefully to the lyrics. The rest of the show faded into background noise. *I have to find out more about this man*, she thought.

A day that had started as a quiet ache was suddenly alive with possibility. An arrow had found its mark.

Back in California, whispers of John's success filtered through a disbelieving jazz scene. John had 'done something' in Europe and now, somehow, he was on the *pop* charts?

'A friend of mine told me that John had a number one disco hit in Europe,' Sam Phipps says. 'I didn't believe him.'

John sent CDs to old friends. Bobby Rivera, his high school buddy from El Sereno, had reconnected with him after hearing the news. John mailed him a signed copy. *Look what we've done*, it said.

Not everyone was thrilled. John heard some of his jazz compatriots were being snobby about his new musical activity.

'They think it's strange I'm running around doing this,' he said. 'They're entitled to their opinion, but the most important thing for me is to have fun – and I'm having a great time.'

In Geneva, bassist Bob Harrison, who played on the *John Larkin* LP, was working at Paul Sutin's studio. Like John, Bob had adapted and played in different genres to make a living. Sutin had worked with everyone from David Bowie to Phil Collins, and tasked Bob with producing dance music.

Do what's on the charts, Bob was told. *It's all about Scatman these days – that's what the kids are listening to.* Bob went to buy the Scatman CD, brought it home, and pressed play. The beat kicked in, and then – *skibidibabopbopbop!*

His mind reeled. *I know this voice.* But he still didn't put two and two together until he flipped the CD case over and scanned the liner notes. There it was. John Larkin.

'I was in total shock,' Bob says. 'I couldn't believe it. It's not possible that John Larkin is some kind of pop star,' he said. 'No way. If all the players of the time had come to vote on who would be the *least* likely guy to become a popstar, it was John. He was such a purist, and an unforgiving purist.'

Still trying to process this revelation, Bob picked up the phone and dialled the last number he had for John. Amazingly, it still worked. Even more amazingly, John was back in California and answered the phone.

'John,' Bob began. 'What the HELL?'

25 MESSAGE TO YOU

Chet Baker and Billie Holiday – John and Judy's cats – padded around the sofa, sniffing and rubbing, as if to remember who they were. John stretched out in jeans and a sweater, chewing nicotine gum. As the cats passed, he smiled and ran a hand over their fur.

Judy lit a cigarette and dropped onto the couch beside him. He'd propped his feet on a wicker basket doubling as a coffee table. Royalties hadn't hit their account, and they were still in the same apartment, seeing no reason to uproot yet.

John was back in California for a few days to rest and plan his follow-up single and debut album as Scatman John. When Bob Harrison had called, John was joyful.

'He was proud of what he was doing,' Bob says. 'His attitude was 100 percent all for it. He said *this is wonderful*. He had broken through the whole paradigm of pop music.'

Bob mentioned the *John Larkin* LP and The Misfit, quoting a line about the bass drum making you numb. John laughed.

'Man, you're the only one in the world who knows about that,' he said, probably because most of the remaining LPs were still shoved in the back of his closet.

'I can't remember those years at all,' John said later. 'And I don't want to try, either. I've come over to the other side. Completely different things matter to me.'

That chapter of his career – of half-empty clubs and albums nobody bought – was behind him. Now, he was about to record something else entirely.

'These kids have never even heard the word "scat," ' John told Bob. What thrilled him wasn't just having success – it was introducing kids to the art form he loved. And they were listening. What else could he tell them?

Usually, he unwound at home by losing himself in improvisations on his compact spinet piano. But John figured he ought to watch more MTV. If Scatman was going to drop in the US, he should know who else was on the charts and what they were saying. At home in LA, he flicked through channels, fishing for a pretzel in the bowl next to him.

The Real McCoy had made the top three earlier in the year with 'Another Night', and Corona's 'The Rhythm of the Night' was close behind. His dance music compatriots were doing okay. So far, so good.

Annie Lennox came on with 'No More I Love Yous'. *There's something special about her*, John thought. Then, the Cranberries' 'Zombie' – a protest song against IRA bombings. He hadn't heard them before, but this was a sentiment John could understand, could relate to. *Great stuff.*

Then the volume spiked. Rappers spitting vitriol about guns, cops, and war on the streets. John sat up.

LA already had a slew of gang trouble, the crack epidemic, and the Rodney King Riots a couple of years back. And before that – Watts. John had seen the wreckage up close. Why would anyone glorify this?

'Gangsta Rap' was at its commercial peak, with explicit lyrics and confrontational posturing that had parents and politicians in a moral panic. Hearing it firsthand made John uneasy. It wasn't about who was rapping. *You're angry*, John thought. *You have every right to be.* He'd built entire performances out of rage himself, and his avant-garde jazz always had teeth. He knew what it meant to clash with authority too – he'd been on the wrong end of police attention most of his life. It wasn't the language either. John cursed plenty – in private.

It was the audience.

This wasn't some underground club where grown adults made their own choices. This was being piped straight to kids on TV, telling them rebellion meant blood. And John hated it.

'How angry those bands sound,' he told newspaper *Heit Nieuwsblad* a few months later. 'It goes like "fuck this" and "motherfuck that". Sometimes the aggression really spatters from the screen. I can understand that aggression, though. The world's in a tragic situation.'

Later, he addressed the artists directly.

'You can call it art,' he said, 'good for you. I don't believe that. I think it's the responsibility of artists – of any age – to try to put whatever insight they've acquired in life out to the people. The world is in utter chaos. We don't need to add more chaos.'

John admitted that maybe he was just an 'old bohemian.' Fine. But if he was going to sell anything, it sure as hell wasn't going to be this.

'Carte blanche,' Manfred says of John's freedom to write lyrics. John had zero guidelines for what his debut Scatman album should be about, other than providing 'more of the same.'

One of the first ideas came as he was driving home through the San Fernando Valley near the Ventura Freeway off-ramp, where he always saw the same homeless woman.

'Every time I pass her, I say, "There but for the grace of God go I,"' John said.

He wanted to talk to her, but sensed she wouldn't welcome it.

'I really relate to her,' he said. 'She's always reading. She has her shopping cart full of books. She seems to have a jug stashed behind the fence. She sits on her milk crate with her dog all day. She never looks up and never holds her hand out. She just sits there.'

He saw her often, but thought about her even more. Later, he wrote 'You're the freeway desperado / And the perfect living model / Of a land that hasn't any good excuse.'

By the time he got home, the song had already started writing itself.

John arrived at his regular AA meeting – a musician-focused group off Lankershim Boulevard, held in a church rec room. The usual quiet chatter filled the space, the smell of coffee lingering in the air. Up front, a small podium stood beneath banners listing the Twelve Steps and Twelve Traditions. He greeted friends and slipped into a seat. Many still had no idea what he'd been up to in Europe.

'Someone, in their infinite wisdom, decided John should read Chapter Five,' John's friend D Jennings says, referring to the preamble that opened every meeting.

John caught the eye of those who knew him well, smirked, and mouthed the word 'fuck.' Sniggers rippled through the room. John got up.

'Ohhhh, here we go!' someone called out. John laughed as he stood behind the podium. Like most people who stutter, he was fine with jokes, as long as he was in on them. He looked down at the text. *Rarely have we seen a person fail who has thoroughly followed our path.*

'Ruh-ruh-ruh-rarely hhhhave w-w-w-we suh-suh ... ' John began, then stopped and exhaled sharply. 'Fuck it, man.'

'We're snickering,' D remembers. '*He's* snickering.'

John tried again, but the words were jammed.

'Fuck it!' he shook his head. 'F-f-fuck it!' The laughter grew – including John's. Then he grinned.

'He starts *rapping* it,' D says.

Everyone clapped their hands in time. Feet tapped the floor. The room was swinging, the AA meeting now a full-on performance.

'He rapped the entire Chapter Five,' D says. 'It was a hoot.'

John gave a little bow and sat down to a storm of cheers and applause.

'Nobody could get serious after that,' D says.

Approaching his ninth year sober, John remained committed to the Twelfth Step – carrying the message of recovery to other alcoholics.

'He really helped me a great deal when I was new,' D says. 'He goes, *you're not fooling anybody*. He taught me to be open about it.'

Most of the group had no idea how famous he was in Europe.

'He was gone a lot, and I didn't know why he was gone a lot,' D says. 'The first six or seven months I knew him, I had no clue what he was doing.'

Since being thrust into the public eye, John often thought about that second 'A' – anonymous. He rarely mentioned AA by name, as was the norm, but he wanted to tip his hat to the program, to pay it forward to those who needed it without breaking cover.

He found a way with a gold pendant: a triangle inside a circle – the symbol of AA. The circle stood for the world; the triangle, for the program's three pillars: Recovery, Unity, and Service. John wore it everywhere, for photoshoots, for videos, or whenever he appeared in public.

Then he wrote a song called 'Time (Take Your Time)'.

Outwardly, it was about slowing down in a fast-paced world. But it was packed with hidden references to AA and the Twelve Steps – messages hidden in plain sight for those who knew where to look.

Heard you're reading Chapter Five / You know how to stay alive / Every morning, hit your knees / Ninety meetings, ninety days …

For outsiders, it was just another song. For those in recovery or thinking about it, it was a signal.

Before returning to Europe, John visited his mother Harriet, and Billy and Sharon. He played 'Scatman' for them.

'We loved it,' Sharon said. The whole family did. Harriet posed proudly with a life-sized, promotional cardboard cutout of John from the record label. John gave Billy and Sharon his first Gold award for sales in Denmark. Johnny, it seemed, had finally done something good. He told *The European Magazine* how he felt. 'I must be doing something right for once in my life,' he said.

But the person who felt most vindicated wasn't John. It was Judy.

'I had never seen my cousin Judy so happy,' her cousin, Mike Metzger, says. Judy never chased the spotlight, but was always there, nudging John in interviews when he got carried away, or snapping photos from the side of the stage as thousands of children threw their arms toward her husband.

'They handled it very well,' her son Lee Newman says. 'She knew. She had an eye for talent. She totally believed in him. And in the end, she was right.'

Thanks to her, when John next set foot in Europe, he wasn't a struggling jazzman hoping for a break but the voice behind the biggest single of 1995 so far.

'Scatman (Ski-Ba-Bop-Ba-Dop-Bop)' had made him a star.

Now the album would decide if he stayed one.

26 SCATMAN'S WORLD

Iris Riemann stood behind the Ramada Hotel reception desk, discreetly watching the peculiar gentleman sitting in the lobby. He was older, mustached, dressed in a trench coat and fedora.

'He looked a little bit like a businessman,' Iris says. 'But on Sundays, you don't have businessmen at the hotel, not until late evening.' Like hotel managers everywhere, Iris tried to guess the stories of her guests. What had brought *this* one to Bottrop, Germany?

A younger man walked in. The two greeted each other warmly before leaving together. *Ah*, Iris thought. *A couple.*

She tucked the assumption away and carried on with her day. Later, when she got to know John and Ingo, she mentioned her first impression of them. They laughed.

It was spring 1995, and 'Scatman' was wedged at number two behind Vangelis's 'Conquest of Paradise' on the German chart, where it would stay for three months. John never mentioned his pop identity when he and Judy checked in. Iris had no idea that the man in the trench coat was about to record the widest-selling album in Europe.

By now, John had figured out what he wanted to say – and who needed to hear it. Fanmail had been pouring in, not just from people who stuttered, but from kids who felt like outsiders. The bullied. The overlooked. The ones who didn't fit in, carrying invisible wounds. The ones ashamed of who they were.

John vowed to answer every letter and sign every autograph, no matter how long it took. Before he left LA, he set up a PO box, never expecting it to overflow within weeks.

The voices in those letters distilled what he already had in mind.

'The world is in trouble. Bosnia, Rwanda, the rainforest, drugs, crime. Try to figure this all out as a young person,' he said. 'They're told to hide their feelings, that sadness is only appropriate for women, that males must be tough, that any sort of weakness is bad and should be hidden. It's a difficult thing to be brought up that way. I know, because it happened to me.'

John knew the world wasn't always safe. He had learned that firsthand. And if reality couldn't offer these kids a sanctuary, he'd have to create one.

So he did.

The album was *Scatman's World*, and at its heart was Scatland.

'Scatland is my metaphor for the child in every person,' John said, 'the pure and the undefiled. Deep inside, we all know how it ought to be. Otherwise we wouldn't be so frustrated.'

With his laptop and notebooks full of songs, John returned to the studio. Tony and Ingo noticed he was more relaxed and centered. Perhaps because this time, Judy was with him.

'They were so down-to-earth,' says Iris, who eventually figured out who John was. 'Scatman', the papers reported, was on the radio more often than the weather forecast.

A few days after John and Judy arrived, a carnival set up across the street from the hotel. One stand played 'Scatman' on a loop – all day, every day. Eventually, a sheepish John wandered down to the reception desk.

'Iris,' he said, 'I'm so sorry. But can we please change rooms?'

Across town, Tony Catania's girlfriend Ilona was closing all the windows in their house. It was booming from neighbors' garden barbecues. Echoing from across the street. Thumping from car stereos. 'Scatman' wasn't just a hit, it was a soundtrack to life itself; a pattern repeating all over Europe and Asia.

With such success came pressure. Iceberg and BMG knew they had to strike again or lose momentum. The follow-up single, 'Scatman's World', had been sketched before John even arrived. Ingo and Tony had the opening line: 'I'm calling out from Scatland, I'm calling out from Scatman's World.' The rest came when John did: 'If you want to break free, you better listen to me.'

Every morning at 10 a.m., John waited in the lobby, ready for pickup. At the top of the attic studio stairs, he paused, panting. His breathlessness had been noticeable as far back as Amsterdam. There was something he hadn't told Ingo and Tony. But for now, he pushed it aside. There was work to do.

'We had complete freedom,' Tony says. 'The concept was simply to showcase John as a jazz musician, and not neglect the things he was really good at.'

The first sound recorded in the studio wasn't music, however. It was John. A deep, steady rumble: *Checking ... one, two.* Always in the same ultra-low voice, his ritual to test the mic. And then there was the chewing. John was addicted to nicotine gum, topping out at thirty or forty pieces a day. He sang with it still in his mouth. Where he hid it, Tony and Ingo never figured out, because when he stopped singing, there it was again. Other times, if he had to take it out, he'd stick it to his laptop, ready to put it back in.

The symbiosis between the three of them – already proven on 'Scatman' – held strong through the album sessions. But now, they had weeks, not months. With a summer 1995 release planned, John was in the studio up to twelve hours a day. Tony and Ingo, even longer.

'The two of us do everything ourselves,' Tony told *KEYS* magazine. 'Plugging in microphones, making coffee, creating samples, dusting, writing letters, mixing, mastering – everything.'

Their process was methodical.

'We always needed two verses of 16 bars. It's like a Eurodance law,' Ingo says. First, they worked on the chorus, or hook line, with John. It wasn't always easy.

'He had problems with the hook lines,' Tony says. 'His melodies were thought out in a complicated way – they were good, but nothing for the masses.'

'What we were doing was way underneath John's musicality,' Ingo adds. 'Sometimes there were chord progressions going on, and he just sat down and said, 'What? This is a minor 6th? You can't do that.'

The album opened with 'Welcome to Scatland', a spoken-word invitation to John's utopia. Then came the potential singles: hook-laden songs designed for dance floors. 'Only You' was a love song for Judy – John's antidote to the codependent themes he disliked in pop music. 'Love is not possession, and it can't be possessed,' it began, paraphrasing a line from *The Prophet*, by Kahlil Gibran. John no longer needed the BPM slowed – his rapping was now naturally fast.

Early cuts of 'Sing Now!' – a high-energy pop number – made their way to BMG and Iceberg.

'Hello, you two magicians,' Manfred faxed Tony and Ingo. 'Sounds great. Positive!'

Like many mid-'90s studios, they ran a hybrid of analogue and digital, side by side.

'We worked a lot with natural instruments – guitars, trumpets, saxophones,' Tony says. They layered these with samplers and computer-edited sounds. John played piano and keyboards.

'This was great for me because I learned from him,' Tony says. 'Especially in Germany, with all the electronic music, nobody could really play anything. So when he came and he was sitting at the piano, I thought, this is unbelievable. I loved it.'

As with 'Scatman', John's lyrics were trimmed for commercial appeal. 'But he was very quick and open-minded toward changes,' Ingo says.

Once the tracks were structured, John could cut loose.

'Free scatting,' Ingo says. 'Wild, creative, unplanned.' Sometimes, the improvisation was so good that it became the song. 'Mambo Jambo' was born this way, with John playing a jazzy riff and half-screaming a line. They left it all in.

What Tony and Ingo hadn't expected were John's other vocalizations that kept coming through the open mic.

'Fuck you, Johnny,' he'd mutter. 'Why don't you go fuck yourself, Johnny? Come *on*, Johnny.' It happened whenever he flubbed a line, missed a cue, or felt pressured. Never John. Always Johnny. His childhood name.

'These John-to-John conversations became routine,' Ingo said. 'Like a third person involved in the recording session.'

Even when he wasn't talking or singing, John made noise – groaning, muttering, or low grumbling sounds to keep his vocal cords loose. But one sound came through louder than the rest: his breathing.

Now that he was recording all day, every day, there was no hiding it.

John had COPD. A progressive, incurable lung disease that made it harder and harder to breathe. His airways were inflamed and narrowed: the tiny air sacs that transferred oxygen were breaking down. Years of tobacco, weed, and hard drugs had eaten away at his breath like a slow-burning fire.

'I could hear him struggling with his breathing many times,' Ingo remembers. John fought it between takes, dragging in deep breaths, then exhaling like he was trying to blow out a stubborn candle.

He'd taken lung function tests, he admitted. The results weren't good; his exhale was weak. Yet when he sang, his voice still spanned three octaves, filling the room with power, gravity, and warmth.

'His voice was dynamic and rich,' Ingo says. 'A pleasure to record.' But nobody knew how long it would last.

During a break, John sat in the studio kitchen, crunching on peanuts and sipping another coffee from the espresso machine. He let out a long sigh, bowed his head, and looked up at Ingo over his glasses.

'Ingoooo,' he said, drawing out his name. 'All I need to do is *surrender*.'

Once the dance tracks were done, John turned philosophical, starting with the song inspired by the woman at the freeway off-ramp back in California. 'Quiet Desperation' – its title lifted from Thoreau's *Walden* – was the album's first break from the dancefloor formula. Listeners expecting another upbeat banger were met instead with a reflection on poverty, isolation, and America's failure to care for its most vulnerable.

Social commentary like this was rare in a genre built on a lyrical landfill of catchy rhymes about partying and sex. But John had never cared for rules.

'I sing about environmental pollution, racism, competition, losers – about things that many people don't dare to talk about,' John said. 'But I also say that you should take everything a little easier.'

Whilst John was recording, Judy passed the time in the hotel lobby, chatting, smoking (unlike John, she hadn't managed to quit), and playing cards with Iris.

'It can't have been easy for her,' Iris said. Once you'd done some shopping and seen the sights, there wasn't much left to do in Bottrop. The two women became friends, and Judy even went over to Iris's house to do laundry. Later, John and Judy invited Iris to stay with them in LA.

At first, John had insisted Judy come with him to the studio, worried she'd get bored. But her presence changed his performance.

'John was distracted,' Ingo says. With a tight schedule, concern grew. It didn't help when, mid-recording, Judy opened a door, forcing them to start over. During a break, Ingo pulled John aside. Bringing people into the studio wasn't a good idea, he told him.

John took it personally. An affront to Judy.

'Fuck you,' he snapped, and stormed out, slamming the door behind him.

Later, John admitted that these blow-ups – especially when he felt cornered – were something he was still working on. It came up again in an interview not long after, when he'd been testy after a long flight:

'I got angry at an airport official earlier. I got a temper, sure,' he said. 'But ... try. We need to learn to love each other. Love – corny word, isn't it? But, man, it's true. We need to try to understand. Try – operative word, try. If we can just try, that will do it. Because all I can do is try.'

Fifteen minutes after walking out, Ingo found John sitting downstairs in the hotel lobby. John looked up, reached across the table, and took Ingo's hand.

'Ingoooo,' he said 'You're my bud.' He apologized, returned to the studio, and it never happened again.

Judy still dropped by sometimes, but only after recording had wrapped, and she didn't like the long climb up to the attic studio anyway. Most nights, John finished by 8 or 9 p.m., and the crew would cross the street to their usual Italian restaurant.

The next morning, they'd start again. Some days, they knocked out two or three songs in a single session. Journalists came by for interviews. The fax machine in the corner spat out contracts, requests, and messages so fast that the paper roll had to be replaced three or four times a day. Yet through it all, the atmosphere between John and his two 'magicians' remained warm, focused, and full of mutual respect.

'He was amazing,' Tony said. 'Really focused in terms of studio work and concentration, really using the time to make the best sound. I've worked with artists big and small, and he was the number one for professionalism I ever saw in my life.'

It was a job, and someone had to do it, which was the theme of the next track: 'Popstar', a send-up of the absurd circus of fame. Self-deprecating and full of musical winks, John lampooned the clichés of celebrity culture, declaring that someone – i.e., him – had to play both hero and clown.

'It's got all these corny sounds, and it really swings, man,' John said. 'I really get down on how serious some of the younger pop stars – who don't know better – take themselves.'

On his Scatman promo tours, John struck up conversations with young bands he shared stages with. They were burning through the industry like fireworks: all heat and spectacle, convinced their moment would last forever. John knew better: none of it would last, not for them, not for him. This awareness was crystallized in 'Everything Changes', a song about impermanence and living in the moment.

He had tried offering a quiet reality check. *Enjoy it while it lasts*, he'd tell them. *But know that the star always falls.* They'd nod or smile to placate him, having no idea that this harmless older dude in a suit had once partied so hard he started getting high in California and woke up in Colorado. Then they'd carry on, tossing hotel furniture out of windows like animals.

John, by contrast, left his own hotel room untouched.

'He never asked for anything,' Iris said, but she gave John and Judy an adjoining room and swapped the bed for a couch, so they'd have a 'living room' to relax in, knowing how hard they found it living out of a suitcase.

Even in Bottrop, John and Judy sought out English-speaking AA meetings wherever they could. When the AA-themed track 'Time (Take Your Time)' was laid down in the studio, it wasn't just a song – it was their way of life. At the Italian restaurant in town, they always asked if there was alcohol in the sauce, avoiding even the remnants left after cooking. Once, John gave his meal away, convinced it had traces of cognac in it.

Rounding out the album was 'Hi, Louis', a joyous, scat-fuelled tribute to Louis Armstrong – and 'Game Over Jazz', a freewheeling, jazzy remix of 'Scatman'. Then there was one thing left to do.

'The Germans say *Quotenballaden*,' says Ingo. *There has to be a ballad.*

'Song of Scatland' pulled everything together. John's unapologetic plea for love, unity, peace, and equality. Originally, John had declared that in Scatland, everyone spoke Scatish – a language of syllables and tones, understood instinctively. Its earthly counterpart was stuttering.

But in a twist of irony, 'I couldn't fit all the words in,' John said. 'When we recorded it, I couldn't fit it into a four-bar pattern.' It was rewritten, removing the reference to stuttering. Instead, John referred to 'those who speak in a tongue of their own.'

Over a twenty-one-day recording marathon, John, Tony, and Ingo had built *Scatman's World*, an album that looked typical on the surface yet was anything but. John didn't settle on one theme. Why should he? He threw them all in – war, homelessness, racism, recovery. And above all, the idea that you could turn inward, confront the darkest parts of yourself, and use them as fuel.

John had spent a lifetime being ignored. Now, in the brief window when the world was listening, he wasn't going to waste it. This wasn't an album, but a personal manifesto, and John was ready to deliver it.

Suddenly, the man who'd been afraid to speak had a whole lot to say.

27 **JOYOUS WISDOM**

'Hey – do you wanna be in a music video?'

These days, if an adult claiming to be working in the film industry approached a 15-year-old on the street with that kind of offer, they'd quite rightly be told to run a mile. Not so in London in May 1995, where, luckily for Laura Hagger and her friend Ruth, the offer was legit.

The teens were hanging out at Roller Express, a skating rink in Edmonton, London, when a scout from Front Line Films approached them. The UK production company was producing the music video for 'Scatman's World', the next single ahead of John's upcoming album.

'Scatman (Ski-Ba-Bop-Ba-Dop-Bop)', meanwhile, had flown past four million sales worldwide.

'I knew it couldn't be stopped,' Manfred says. 'Like a snowball, like a pandemic.'

Laura and her friends hadn't been given many details, so it wasn't until they arrived at the first location – Liverpool Street Station – that they realized they were working with the Scatman. Judy was there too, in a sharp pair of cowgirl boots. John wasn't what Laura expected – there was no ego, and no pop-star detachment.

'He was really lovely,' she remembers. 'He made time for every single one of us. He was stammering, and we were just patient with him.'

Every kid on set had heard 'Scatman'. It was still #3 on the UK chart. They circled around him, curious. The scat-singing couldn't possibly be real – it must be a studio trick, right?

John smiled. Then he fired off a verbal bullet train of syllables. Their jaws dropped. *How does he do that?*

The title track of the album, 'Scatman's World', was Eurodance with a twist. Its bassline followed a descending, cyclical progression from the '70s anthem 'Go West', which, in turn, traced back to seventeenth-century classical piece Pachelbel's Canon in D; a warm, anthemic foundation for John to open the door to his world – and invite everyone in.

Part of the song's message came from a conversation John had about racism with soul singer Billy Paul. John was struck when Paul said, 'Soul ain't got no color, man.' That line became the seed for one of the song's most powerful lyrics: 'Scatman, fat man, black and white and brown man – tell me about the color of your soul.'

John also wove in environmental worries, his yearning for truth ('My intention is prevention of the lie'), and the fundamentals of mindfulness ('Be a human being, not a human doing').

Bringing this vision to life on screen in the '90s meant going bigger and bolder. Video had launched John into the mainstream, and in 1995, it was king. Without a strong visual, even the best song risked vanishing in the flood of content on MTV, VH1, and VIVA.

The job fell to director Zowie Broach, known at the time for her work with Danni Minogue, Kula Shaker, and other '90s artists.

'I was pretty young,' she says. 'Probably quite vulnerable as a woman, as a director.' But she had an instinct for what John was trying to say. 'A world of spirituality in nature juxtaposed with cynicism, power, and greed,' her pitch read. 'John will put the world under a microscope. Through the eyes of a child, he checks things and people, knowing his world exists.'

'We were naturally inclusive,' she said of her team. 'One of my assistant directors had a stutter.' The problem, as ever, was money.

'At the beginning of the '90s, record companies spent less money than they did in the '80s,' she explains. 'So you had to be very resourceful.'

Unlike the black-and-white debut, this video would be vivid and narrative-driven: less a music video, more an experience. 'In his world was magic and energy and positivity,' Zowie says. A skeptical news reporter interviews a bored teenager, who then steps into Scatman's World, triggering a dreamlike plunge into a boundless wonderland. At least, that was the plan.

'We wanted much more surreal locations than we actually got,' Zowie says. 'I remember trudging around gardens, looking for places where he could stand under leaves. Pretending to be in different places around the world – but obviously restricted to around the edge of London.'

The busy UK capital, however, became the perfect backdrop for John's message. On London Bridge, commuters rushed past, too busy to notice the man standing still in their midst. At Oxford Circus, John stood in the center of swirling city traffic, untouched by the chaos. In Greenwich Park, a field of buttercups doubled as a technicolor utopia – except, in reality, it was another rainy London day. The crew snapped stills of John standing in the mud, arms thrown wide, beaming.

John didn't need much to make a shot work. 'His physicality was so amazing,' Zowie remembers, likening his performance to jazz: all spontaneity and responsiveness. 'You could have filmed him in a desert, and he'd have still been exciting.'

The kids skated, jumped, and circled John across multiple takes.

'It was very playful, the whole process. I loved him lying on the floor and going crazy with the kids,' Zowie remembers. 'It was kind of wonderful.'

She knew from experience that artists could get frustrated by the repetition and the long hours on location. But John didn't.

'He didn't go away or anything,' Laura Hagger remembers. 'He made sure we enjoyed ourselves, making the day fun instead of getting bored. If other kids wanted to go up and talk to him, he'd talk to them.'

Judy was the same – she was never distant, never performing the role of a celebrity's wife. She chatted with extras and often checked if everyone was okay. Laura and her friend Ruth had started asking questions about the filming and the process. John noticed their curiosity and made an offer.

'Do you want to come to Oxford Circus and see how it all works?' he asked. Laura still remembers how unexpected that was.

'I think he could sense that I wasn't the most confident teenager,' she says. 'I think that's why he probably said it.'

Even though they weren't needed on set, Laura and Ruth spent the day with John and Judy.

'We stood there for hours, just talking,' Laura says. 'He was super happy, just himself. A really kind, nice man.'

They watched as the crew captured stop-motion footage of John's fedora perched on a vintage microphone after he'd tossed it there. 'One of my favorite shots,' Zowie says. 'That was his energy. His little quirkisms.'

Post-production was a leap from the minimalist debut video. This time, they pushed the color grading to its limits in the telecine suite.

'It was one of the ways we could make it more surreal, more vibrant,' Zowie says. 'We were right on the edges of what the machines should do.' As a nod to the first Scatman music video, some shots of John remained in black and white, set against blazing, hyper-saturated backgrounds. Asked to describe John's essence, Zowie didn't hesitate.

'Joyous wisdom,' she said.

With the video complete, John went straight back into the promotional grind with stops in Finland, France, Germany, and the Netherlands. The schedule was hard work, but sometimes, it felt like play.

BMG Ariola Hamburg's Senior A&R Janine Ramond traveled with John to a German theme park for a children's autograph session. The park had closed for the day, and after the last kids left, John was given the run of the place.

'We were like small children, running from one roller coaster to the other,' Janine says.

John became fixated on *Bobbahn*, a bobsled coaster that had opened eighteen months earlier. With no one else around, he waved to the ride operator: *Send us again.* And again. And again.

After sixteen consecutive rides, Janine cried off with a headache. John looked ready for sixteen more. But this was the problem – he had no off-switch. He was also ricocheting across the Atlantic, sometimes home for just days between flights.

'It's completely knocked me off my feet,' he admitted. 'I've been on the road for months, and it's exhausting. If my wife hadn't been there all the time, I would have given up.'

With a second single and full album about to drop, he made one thing clear: Judy had to be there – every show, every tour, and every interview.

'If she chooses not to come, that's her option,' John said. 'I need her now in every way.'

Judy saw what was happening long before John did. He was saying yes to everything, eager to prove himself. But the cracks were starting to show. The day after John returned, exhausted, from another trip, she picked up the phone and called Iceberg Records.

'Manfred,' she said. 'You've got to start looking after John's health.'

Manfred agreed, but said that John's 'splendid' way of presenting himself on radio and TV was the engine behind his success. No promotion? No momentum. But he capitulated and reprioritized the schedule. John finally got something he hadn't had in months: a break.

He and Judy flew home to Los Angeles just in time for a milestone. Judy's son – John's stepson, Lee Newman, was about to release his own album, *Relatively Singing*, a tribute to his great-grandfathers Eddie Cantor and Jimmy McHugh.

'I was playing clubs like the Troubadour, the Whiskey A Go Go, and the Roxy,' Lee says. 'They would come to those shows, and he was very supportive of me.'

Since Lee was already in his 30s, John had never tried to be a father figure – just a friend. 'I'm a stepson,' Lee later said, 'but a *happy* stepson.' They bonded over music. 'We would sing together, and we would jam together,' Lee said. When John was home, they traded recommendations, often swapping songs and albums.

Meanwhile, royalties had finally started coming in, and John and Judy went to view a four-bedroom house in Studio City, tucked into the greenery of Fryman Canyon. They both loved it – John especially. It was rare to find a home in LA with direct access to a nature trail. The secluded setting sealed the deal, and they agreed to buy it.

For the first time in his life, John wasn't renting. He was buying a home 'for my family and my cats,' he said.

But there was little time to settle in. The ink on the real estate paperwork was barely dry when John had an important engagement: the National Stuttering Project's 1995 convention in San Diego.

Months earlier, when he was still an unknown jazz musician, John had agreed to be the keynote speaker. Now, on a warm July day, he walked into the convention hotel as a star.

He had a tan and looked rested when he sat for an interview before his performance. He cracked jokes that only stutterers tell each other, smiling as he told reporters the conference would have to be extended by two days just so everyone could finish their sentences.

People used to tell him he should just sing everything he wanted to say, John said.

'I think I would sound pretty silly if I went through life talking like this,' he sang in an exaggerated trill. 'They'd say, *oh God, you better just stutter!*'

John met Nora O'Connor at the convention – the teenager he'd written letters to in 1992 – but she was in the midst of a drug and alcohol relapse. 'John didn't scold me for my intoxicated state, nor did he take it lightly,' she remembers. 'He let me know I had the answers within me if I chose to look for them.' She sat down for John's keynote speech, which would later leave her in tears.

Judy had bought a camcorder for the occasion and sat in the front row for John's talk. She hit record as the 'Scatman (Ski-Ba-Bop-Ba-Dop-Bop)' music video played on screen for an American audience that had never heard it. The US release wasn't set until August.

As the final notes faded, the room erupted – hundreds of stutterers on their feet, cheering, clapping, roaring.

John wasn't ready for it. He started to cry.

Oh my God, he mouthed.

In the front row, Judy leaned forward.

'I love you, honey,' she whispered. Later, she'd say she had never seen him so raw.

John wiped his eyes with a wad of tissue and stepped up to the microphone for what would become one of the shortest keynote speeches in NSP history.

'I've been stuttering since I've been speaking,' he said. 'Now all of a sudden – Jesus Christ – I'm a pop star.'

Laughter rippled through the room.

'Wait until they find out who I *really* am!'

More laughter. John paused and thought for a moment.

'Spit it out, John!' someone called from the crowd.

He chuckled. The audience erupted again.

Then, after a beat, he got serious. He spoke candidly about his shame. His years of alcoholism. The heroin addiction.

The room fell silent.

'You are l-l-l-l-looking at a walking, talking miracle,' he said. 'Because I should be dead.'

After a condensed version of his life story, John moved on to the way he communicated best. He hopped down from the podium onto the stage where an upright piano waited. His buddies were there with bass and drums. He rolled up his sleeves and tore through jazz standard after standard, weaving in extra bursts of scatting for the whoops and cheers of the crowd.

In the audience, ten-year-old Daniel Kremer sat wide-eyed. *This guy is the real deal.*

'He was electric. On fire,' Daniel remembers. 'I had never seen another stutterer be this dynamic in front of an audience. It was something hopeful, and I was very impressed.'

Daniel had come with his brother, who also stuttered, and their mother.

'That conference changed my mother's life,' he says. 'She'd walked in feeling pretty hopeless about how we'd make our way in the world – not being able to speak with any kind of fluency.' But over those few days, they met people from every walk of life. Happy people. Successful people. Who just happened to stutter.

And there was John. Onstage. A multi-Platinum artist *because* he stuttered.

Before taking his seat at the piano, John talked about the whirlwind: the charts, the TV, the interviews, and the *if I can do it, so can you* heart of *Scatman*.

'You've got to figure, with all those copies sold,' he said. 'There's got to be some stutterers out there who hear it.'

What he didn't know – what he couldn't know – was that at that very moment, halfway across the world, his voice had become somebody's only refuge.

28 WELCOME TO SCATLAND

Five thousand miles from where John stood behind the podium in San Diego, Eloise Pitchford cranked the volume up on her Walkman, trying to drown out the voices.

'Hey moron!'

'Why won't you speak?'

She flung another newspaper onto a porch, eyes locked on the sidewalk. The bullies followed in a loose pack, just far enough behind that the homeowners wouldn't notice. Occasionally, a stone would fly past, making her flinch. She didn't say a word. Not speaking meant not stuttering, so it was easier to be mute.

Imagine a land of love, John's low, steady voice said. *Where people have time to care*. She turned the volume dial again, adjusting the cheap orange headphones she wore like armor.

At school, though, she had nothing. Her tenuous circle of friends evaporated the moment the head bully showed up. She made the mistake of bringing a *Smash Hits* magazine to class because it had the lyrics to 'Scatman' in it. A hand shot out and snatched it away, then it was slowly and deliberately torn in two in front of her face. The pieces were now in a box under her bed, along with the hidden diary where she wrote how she wished she was dead.

The voice on the tape, though, he sounded like he wanted her to carry on. 'Keep living in the moment,' he sang. She swallowed hard. *I'll try*, she thought, and quickened her pace.

That July, the 'Scatman's World' single – with John on the cover this time – shot to number one in Germany, France, and Belgium, and cracked the top five across nearly every other European chart. In Switzerland, 'Scatman (Ski-Ba-Bop-Ba-Dop-Bop)' had only just been released, so both songs squatted in the top five at once, holding the charts hostage and blocking U2, Celine Dion, and Bon Jovi from climbing any higher.

The music video was everywhere – MTV, VIVA, The Box. Laura Hagger and her friends taped it off TV, then rewound and paused the VHS to catch themselves mid-jump or mid-wave, shouting along with John.

MTV Europe nominated John for Best Male Artist of 1995, placing him shoulder to shoulder with Michael Jackson, Dr. Dre, Neil Young, and Lenny Kravitz. They didn't just want him at the awards, either – they wanted him live.

John performed both 'Scatman' and 'Scatman's World' on the channel's *Most Wanted*, ditching playback for a jazz-heavy reinvention with a live band, injecting the songs with energy the studio recordings could only hint at.

But when it came time to speak to presenter Ray Cokes, John slipped into a cartoonish voice, playing along with the irreverent vibe. He'd heard all the jokes about 'scat' meaning animal poop, so he beat them to it – calling Scotland 'Crapland' instead. But the histrionics weren't just for laughs. 'I'm trying not to stutter,' he eventually admitted – and then used that honesty to talk about it.

Back in the saddle of the promotion machine, John bounced from country to country, stage to stage, camera to camera. One journalist joked that demand for John was so high, the only practical solution would be to clone him. Another caught him backstage, but before he could begin a question, John asked, 'Where are we again?'

The Swiss town was pointed out on a map, by which time John was whisked away, saying, 'I only sleep in my spare time.'

The question of whether he really stuttered was joined by another kind of skepticism after interviewers connected the dots between Scatman John and John Larkin, jazz pianist. Had he sold out?

'Everything is jazz,' John countered, tapping the table in time. *One, two, three, four*. All variations of the same thing, the roots unchanged. Scat, he reminded them, *was* jazz. His hero Coltrane once said: *You can play a shoestring if you're sincere*. John agreed.

'If you mean the music you're playing, it's good,' John said. 'If you don't mean it, it's not.'

French magazine *Entrevue* didn't sugarcoat it and accused John of betraying jazz for fame and money.

'Quite the contrary,' John shot back. 'You know how many jazzmen make a living from their music? Not even one per cent. Playing as Scatman lets me play the piano again. The world has betrayed real, pure jazz,' John said. 'Not me.'

Having shed the one-hit-wonder label, John accumulated so many Platinum and Gold certifications over the summer of 1995 that BMG threw him an award party in Hamburg. At the door, every guest was handed the same plain white painter's overalls – a symbolic equalizer to show that in Scatman's World, status didn't matter. Not even at a music industry soirée.

Reality, however, clashed with this message when the awards were handed out, and John noticed an omission. He found Janine Ramond and pulled her aside.

'Why didn't you get an award, Janini?' he asked.

Janine explained that's just how it worked. The company received the award, not her, and it would probably end up on the office wall.

'But you work with me around the clock,' John said. 'I can't believe you don't get one.' Janine explained that yes, it was disappointing, but perfectly normal.

The next morning, Janine was mid-meeting in her office with Axel Alexander when the door swung open. John walked in, holding his first Platinum award for 'Scatman's World'.

'Janini,' he declared. 'This is your award.'

Janine tried to refuse. John wouldn't hear of it. She took it, unable to hold back tears.

'Don't worry, Janini,' John smiled. 'It'll go double Platinum. I'll get the next one.' He was half-joking. But he was right.

In Denmark, Iceberg Records was in overdrive. Manfred and Mette hadn't had time to even consider signing new artists, and brought in extra staff just to handle the avalanche of Scatman requests: movie roles, interviews, festival bookings, concert tours, charity galas, and compilation albums fighting to include the track.

Most had to be declined – there simply wasn't time. But one high-profile collaboration John did accept was with David Bowie, Phil Collins, and other music legends: a limited-edition Scatman John Coca-Cola can, with his image and signature, released to benefit Nordoff–Robbins, a charity funding music therapy for children.

Licensing requests were coming in almost daily, and everyone from car manufacturers to airlines wanted a piece of Scatman. One was from Good Humor, the iconic US ice cream brand, offering a hefty paycheck to turn 'Scatman' into a jingle for their latest TV ad. John agreed – until he saw the lyrics.

They were packed with syllable repetition. Words like 'Goo goo goo Good Humor.' Was it a reference to stuttering? John couldn't be sure, but he wasn't taking chances. A fax landed on Manfred's desk at Iceberg. It was from Judy.

'Manfred, John is not pleased about an actor imitating a stutterer,' she wrote. 'Hold off for now. He does not agree.'

Manfred reassured them that no one was mocking John or trying to be a soundalike. But then he checked the original proposal. Sure enough, the lyrics had repetition. John drew the line. If a fluent actor was going to fake a stutter, he was out – six-figure deal or not.

Manfred backed him. 'If the production were to imitate or parody a stutterer, Scatman John would never allow this,' he told the Good Humor team, adding that if the words were simply scat-like or rap-inspired, no problem. Better yet, John offered to do the vocals himself.

But his schedule got in the way. When it became clear he wouldn't have time to record it, John insisted on final approval of the lyrics. Most of the repetition was cut, and the ad was eventually greenlit.

Meanwhile, the *Scatman's World* album was flying off the shelves, selling tens of thousands of copies a week. John refused to take all the credit.

'Tony and Ingo are the architects of Scatman. They made a hell of an album here,' he said. 'It's great. I even like it. And that's something else, because I'm a critic.'

The external critics were less unanimous. The strutting cynicism of the '90s was alive and well, with UK journalist Stuart Maconie dismissing *Scatman's World* as 'full of homilies about universal tolerance and really rather grisly.' Others called it a one-trick pony. But then there were those who got it.

'It might sound like the last vestige of flower-power free spirit,' one journalist said, 'but John Larkin – Scatman, as he's called – has caught me, Denmark, and the rest of Europe with their pants down with his positive persona.'

Music reviewer Michael Smiley agreed. 'Scatman John was a slave to drugs and alcohol for twenty-five years. Today he gives good advice to young people,' he wrote. 'Scatman John is not bullshit. If you are young, confused, and angry, there is plenty of good advice to be had.'

Those expecting just another Eurodance album found something more, too.

'Hip-hop, Euro-disco, mambo, jazz, and fairy tales in a witty and lively way. It's a joy to behold.'

Tucked inside every copy of *Scatman's World* was a blueprint for Scatland, John's imagined utopia where trust replaced laws, where power belonged to those who gave the most, and no one was left behind.

In hotel rooms between interviews, hunched over his laptop, John distilled months of thought into his liner notes. The dedication was part disclosure, part declaration.

'My name is John Larkin,' it began. 'I am a person who stutters.'

His stutter, he wrote, had 'haunted' him, until he realized it was 'a source of strength, and a source of humility in disguise.' His life had changed. He had stopped living in the problem and started living in the solution. What was the solution?

'To try to help all of us kids out there who are struggling,' he said. 'That is why I dedicate this album to all who have problems, living in a confused world … which includes those of us who stutter.'

Hundreds, then thousands, then millions of kids unfolded those same notes, and read those same words. Maybe their emotional pain wasn't from a stutter. Maybe it was something else. But they understood. They weren't alone. 'As long as you need me, I will be here for you,' John wrote. 'You are all my children.'

Some critics scoffed. Some rolled their eyes. John didn't care.

'I hear people blame me that my music and lyrics sound far too optimistic. Yes, even naïve,' he said. 'I don't agree. A lot of young people use music as an exhaust valve for their incomprehension and inability. I don't have anything against that. My music has nothing to do with aggression. Instead, it has everything to do with love and solidarity. I fear that by only focusing on the negative things in the world, we're losing our faith in the fundamental kindness of mankind.'

'And that,' he concluded, 'is a disaster.'

By the fall of 1995, John had spent weeks atop *Music & Media*'s Border Breakers chart as the artist who'd reached more countries than any other.

'A more convincing triumph is hard to imagine,' the magazine announced. The *Scatman's World* album had cleared two million copies. The debut single? Another two million. The follow-up? Over a million.

Then there was Japan. John had crammed more than fifty radio shows, TV appearances, and interviews into a two-week promotional blitz. The country responded in kind. *Scatman's World* was barreling toward a million copies sold there alone – a rare feat for a foreign artist.

But just as *Scatman's World* conquered Europe and Asia, America shrugged.

'Scatman (Ski-Ba-Bop-Ba-Dop-Bop)' finally hit the US in September, entering the *Billboard* Hot 100. It climbed, paused, and stalled at #60.

'Dance music in the US has been backed into a corner,' RCA's dance crossover manager told *LA Weekly*. Music producer Peter Lorimer agrees. "America was in a rock phase going into a hip hop phase," he says. "Dance music was really only played in the gay clubs and the Latin clubs." To American ears, Eurodance often sounded like 'that cheesy disco shit' as writer Rolf Potts put it.

US radio was still feeling the aftershock of the 1979 Disco Demolition, when a crate of records was blown up on a Chicago baseball field, and dance music was driven off the air. Eurodance, a direct descendant, bore the brunt of that stigma well into the '90s. And unlike post–Cold War Europe, America had no reason to embrace a genre built on escapism and unity. 'The first single just didn't connect here the way it did in other countries,' RCA admitted.

They tried to fix it. A year earlier, Arista had turned Swedish band Ace of Base into a US juggernaut by repackaging *Happy Nation* as *The Sign*, adding tracks and remixing it. Hoping for similar magic, John, Ingo, and Tony flew to LA's Enterprise Studios to record a new track, 'Hey You!', and tweak others with added female backing vocals to make them sound more 'American.'

It didn't work. Manfred watched the charts and faxed a warning: 'America goes at a snail's pace.' If 'Scatman' didn't crack the top fifteen soon, he said, launching the album in the US would be commercial suicide. It would be swallowed by the holiday sales rush.

Just over a month later, it vanished from the charts.

That was that. The US release was scrapped.

'A disappointment,' Judy said. John had already complained that America didn't 'look after' its jazz artists, and now his home country had rejected him again. But with time, he admitted he might have the best of both worlds. 'John liked his anonymity,' Judy said, pointing out that he didn't mind being a megastar abroad, yet unknown at home.

As 1995 drew to a close, one final fax arrived at Iceberg Records. *Music & Media* had tallied the year-end stats.

John had done it.

He was the top male artist in Europe. Michael Jackson came second.

'I beat out Michael Jackson!' John laughed. He framed the fax and hung it on the wall of his new house. But there was no time to celebrate. Something much bigger was coming.

It was time to take Scatman John on tour.

29 **JOHNNY JETLAG**

John ducked behind the curtain and reached for the mask. The band hit the bridge, sax wailing, bass thumping, enough to buy him thirty seconds. He clamped it to his face and inhaled. The oxygen hissed, dry and metallic. Nothing like the air out there, charged with heat and sweat.

His chest heaved, fell. Rose again. *Twenty seconds.* He looked at the gauge. The needle twitched down. *Ten.* He flung off the mask, wiped his hands on his pants, and shoved the tank out of sight. The sax solo climbed, stretched, and looped back. Almost time.

John straightened, turned, and stepped back into the lights.

'Everybody's from Scatman's World!'

Thousands of voices roared as a human wave surged forward. From the side of the stage, Judy watched, camera in hand. Too far for the lens to catch the sweat pouring off John's forehead, soaking the lining of his fedora.

There was no slowing down. No time to breathe.

When tour planning began, John made not just one request, but two. This was rare. One BMG exec once joked that as long as John got eight hours of sleep and three meals a day, he was content. But now he had specifics. On stage, there had to be a saxophone player. And off it – an oxygen tank.

Tour manager Ulrik Hinsch had handled John's 1995 promo events, and now, in January 1996, he was tasked with a full-scale live tour, spanning two continents and ten countries, with barely a pause between gigs. The oxygen, Ulrik knew, wasn't optional. Without it, 'He couldn't do 75 minutes,' Ulrik says, 'Or even two times 45 minutes.'

Manfred asked bass guitarist Steve Brzezicki, a musician he trusted, to assemble not just a band but a balancing act, finding musicians capable of fusing Eurodance, pop, rock, and jazz.

'As soon as I heard John, I knew he was an accomplished jazz pianist,' Steve says. 'I put the band together with a sax player that could also double on keys.' That sax player was Steve Hamilton, who had keyboard chops and could also play the EWI (Electronic Wind Instrument), which was essential for recreating Scatman's studio sound live.

Back in LA, John rang in the new year with Judy, Lee, and their new golden retriever puppy, Winston (named after Churchill). Then he left the California sun behind and flew to the UK. His friends had a name for him during stretches like this: *Johnny Jetlag*.

Waiting for him in London were the final pieces of his touring band: keyboardist Tim Best, drummer Steve Williams, and guitarist Paul Dunn. None of them had met John before.

'It was great fun. He was lovely,' said saxophonist Steve Hamilton. 'Very nice fellow,' added bassist Steve Brzezicki. 'Very warm.'

With only one album to draw from, John filled out the setlist with a handful of covers. Gone was 'Song of Scatland', which had been released as a Christmas single and briefly charted in Germany before fading – a rare misstep in an otherwise unstoppable run. In its place was Louis Armstrong's 'What a Wonderful World'.

He threw in Bobby Troup's 'Route 66', and 'Get Back' by the Beatles ('incongruous, to say the least,' Steve Hamilton says), but the latter's long solos gave John time to duck backstage and load up on oxygen. The result was a set that zipped along, genre-hopping in a way that made as much sense as a jazzman in a fedora storming the dance charts.

John grumbled about the cold. 'A foggy day in London town,' he said of the January rehearsals. He stayed a few nights with Steve Brzezicki and his wife, mostly keeping to himself, except to ask for an internet connection so he could look up local AA meetings. Then, every morning at 11 a.m., the band convened.

'He wanted to put a band together to enjoy themselves rather than rehearse,' Steve Brzezicki recalls. 'Loosey goosey,' John told them. Nothing too strict. Their main job was to nail the starts and ends of songs because the middle was whatever John felt like in the moment.

The second challenge was blending electronic elements into the live show. Samplers were wired to a sound module powered by an Atari 1040, triggered by Steve Williams on drums. After a week of rehearsals, it was time for the opening night.

The tour got off to a rocky start in Kyiv, Ukraine, with late January temperatures around 13°F (-25°C). John, Judy, and the band arrived in heavy ice and snow, bundled in *Scatman's World* tour jackets that barely kept out the cold. Then the first hassle: luggage carts cost extra, and they were told to pay or haul everything by hand. So they paid. A police escort flanked their bus as they set off through frozen streets. At the venue, things went from bad to worse.

The wrong electrical converter plugs had been packed. Tour manager Ulrik dashed out to find replacements while the band tried to stop the gear from freezing.

'I couldn't touch my saxophone because it was frozen,' Steve Hamilton says. 'It was so cold the metal was sticking to me.'

After blasting the instruments with hot air blowers, the band finally took to the stage, hours behind schedule. Halfway through the set, people started walking out.

John panicked. *They hate the show.*

Then someone explained: the last bus was leaving. The city's transport curfew was strict. If people stayed, they'd be stranded in the cold, so most of them left.

'Insanity,' John called it.   And that was just the beginning.

Next up was Moscow, Russia.

'I was petrified,' said John's business manager, Michael Schur, when he found out where John was headed. 'I got escape and evasion insurance.'

As their plane descended, Judy glanced out of the window and saw big crowds of journalists, press, and security waiting on the tarmac. *Someone really important must be arriving*, she thought. It was only when they landed that she realized – it was John.

Armed guards escorted them to the hotel and swept an entire floor. In the evening, the band arrived at Metelitsa, Moscow's premier post-Soviet playground for the elite.

Inside, heavily made-up women lined one side of the room, and men swaggered and knocked back champagne and vodka on the other. Steve Brzezicki watched more file in, casually checking their guns at the door.

'It wasn't an audience,' he said. 'It was people at tables, eating caviar.'   Payment, Manfred recalled, arrived in a shoebox stuffed with used notes.

John played two nights there. Later, he never said why, but made it clear that no amount of money would persuade him to return.

Then, just as the band was starting to find its feet, John slammed one of his in a hotel door. It swelled so badly he couldn't get his shoes on for the gig at the Hungexpo in Budapest. But John didn't like wearing them anyway, so he walked onstage in his socks.

The delay gave the audience more time to drink. Among them was photographer Ákos Hegedűs, aka Morpho, who'd been chasing beer with vodka. When John finally appeared, 'I had every reason to believe I was the weakest link among the people working in the hall,' he said. 'But it soon became clear the artist was also standing on relatively weak legs, in socks and no shoes.'

John wobbled, laughed, then lifted his foot and wiggled his toes for the crowd. *Click.*

By morning, the photo was splashed on the cover of *Kurír*. 'He was the best performer of the past year,' the tabloid wrote, applauding John's attempts to teach the raucous crowd how to scat-sing, though how well that went was anyone's guess.

No one noticed the effort behind his breath. Not even the band.

'At some point, I realized there was oxygen around,' Steve Brzezicki says. 'I had no idea what was going on. I didn't know John had a condition.'

When asked why he insisted on singing everything live, 'I'm from the world of jazz,' John said, 'where playback is completely unknown.' That was about all the press got before, as one paper put it, 'his army of bodyguards took him away.'

That army had a new job now – crowd control. John was constantly getting mobbed.

It started in a restaurant. A few teenagers spotted him eating with Judy. Minutes later, the place was packed. John barely touched his food, too busy signing anything they put in front of him.

Even after shows, exhausted, he refused to turn anyone away. BMG printed pre-signed postcards to save time, but he defeated the purpose by personalizing them anyway. Manfred noticed John trying to reply to fan mail in between gigs, in his hotel room.

Eventually, John and Ulrik struck a deal. After a while, Ulrik would drag John away and absorb the backlash. John would throw up his hands and say, 'I can't! Look how mean he is …'

It worked. Left to his own devices, John would have stayed all night.

By the time the crew reached Germany for six back-to-back shows, the tour had finally hit its stride, though not before one last hurdle in Warsaw, Poland.

John took the stage flanked by dancers and fireworks, a way to keep the visuals interesting, since he often played from behind his keyboard. He opened with 'Sing Now!' and 'Scatman's World', whipping the thousands-strong crowd into whirling groups, their jackets and T-shirts flying.

Then the lights dimmed and John, alone in the spotlight, performed what the press called his 'sensational version' of 'What a Wonderful World'. The audience swayed, holding up lighters.   Ulrik spotted blinking red and green lights among them. Recording devices.

The local record promoter had cut a deal: recordings were allowed, but only for the first two songs. They were well past that now. Ulrik waded into the crowd, ordering people to shut it down. This pissed the promoter off so much he retaliated by withholding the band's plane tickets out.

They eventually departed, late again. But John never complained, Ulrik said. Not once.

'He was always full of joy, positivity, and loving what was happening,' Steve Brzezicki says. 'He loved to get out and play.'

In Germany, the schedule finally smoothed out, and John, mindful of his energy, mostly kept to himself with Judy. They ordered room service, ventured out for nicotine gum or AA meetings, and skipped the nightlife.

'Because of the addiction issues he'd had, if we went out to a club, he wasn't going to be there with us,' Steve Hamilton remembers. 'There was a natural segregation.'

But soundchecks were different. One afternoon, Steve Hamilton started playing 'Black Narcissus' on his sax, a 1970s jazz piece by Joe Henderson. John heard it.

'He completely surprised me by just joining in and playing it all the way across,' Steve remembers. 'We jammed quite often. He was an incredible musician.'

They crisscrossed 1,500 km of German countryside in a luxury tour bus once used by Paul McCartney. Out of respect – and amusement – they left a front seat untouched, calling it 'Paul's seat.'

After nearly three weeks of European gigs, Manfred boarded a flight to Japan in mid-February, ready to join them for the biggest leg of the tour. Every single show was sold out. *Scatman's World* had moved almost two and a half million copies there, putting John in the company of the Beatles, Queen, and the Eagles.

Manfred rode with John through Tokyo's neon-lit streets, headed to Liquidroom – an industrial venue on the seventh floor of the Humax Pavilion Shinjuku complex. John had played to packed houses before, but Japan was different. He knew the numbers, knew the records he'd broken. But nothing prepared him for what he saw as the car turned the corner.

Thousands of fans snaked around the block and into the distance. The second they spotted him, the noise detonated – screams, shouts, hands slamming against barriers. Security guards strained to keep the wave of bodies from spilling into the street.

'I don't want to get out,' John said, eyeing the guards barely keeping the crowds back. He said it again as the car stopped at the artists' entrance.

The door swung open. Manfred smirked, put his shoe against John's backside, and playfully nudged him forward.

'You're the bloody pop star,' he said. 'Out!'

John laughed – and stepped into the storm.

'John!' people yelled at the closed curtains.

'Joooohn!'

It was uncharacteristic of a Japanese audience to do anything but sit politely, waiting in respectful silence for the performer. But not this time.

Steve Brzezicki peeked out. He had never seen so many women wearing hats and mustaches.

John walked on, and for the next ninety minutes, he powered through his set, his roaring stage presence masking a body barely keeping up. At least here, he had help. He turned the mic to the crowd. Everyone in the place knew every word.

'A better high than my old world,' he later said. 'To see some of their faces – their beautiful faces – screaming, "Scatman, Scatman." As if you could reach such innocent beings.'

For Japan, the band had rehearsed the English version of 'Sukiyaki' by Kyu Sakamoto. But rehearsals were only ever a sketch.

'John, bless him, was never really interested in how the songs *should* be,' Steve Brzezicki says. 'He would rather just wing it.'

The result was glorious chaos.

'Steve!' John would shout. 'Solo!'

Except three of the five band members were called Steve, so they'd glance around to see which way John was pointing – usually at Steve Hamilton on sax. But with a stage full of seasoned musicians, it didn't matter. They ran with it, had fun with it, and had a roadie standing by to reset the sequencer whenever John veered off-script.

John told fans in every country, 'I love you.' He learned it in every language. In Tokyo, before 'What a Wonderful World', he addressed the crowd.

'I want you all to hold your partner's hand,' he said. 'Boy, girl, it doesn't matter.'

By now he was too emotional to say it, so he sang it: 'There I go again, feeling love, and trying so hard not to show it. That's only for children …'

Later, someone in the crowd shouted, 'We love you!'

John's face crumpled with joy. He dropped to his knees and took big, exaggerated bows towards the audience. When he rose, even those at the back heard him yell, 'I don't need a microphone to tell you I love you!'

He jumped around, tossed his hat aside and slapped his bald patch to the crowd's cheers. After decades of being told to keep it down, to rein it in, John scatted, screamed, shouted and howled with the abandon of a man who had waited a lifetime to be unchained. The more he did, the louder they got.

This wasn't a tour – it was a victory lap. John gave them every ounce of breath, burning himself down to the last ember, leaving it all onstage.

Which is why, after a grueling ten-thousand-mile round trip from Japan to Germany and back for yet another award show, something had to give.

On the morning of 27 March 1996, with the tour over but weeks of promo still ahead, everyone connected to the Scatman project received a fax.

'I am exhausted,' John wrote. 'By the time I return, I'm going to be ready for a rest home. You know I always give my all,' he continued.

'But I can't do this.'

30 JOURNEY OF FANTASY

John lobbed the tennis ball into the pool, laughing as their golden retriever puppy, Winston, launched himself after it with a splash.

It was spring 1996. He and Judy had owned the house for six months, but John had barely been in it. Between touring, promo, and press, the place still felt new. Now, finally home, he began hanging his twenty-five Gold and Platinum records in the hallway – and quickly ran out of wall space.

This wasn't the first time he'd had to step back. After the summer of '95, Mette Zähringer had canceled a stretch of appearances. She apologized to networks, saying John had to back out 'due to poor health and because he is quite exhausted.' Now it was happening again.

He was supposed to be in Bottrop, recording his second album, *Journey of Fantasy*. Instead, he was in his backyard, trying to remember what normal life felt like. Judy watched as he took the tennis ball from Winston's mouth and threw it again.

'Championella!' John yelled. He'd always had trouble with Ws. If your name started with one, chances were, you had a nickname.

After the European and Asian tours, John had gone straight into another round of promotion in Korea and Japan, where Scatman had gone from a hit to a cultural phenomenon. Comedian Kato-Cha covered 'Scatman (Ski-Ba-Bop-Ba-Dop-Bop)', and even the superhero Ultraman gave it a go.

By the time he flew home, two commercials were set to air in Japan. In one, John co-starred with actress Honami Suzuki for Kanebo cosmetics, singing a new jingle: 'Su Su Su Super Kirei' – meaning 'super beautiful'. The stuttered syllables were deliberate this time, since John was the one singing them. He'd recorded both the song and video in LA. Between takes, he surprised the crew by sitting at the piano and playing a stripped-down acoustic version of 'Love Me Tender' that was so good, BMG Japan snapped it up as a bonus track.

Then there was 'PriPri Scat', a jingle for Glico's Pucchin Purin, a popular pudding dessert. He'd written it, sung it, and starred in the ad, recorded in February straight off the road. Both jingles became singles. Both were hits, totaling over 200,000 copies sold.

The tennis ball bounced along the pool's edge. Another new dog – a King Charles spaniel called Charlie Parker – skittered after it, barking at Winston.

On 13 March 1996, John had turned 54 in a Paris hotel room, surrounded by flowers, having just landed after another long-haul flight. Somewhere between touchdown and the room service tray, he learned his global sales had passed six million. A popularity poll had ranked him the seventh most famous person in Japan.

Yet back in Los Angeles, nobody looked twice at the middle-aged man in a T-shirt and sweatpants, throwing sloppy tennis balls for his dog.

'It was like nothing,' says John's business manager, Michael Schur, of John and Judy's sudden leap from scraping by to millionaires. 'It didn't change their lifestyle. They just kept doing their normal life.'

John didn't really know what to do with the money. He started with the basics – things most people took for granted, things he'd never had, like a new car. He picked a black Cadillac Eldorado, loaded the Bose sound system with jazz and Scatman cassettes, and drove it to friends' houses just to show it off – even if they'd already seen it.

'I've got a home, some cars, and a computer,' John said. 'I know it sounds corny, but sometimes I tell myself I don't deserve all this.'

That computer went everywhere with him, lugged across continents on tour. He racked up so much time on dial-up internet overseas that his label eventually made him pay his own phone bills. Late at night – jetlagged or buzzing from shows and too wired to sleep, he'd log onto AOL or AltaVista and wander the early corners of the web. That's where he stumbled across a couple of fan-made websites devoted to Scatman John.

One of them was run by Elson Trinidad, who'd first heard John's music while in France but, ironically, lived just half an hour away in LA. They connected first by phone ('At times he'd apologize for his stuttering,' Elson recalled), and later in person, when they went to see one of John's heroes, Coltrane's pianist McCoy Tyner, in concert.

'John was too shy to talk to him,' Elson says.

Soon, John began using Elson's site to reach his growing fanbase, posting updates and trying, unsuccessfully, to reply to the torrent of messages.

'Hello to you all,' he wrote after returning from the tour. 'Just returned from Asia where the Scatman project has soared. The kids there are beautiful … I can't tell you the joy it is to hear them say "I love you, Scatman." Not having children of my own, I think I'm experiencing the feelings of a father …'

He kept in touch with stuttering organizations around the world, and when they asked to use his music in educational materials, the answer was always yes. He told Iceberg and BMG not to charge.

In Japan, members of the Japan Stuttering Genyūkai Association visited him at his hotel. He invited them backstage at his concerts. When he won the Grand Prix award for New Artist of the Year – along with its million-yen prize – he donated the money straight back to the association.

Back in LA, John walked the wide, dusty trails of Wilacre Park behind his house, up past scrubland and oak trees, taking in views of the valley. Time to think. He was once asked what drove him. 'A constant evaluation of my values,' he told journalist Honda Jorgensen. 'A search for what my motives really are.'

How can I fulfill the purpose of my existence? He thought. *How can I help others?*

Fame hadn't solved everything. If anything, it had exposed the work still to be done. Stuttering was still horribly misunderstood. The public didn't always get it. The press didn't either.

In Finland, a TV host had laughed and imitated his stutter. Today, it would be unthinkable to mock someone's disability on air. But in the '90s, it wasn't rare – and it wasn't the only time, either.

In the summer of 1995, John was onstage in Portugal, having what he later called 'a very bad day' with his speech. He was stuttering on nearly every word. But he kept going.

'If you've heard the words to Scatman, it's all about sttttuttering,' he said. 'I'm up here, sttttuttering. And I ask all the y-young kids, if you have a problem that you think is holding you b-b-b-b-back …'

Laughter broke from somewhere in the crowd. John stopped.

'I know, it's cute, isn't it?' he said, flipping the moment. He threw an arm around the presenter, taking control of the stage.

'If you have a problem that is holding you b … ack. There, I said it!'

Now the audience was laughing with him, not at him.

'You can tap into that problem,' he continued, 'and it can become a source of strength, and a source of power.'

He was invited to play piano. As he took his seat, his hands trembled so much that he had trouble getting the mic onto its stand. But then his fingers touched the keys for 'Route 66' – and he slipped into jazz like he was home.

Mid-song, he glanced at the crowd. There it was. The look. The same one he had in high school. The same one he had every time someone had laughed at him.

I may stutter, that look still said. *But watch this.*

He quieted the band and took a rollicking scat-singing solo. The audience cheered, whistled, applauded. He had won them over. Not by hiding his stutter. But by owning it.

That was it. He knew where his money needed to go. Stigma was high, awareness low, and shame ran deep. Much of the world still held the 1950s mindset John had grown up with: fix the speech, hide the rest.

He began the paperwork for a nonprofit, The Scatland Foundation, 'serving the worldwide community of people who stutter.'

Looking for direction, John reached out to the new International Stuttering Association – and inadvertently stepped into a long-standing divide. Some wanted to pursue greater fluency. Others pushed for self-acceptance. John leaned toward the latter.

'When I accepted that I stuttered, I no longer let it control me,' he told the committee. In an interview with the Japan Stuttering Genyūkai Association, he hinted at a yet unnamed movement: stuttering pride – the idea that stuttering isn't a flaw to hide, but a voice to reclaim.

'What I've tried to achieve,' he told them, 'is to stop trying not to stutter – and instead stop being ashamed of it. If you think your "real self" is the fluent one, you'll feel more ashamed when you stutter. Of course, that's just my opinion – everyone should have their own approach to stuttering and how to face it.'

John's personal preference was towards acceptance, but publicly, he didn't pick a side. In his exchange with the International Stuttering Association, 'If you wish to acquire more fluency, then that's the priority,' he wrote. 'If you wish to acquire self-acceptance, then that's the priority. There are as many opinions as there are people who stutter. Open-mindedness and respect for other opinions are essential.'

There was no single path forward. And that was the point.

'The Scatland Foundation has an open mind,' he said. For John, acceptance didn't mean giving up. It meant showing up. Because one thing, he insisted, was nonnegotiable: *educate the public*. The myths – that stuttering meant low intelligence, poor thinking, or lack of ability – had to go. 'We need to let the world know that stuttering isn't psychologically or physically abnormal,' he said.

John gathered his research, filed the papers, and waited.

He was due to fly back to Bottrop in April 1996 to begin recording. But first, John took his new car and drove to collect the fan mail from his PO box.

Later that afternoon, Judy found him in his new downstairs office. Bags and bags of mail were strewn around the floor. John was sitting in the middle of it, his head in his hands.

'I can't answer it all,' he said when she asked what was wrong. Judy tried to reassure him that it was okay – no one expected him to reply to everything.

John looked up. She saw he was on the edge of tears.

'What if there's another me?' he said.

31 EVERYBODY JAM!

Oh shit.

Manfred looked everywhere: backstage, out in the crowd, in the dressing rooms. No John.

It was March 1996 – days after John had told the label he couldn't do this anymore. He was minutes from going live on national TV at a major concert hall in South Korea.

Earlier, a local jazz band had taken the stage. Manfred noticed John watching them.

'I could see something in John's eyes,' he said. Now John had vanished.

'I feared the worst,' Manfred said. 'And the worst happened.'

The curtain rose. There was John at the piano, the trio's bassist and drummer beside him.

'Oh shit,' Manfred said – out loud this time – as John began playing Thelonious Monk's 'Well You Needn't', throwing in the occasional 'I'm the Scatman!' like punctuation.

This was absolutely not what he was booked to do. It was a promo event. He was supposed to be miming Scatman tracks.

Instead, John burned through three or four times his allotted segment – on live TV – then finally closed with a couple of playback Scatman songs.

He got a standing ovation.

'In any other country, he would have been stopped,' Manfred says. 'And fired.'

The industry's inability to put John back in his box showed up in the brainstorming for the next album. *Journey of Fantasy* was pitched as a trip around the globe, each track built around a different cultural or musical influence: African rhythms, gospel, Indian and East Asian motifs, and – much to John's happiness – jazz.

BMG Ariola Hamburg's A&R team drew inspiration from movies like *The NeverEnding Story* and *Momo*, asking for 'childishly naïve simplicity, adventure, joy, infinity, curiosity,' to be threaded through the album with 'togetherness, love, and respect for life.' John liked the idea.

In April 1996, after his precious few weeks off, John and Judy flew back to Bottrop. The album was already behind schedule. A new single was the priority

– Iceberg had already lost at least one major sync (media licensing) opportunity because there hadn't been a new Scatman release in months.

John returned to find an upgraded setup.

'To speed up the workflow, we needed another studio,' explains Tony Catania. 'One for recording – like vocals – and the other for editing.'

The apartment beneath them had changed hands, too. The elderly lady was gone, replaced by a younger man far less tolerant of the *thump-thump-thump* of techno above him. On occasion, he'd even cut the power in protest.

Ingo and Tony had sunk thousands of Deutsche Marks into new gear. When Tony ran downstairs to help unload their biggest delivery yet, the neighbor helped to carry the box in. He asked what was in it. When Tony told him it was a new mixing board, 'He looked at me like he wanted to kill me,' Tony laughs.

John and Judy settled back into their familiar routine at the Ramada, warmly greeted by Iris, whom they now considered a friend.

'I've been to many places in the world in my life and have seen the most famous and expensive hotels,' John said. 'But when I come to Bottrop, it's always a bit like coming home.'

As usual, he hogged the room's phone line, plugging in his laptop to post updates to the Scatman website.

'Some of your letters were so beautiful,' he wrote. 'It breaks my heart that I cannot be personal to you all and answer the letters individually … but there are simply too many of you out there to do that.' For now, John thought, the best he could do was keep creating the kind of songs that seemed to resonate with them.

The first album had flowed, free of the weight of expectation. But now, 'the performance pressure was enormous,' John said.

He spent three weeks in the studio, spinning childlike themes into songs with bite. He paraphrased Gandhi in '(We Got to Learn to) Live Together' ('an eye for an eye has made the whole world blind') and went full anti-war in 'People of the Generation' ('they gave a war / nobody came / imagine all the fuss / they'd have to send themselves / instead of sending us').

'Not bad for an old fart,' John would occasionally say when he nailed a take. He stood at the mic – always in socks, never shoes – singing between ragged gulps of air, his hands clamped over his headphones. The rest of the time, his jaw worked a piece of nicotine gum as he mumbled and murmured through his notes on his laptop, still swearing sharply at himself from time to time.

'We really had fun preparing "Shut Your Mouth and Open Your Mind",' says Ingo, who co-wrote the scathing indictment of politicians ahead of the 1996 US presidential election. '*Your lips keep movin', talkin' as you walk / But everybody knows you're not walkin' what you talk*,' John rapped, in what Ingo called an 'almost affected, serious voice.' Whether John had anyone specific in mind, he didn't say.

'We never spoke about politics,' Ingo adds.

Later, journalists noticed and would try to bait John.

'You're not a communist, are you?' one asked.

'I hope not,' John replied. 'No, I'm somebody who wants to be part of the solution instead of part of the problem. I'm not into any politics.'

'Are you religious?' another prodded.

'No. No … I think religions create division,' he said. 'Spirituality, on the other hand, teaches the world to support each other.'

When one DJ tried to politicize his vision of Scatland, John just smiled and offered noncommittal 'Mmm-hmms' until they gave up, choosing instead to wave and grin at the kids gathered outside the studio window.

Having had direct contact with his audience, John wanted to share his first love with them.

'I'm giving kids a little jazz, like a flower,' he said. 'One petal at a time.'

John name-checked no fewer than nineteen jazz musicians in the song 'Jazzology'. Next, John, Tony and Ingo began work on a demo called 'Jazz Jam', using modern sampling to build a cross-generational conversation between John and his idol, Louis Armstrong. Ingo combed through more than fifty Armstrong CDs, listening not just for trumpet lines, but for scraps of speech that could become an imagined exchange between two men who had never met, but spoke the same scat-singing language.

In April 1996, John had to pause recording and rejoin the promotional circuit. Even with no new single to push, he was still flown back and forth to Japan, 'so the buyers don't forget him,' the label said. He was now BMG's biggest foreign asset.

Mix magazine columnist Knud Løkke caught up with John in Tokyo and marveled at what was, supposedly, a light day.

'If this promotion belongs on the easy end,' Løkke wrote, 'I really don't want to be there when it's hard.'

He described a schedule that put John in front of cameras and microphones 'every eternal and single day' – from headlines and talk shows in the morning to late-night television. That's how it had been for days before Løkke arrived, and it was how it would be for weeks after he left. Yet John was still game.

'Man, I've thrown away so many years by filling myself with booze and drugs,' he said. 'I want to catch up.'

John's only complaint was that pre-recorded radio shoutouts always ran overtime because no one had accounted for his stutter. Then and now, people who stutter need such time adjustments – and rarely get them.

Despite the schedule, John always made time for Satoru Hanazono, a fellow stutterer from Tokyo. They'd met earlier that year. John's fame had skyrocketed in Japan, but 'he didn't change,' Satoru recalls. 'He took the time.' When Satoru called his hotel room, John always came down to see him, even for just half an hour.

After this stretch on the road, though, John was back on the phone with his team, asking for more time at home before the album resumed.

'He started to get stressed,' Tony Catania says. 'He said, I can't come to Bottrop. You need to come here.'

In May, a few days before Tony and Ingo were due in LA, John walked into David L. Abell's storied piano shop on Beverly Boulevard, a few miles from his home. To most of Los Angeles, Abell was 'Piano Dealer to the stars.' To John, he was a fellow jazz devotee. Abell understood: a piano wasn't a transaction – it was a relationship.

John sat at a Yamaha DC3II Disklavier grand in gleaming, polished ebony. His fingers punched out storms of sound, the lows thundering, the highs tinkling like shattered glass. 'It's like kissing the heart of God, man,' he said later. The piano was acoustic but had electronic guts. It could replay performances from floppy disks and CDs, sync to MIDI, or slot straight into a studio setup. It was perfect.

Eighteen months into being Scatman, John finally had both the time – and the money – to buy it. His small, well-worn spinet went to his mother's place, so when he visited, he'd have something to do other than talk.

The piano had been delivered by the time Ingo, Tony, and Tony's wife Ilona landed in LA, but there wasn't much else to work with. They rented a couple of keyboards and made do with an old eight-track machine, but it was a struggle.

'The atmosphere was terrible,' Ingo remembers. John seemed out of sorts and told Tony that he didn't want Ilona at the sessions, perhaps remembering how Judy's presence in Bottrop had distracted him. 'But I understand that,' Tony says, 'in the professional way.'

Judy tried to lighten the load – handling calls, faxes, and paperwork with their business manager. Over in Denmark, Manfred was busy cancelling gig and promo invitations to carve out some breathing room for John. One evening, he called the house, hoping to hear some new material. But John was asleep.

'Don't wake him,' Manfred said, not yet aware John was losing the ability to bounce back.

Tony and Ingo returned to Germany to start mixing, but BMG was getting anxious about the delays. When early demos went out, the reaction was tepid.

'Expectations were extremely high,' Ingo says. 'The lightness of before had disappeared.'

Interruptions came nonstop – calls, couriered memos, faxes, and uninvited visitors buzzed toward the Bottrop studio.

'Too many people with different opinions,' Tony says. 'They expected something even better, but how do you top it, with the same idea? It's not fresh anymore. So you need to reinvent yourself.'

When John learned about the interference, he was furious.

'All of a sudden, everybody became a Scatman expert,' he fumed. 'They are not the kids. They don't know! The kids want to hear REAL music. The kids love Scatman because of the integrity of the first album, and that same integrity is on the second album. I hope you guys hear what I'm saying here,' he wrote. 'I have had firsthand exposure to these kids.'

In August, after yet another trip to Japan, John returned to Bottrop to finish the record and cut one of its final tracks – a cover of Queen's 'Invisible Man'. Germany's biggest paper, *Bild*, came by, and John made it clear whose corner he was in: 'Without the two of them,' he said of Ingo and Tony, 'there would be no Scatman. They made me a star.'

But the meddling persisted. 'Everybody got their souls broken trying to make this second album,' John said. 'I got angry. They were all in the studio, and I told them, guys, get out of here, let us make the music, please.'

Eventually, 'Jazz Jam' became 'Everybody Jam!', and it was chosen as the lead single and album title. The lyrics were a tribute to Louis Armstrong, built around the reconstructed conversation between the two men and born of John's childhood spent watching 'Satchmo' smile through the TV at him, free and joyful.

'Satchmo's message was love,' John said. 'Even though he was Black and oppressed. He won people's hearts that way. I wish I had his courage. I'm working on it.'

Before the video shoot in New Orleans, John made one last stop. In September 1996, he flew to Washington D.C. to accept the Annie Glenn award from the American Speech-Language-Hearing Association.

Annie Glenn – the wife of astronaut John Glenn – had a lifelong stutter and later became a powerful advocate. The award in her name honoured those who raised public awareness of communication disorders. Now John was one of them, joining the ranks of the first recipient, actor James Earl Jones. The two met and swapped stories about life with a famous voice – and a stutter.

'Such a nice man,' John said afterwards.

When he got home, John placed the heavy glass globe on the shelf across from his laptop, where he could see it every day. Among the Gold, Platinum, and framed milestones on the walls, it was always the one he pointed to first.

'This,' he said, 'is the one that means the most.'

The music video for 'Everybody Jam!' entered its final planning stages with director Hannes Rossacher of DoRo Film in October 1996. BMG threw everything at it – $200,000 and a full-blown extravaganza in Louisiana, hoping it would rocket Scatman back into the spotlight.

John's youngest nephew, Steve, had just started his first job out of grad school in New Orleans when his parents mentioned that Uncle Johnny was in town filming a music video. On his lunch break, Steve walked over to the French Quarter to see what was going on.

Madison Street had been shut down and overtaken by a hundreds-strong crew. 'A completely crazy, shrill mix of Dixieland and Love Parade!' one magazine wrote. The parade thundered through: marching bands, dancers, a fire engine, a horse-drawn carriage, and a 1950s Cadillac carrying John and a Louis Armstrong lookalike playing trumpet. Crowds lined the route, cheering and waving Scatman flags.

As Steve made his way toward the maelstrom, his uncle spotted him.

'Wardrobe!' John yelled.

Two women swooped in and led Steve into an old theater, where they brushed glitter across his cheeks and dabbed makeup at his temples. Before he could object, they'd strapped him into a bubble-wrap vest and six-inch platform boots and sent him back outside.

He danced up and down the street all afternoon among musicians, floats, and confetti cannons. 'The video director kept asking me to loosen up, but it wasn't easy for me,' he said. 'Johnny, though, went out of his way to make sure I was clearly in the video, saying family had to be involved.'

Later, in John's trailer, it was just the two of them. 'He talked about how strange all of this was, that it was really quite unbelievable what life had given him,' Steve remembers, 'but also how much fun he was having being Scatman John.'

Steve tried to go back to work. He'd only meant to step out for lunch. But when he looked in the mirror, his eyelids glittered no matter how much he tried to scrub them.

For the rest of the week, if the light hit just right, he'd catch a tiny sparkle on his cheek or nose and brush it away. 'I really appreciate Uncle Johnny letting me into Scatman's world that day,' he says.

While John rode confetti floats in New Orleans, some of the BMG Ariola Hamburg team were on the ground too, mapping out the release of 'Everybody Jam!'

Even without a new single in nearly a year, the European press still came calling when John returned to the continent to promote it. Journalists joked it might become 'the new national scourge,' just like 'Scatman' and 'Scatman's World' had before it.

John didn't need much prompting to gush about the title track. 'To have the opportunity to present Louis Armstrong to kids who may not have heard him is an honor,' he said. 'To bring him into pop music and actually have one of his solos on my single? That's just wild. It doesn't get any better!'

John's ten-year sobriety birthday was approaching, and his mind turned to deeper things. He had started to call his audience 'children of all ages', to acknowledge not just kids, but anyone dragging around a wounded inner child, like he had. Maybe because of that, he was allowing himself to be more open. But not all the way.

When asked about the worst moment of his drug years, 'Damn, there are tons,' he said, before describing his heroin overdose and resuscitation.

'I don't know if you can print this,' he said. 'If it helps, print it. Kids need to understand that this is an abomination.'

He came close – more than once – to breaking his silence about childhood sexual abuse. Sometimes he would begin: 'I had some experiences in early childhood that …' and then stop, never quite able to continue. Other times, he'd minimize it: 'Maybe not worse than many others.'

For a man from the Silent Generation, opening up about sexual abuse in the mid-'90s came with real risk. It meant exposing not just personal pain but inviting judgment from a world that, John knew, wasn't always ready to listen. Chipping away at the stigma around stuttering and addiction was hard enough. Adding this felt insurmountable.

But the unspoken truth was on John's mind. It showed up in the new album's lyrics, in more autobiographical songs like 'Let It Go': *I'm holding on to secrets that are too hard to see / and I'm thinking everybody is better than me.*

For now, though, John focused on the new album. The promo tour ended with a one-hour special on Germany's *VIVA Jam*, where he was more candid than ever.

'I'm not complete yet, kids,' he said. 'I've still got those feelings of inadequacy going.' He told journalist Morten Lind something similar.

'Intellectually, I know I'm okay. But I'm still driven by wrong ideas, old images that pop up, old tapes that play in my head. But now I know – that's not the real me,' he said. 'It can't be.'

'Everybody Jam!' finally arrived in November, months behind schedule and thrust into the competitive Christmas market – exactly as John's breakout single had been.

'Let's hope the god Fortuna is smiling on us again,' Manfred said, not knowing that in just over a year, John would be fighting for his life.

32 ONE CONFUSED SOUL

Eloise Pitchford tore open the parcel and shook out a cascade of exotic, shrink-wrapped jewel cases covered in unreadable Japanese text. Among them: *Everybody Jam!*, the Japanese edition, loaded with bonus tracks.

In the UK, Scatman fever had cooled. But Eloise was still listening, spending her paper-round wages on pricey imports from overseas. After turning 16, she picked up extra shifts at a local takeout to scrape together more cash. But she was fired for not repeating orders back to customers when her usual word-swapping failed her.

Trying to distract herself from bleak thoughts about the future, she booted up her clunky old PC. One of the magazines she delivered had a free America Online CD-ROM glued to the cover, with a trial offer for internet access. She installed it and listened to the modem screech as it connected.

While she waited, the Japanese CDs played in the background, John's voice filling the room. When the AOL interface loaded, she acted on impulse and typed 'John Larkin' into the member directory.

The screen blinked. Then: one result.

Username: Hapnintwo. Name: John Larkin. Location: California. Occupation: Jazz.

Couldn't be.

But what if?

She took a breath and wrote a long, careful message. Then hit send.

Across the ocean in Los Angeles, John was packing for Germany. He'd been invited to perform at Sounds of Frankfurt, a festival expected to draw 300,000 people.

'I guess Scatman isn't dead yet,' he told Manfred. 'Of course, I'll do it.'

1997 had opened with a mix of hope and frustration. The good news: The Scatland Foundation was now officially a nonprofit. The bad: the 'Everybody Jam!' single was struggling, except in the Czech Republic, where it was climbing toward #1, and in Hungary, where it had cracked the Top 10.

In Japan, the album had already sold half a million copies, and Scatman John dolls were being given away as prizes. A remarkable feat for any foreign artist –

unless you were the same foreign artist who'd moved over two million copies of your last album. Then the label was disappointed. But John wasn't.

'I don't think about failure or success,' he said. 'If I can help just one confused soul, I'll show up.'

There were reasons to stay optimistic. Disney had expressed interest in a collaboration, and 'Everybody Jam!' – with its New Orleans roots – was pitched as the best shot at finally cracking the US market. Logic Records was launching the single in the US, and after Frankfurt, John was booked for a North American promo tour.

He had new US representation: Entertainment Attorney David Helfant, alongside Jan Roeg, a manager and talent scout with major-label experience. Logic faced a tough task to reintroduce Scatman to a country that had already turned away once. So John cleared his calendar and canceled appearances at three stuttering conventions and a jazz festival. He didn't like backing out, but if this was the chance to finally reach his home country, he wanted to do it right.

His visibility ticked upward when, alongside KISS and Lauryn Hill, he lent his voice – and the 'Scatman's World' video – to a national anti-drug PSA for the Musicians' Assistance Program, run by his friend Buddy Arnold.

'Life's about living, laughing, loving,' John said in the voiceover. 'Drugs, baby baby? They ain't about nothin''

On the surface, things looked good. But then John began asking for things that had already been sent. He started misspelling 'Iceberg' in emails. When Manfred pointed it out, John blamed his 'brain cell situation,' offering no further explanation.

But others had noticed, too.

'It got to where he would forget stuff,' says friend D. Jennings. 'Which was unlike him. At first, everybody thought he was just overdoing it. They wrote it off to older guy fatigue.'

Most of the time, though, he seemed fine. Not long after John's March appearance on Hollywood's Radio AAHS – part of the national children's network – there was a *tap tap tap* at his front door.

That alone was strange. No one knocked at John and Judy's place. Jazz musicians, neighbors, and AA friends came and went, often letting themselves in. John and Judy kept a spare room and an open house, whether for one night or for the months it took someone to get on their feet again.

Judy looked out and saw a group of young kids clustered on the porch. She called John. He padded over and opened the door. *We've come to see Scatman*, they said, staring up at John in his socks, shorts, and T-shirt. No hat.

Judy's son Lee watched from the hallway as his mother welcomed them in. Within minutes, John had cued up some Scatman CDs, fetched the fedora, and was dancing around the living room.

'It was the sweetest thing I ever saw,' Lee remembers. 'He held their hands, and they were in this little circle, just looking up at him like, Oh my God. They couldn't believe it. And he loved that. That meant the world to him.'

Relishing the rare time at home, John began building a home studio and invited players around. 'I gather my jazz quintet every Sunday,' John said. 'We have our own little workshop that keeps me alive.' The lineup changed, but regulars included playwright Julian Barry on tenor sax, longtime friend John Lasonio on bass, and Dick Forrest on trumpet.

Other friends dropped by to listen, remembering the old days of John hammering out tunes on battered pianos, some with broken keys, one famously smeared with cheese after a gig at a Chuck E. Cheese restaurant. Now they watched him beneath a wall of awards, adding flourishes to Miles Davis's 'All Blues' on his grand piano, recording for the joy of it.

In his Radio AAHS interview, between jokes and riffs, John explained why the Scatland Foundation mattered.

'We need to change the social understanding of it,' he said. 'The most important thing the world should know about people who stutter is that we only stutter when we talk. We're not mentally defective.'

He also plugged 'Everybody Jam!', earning an unlikely thumbs-up from Weird Al Yankovic, who covered it on accordion.

Everything was going well, until it wasn't. Partway through the interview, John lost focus.

'I'm sorry,' he said after host Bruce Barker asked a question. 'I couldn't follow you. I just about passed out.' He blamed the heat in the studio. Barker threw to a break.

John pulled himself together, as he always did, and ignored the alarms his body was sounding. As he always did.

Before leaving for Frankfurt, John sat down to check his email. Buried among the usual messages from Billy, Sharon, Iceberg, and his five webmasters, one stood out: a long email from a British girl named Eloise.

Dear John, it began. *I'm not sure this is really you, but in case it is …*

He kept reading. Depression. Suicidal thoughts. There was no doubt: this was a cry for help. It wasn't unusual in the stuttering community. He and Judy already knew of two suicides, and he understood exactly what this message could mean. But he was halfway out the door. He typed quickly. Later, he would say he had a gut feeling he should reply.

Dear Eloise,

Your mail deserves quality time with a quality answer. I would love to give you both, however, I don't have either right now. I am off to Frankfurt. I will answer your mail soon when things calm down.

I will get back to you ...
Love to you ... John
He hit send, and hoped it was enough.

When Ingo Kays and Iris Reimann heard that John had arrived in Frankfurt, they came straight to meet him. After sleeping off some of the jet lag, John arranged for his driver to pick the three of them up and take them out for the evening.

They were chauffeured to a beer garden set along the banks of the Main River. The sun was setting, gold slipping into blue, the air warm with the tail end of the day.

As they walked through, a saxophonist played beneath a tree. John stopped and listened. Ingo paused beside him. Then John began to scat-sing along.

When the song ended, he struck up a conversation.

'They started talking about John Coltrane,' Ingo says. 'Raved about him.'

The saxophonist began a Coltrane piece Ingo didn't recognize. John joined in, scatting the exact same lines, note for note.

'I'm not dumb musically,' Ingo said, 'but I have no idea what they were doing. Complex scales with really strange accentuations and pauses. Totally precise and completely in sync.'

Ingo stood back, shaking his head. 'It was a beautiful experience,' he says. 'At that moment, John didn't care about anything else; only his jazz homie mattered.'

Later, they found a table near the water. Night rolled in. Ingo and Iris drank beer, and there was an apple juice spritzer, as usual, for John.

The next day, John visited a local school for kids who stuttered. It was filmed for a segment to slot into the live *Sounds of Frankfurt* broadcast, to run while the stage crew swapped out his mic and keyboard. The visit was 'at his own request,' the voiceover said. 'Not only a man of his word, but also a man of action.'

Before the visit, John kept asking for the school's name. 'This is very important to him,' Manfred stressed to the organizers. But John may never have been told. The school was the *August-Henze-Schule* – named for a Nazi-era educator whose legacy, in 1997, was turning toxic.

The school's philosophy was modern and inclusive. Inviting John reflected that. But Henze had defended special education as a means to prevent 'impaired' children from becoming a burden on society – and had praised the 1933 Nazi sterilization law.

Inside that building, Scatman John pulled up a chair in front of a classroom of teenagers who stuttered and said, 'Accept yourself as you are. You have so many positive qualities. Your stutter does not erase these qualities. It is just your way of speaking.'

He told them his own stutter had made him stronger. That he wasn't a star despite it, but because of it.

Weeks later, a public exposé led the school to drop Henze's name. Had John been born in Nazi Germany instead of Los Angeles in 1942, someone like Henze might have marked him – and those kids – for sterilization, segregation, or worse.

But on that warm summer afternoon in 1997, none of that was on John's mind. He sat at the teacher's desk, laughing with the students, focusing not on the past, but on reshaping their future.

That night, in the dusky Frankfurt heat, hundreds of thousands of kids screamed as John took the stage well past 2 a.m. for a 25-minute half-playback set of Scatman hits. He duetted with a labelmate, British singer-songwriter Andrea Black.

'A wonderful, great, open-hearted man,' Andrea says. 'Very warm, very hospitable, very kind, very supportive.'

Though they pulled it off, they hid the true chaos behind the performance.

'There was no chair. One microphone. One keyboard that's rolling down the stage,' Andrea remembered. 'We're both desperately hanging onto the keyboard, handing the mic back and forth, smiling … You couldn't tell any of this was going on.'

Backstage, they laughed at the absurdity of it. Then John slipped away, back to his hotel.

The next morning, he plugged in the laptop and logged in under his usual handle: Hapnintwo. Eloise had replied.

Now, his attention shifted from 300,000 kids, to just one.

She was online. An instant message popped up.

Eloise sat alone at home, the phone cable trailing from her father's bedroom. She wasn't supposed to be online – it cost too much per minute. But when 'Hapnintwo' logged on, she forgot the rules.

Hi John, she typed, her hands trembling slightly.

For the next two hours, she told him everything she'd never told anyone. Her shame, her isolation, her fear that her stuttering – or stammering, as the British called it – didn't count because she hid it so well. Was it still real if nobody knew?

Of course it is, John typed. *Your feelings are what matter.*

There was no small talk. He went straight to the heart. *How are you feeling?*

No one had asked her that in a long time.

As she typed, she still couldn't believe this was him. The man whose songs had kept her going. But it felt real. He wasn't being weird or inappropriate. He was kind and open and honest.

Back then, no one worried about who you were talking to online. But this man turned out to be exactly who he said he was. The voice in the lyrics – *You're enough. Don't beat yourself up. You're not alone* – was now here, typing directly to her.

'Isn't messaging great?' he wrote. 'Artificial fluency!'

They talked about everything: emotionally distant fathers, school pressure, the madness of the world. She admitted she'd shied away from the stuttering community and had avoided speech therapy after one bad experience.

'They'll think I'm too fluent,' she wrote.

John corrected her. 'You belong with us,' he said. He explained covert stuttering: the same neurological wiring, but where the stutter is hidden thanks to swapped words, dodged sounds, situation avoidance, and constant, exhausting mental gymnastics. That kind of masking, he told her, would steal her life if she let it. 'Trust me on this one,' he added. Then he gave her the email of the British Stammering Association.

'Tell them you're a friend of mine,' he said.

A friend? Her heart nearly burst.

Eventually, he had to go. *Keep in touch*, he told her. *You'll be okay*.

When she logged off, she sat in silence. For the first time in months, she thought, *maybe I will be.*

33 CALLING OUT

At 5 a.m. on a Thursday morning in February 1998, a phone shattered the silence in Edesio Alejandro's home in Alamar, Cuba. Half asleep, he grabbed the receiver and pressed it to his ear.

A German voice introduced himself. If Edesio could get to Hamburg by the following Monday, the voice said, he could compose and produce a new track for Scatman John.

Edesio hung up, shot out of bed, and tore around the room screaming, 'Ski-ba-bop-ba-dop-bop!'

His wife Idolka jolted awake.

'What's happening?' she yelled. 'Edesio, *what's happening?*'

'Ski-ba-bop-ba-dop-bop!' he shouted again, spinning with joy. Then he told her: he was going to work with one of his idols.

The paperwork fax arrived that morning. Edesio dashed out past concrete blocks and the scent of frying plantains straight to the German embassy in Havana. By afternoon, his visa was approved. He picked up the phone and called the number back.

'I'll see you Monday,' he said.

That weekend, he and his musicians locked themselves in the studio, sketching out demos. By the time Edesio boarded the flight to Hamburg, he had a dozen ideas ready to go.

At the airport, two men greeted him: Eduardo, the voice on the phone, and Ricardo, another Cuban musician brought onto the project. They went straight to a meeting.

The brief was to use a classic 120-BPM dance beat but mix it with mambo. Edesio was chosen for his skill and reputation in fusing electronic music with Afro-Cuban rhythms. He went away and delivered a rough cut within twenty-four hours. But then the execs changed direction and asked for something slower. The next day, he brought them that, too.

'Now try a reggae,' someone said. Edesio lost it.

'That has nothing to do with mambo,' he snapped. But no one wanted to lose their job. Under protest, he stitched together a strange fusion of mambo, dance, and reggae – 'like a circus,' he would later say, and then caught a few hours' sleep.

The next day, they heard that John Larkin was flying in. They would finally meet him. And then they would play him the music.

A few months earlier, John walked out of a German TV studio, head down, a folder still clutched in his hands. Crisp and freshly printed, it read *Scatland Foundation* across the front. It had stayed on the table for the entire segment. No one asked about it. Not once.

The show was about stuttering, but John was the only guest who did.

'The more I tried to stop stuttering, the more I stuttered,' he said, facing a live studio audience. 'It was through self-acceptance that I began to overcome the shame and the horror and the fear of being a victim of my stuttering. I'm not a victim anymore.'

He held the folder as he spoke, hoping the host might bite. He'd already drafted the first newsletter, *Calling Out*, and made it clear the foundation supported both speech therapy and acceptance, whichever path someone chose. But it was 1997, and fluency alone was still the media's gold standard.

John sat, polite and smiling, while a fluent actor who had once stuttered was praised for 'conquering' it and speaking 'flawlessly'. Another guest said hypnotherapy had erased his stutter in five days. John knew the odds of that: lottery-ticket rare.

John lit up when cameras cut to a boy in the audience who stuttered, seated beside his mother. But the boy talked about being teased.

'Now's your chance to tell a lot of people how you'd like to be treated,' the host prompted. 'Just normally,' the boy said. 'Like anyone else who speaks fluently.'

John's earpiece was faulty, and he missed what came next – the host wrapping the segment by suggesting that stuttering could be beaten by strength and will. That maybe the boy could come back one day, once he'd found a 'way'.

Back at the hotel, John was livid. He fired off emails, furious at the media, the moment, and himself.

'If I had been more aggressive and assertive, I might have been able to say more,' he wrote. But he didn't feel he could. He was there to perform 'Everybody Jam!', after all. 'They need the monkey for the promo,' he said of these events.

He hadn't even been sure he wanted to make the Foundation public, but since it was the show's topic, he decided he would. And it had been ignored.

Supportive messages flooded his inbox. One of the first was from Eloise. Another came from Shinji Ito, a leader in Japan's stuttering community. It was enough, he said, that John had stuttered openly on TV. That alone was rare.

John cooled down.

'In these days of career turbulence, I can sometimes forget or minimize the importance of the more enduring values of life,' he replied. 'I thank you for reminding me of the importance of non-aggression.'

But the media coverage he'd hoped for wasn't materializing. A new single, 'Let It Go', had just been released in Europe and became the first not to chart at all. *Petra* magazine in Germany named John 'Good Man of the Month' for his philanthropy, but without a chart hit to anchor the story, few journalists followed up.

John had always said that when the Scatman star faded, he would step out from behind. 'Celebrity positions, especially in the dance/rap recording field, tend to rise and fade very fast,' he acknowledged. Now he wondered if that moment had come.

Back across the Atlantic, he was poised to promote 'Everybody Jam!'. Logic Records had booked John into smaller venues in the US, and he tried to meet them halfway. But his symptoms – chalked up to stress and overwork – were becoming impossible to ignore.

'My health is still the single most important item,' he told BMG. Doctors had warned him to slow down.

'I expect sane working hours,' he said. 'I have the option to cancel if any part of the schedule is absurd.' And yet, he was stepping onstage as late as 1:30 a.m., playing nightclubs in Toronto and New Jersey. To cope, he relied on the same tools he'd used since the '70s to stay centered.

'Are you ready, John?' his co-manager, Jan Roeg, asked before one show.

'I'm ready,' he said. 'But I need to get in touch with the Creator. We need to sit in quiet for half an hour.'

She offered to leave. No need, he said. If she could sit in silence, too, they could do it together.

'He just shut his eyes and connected,' Jan says. She remembered thinking *Whoa. This is good.* Years later, after managing major artists across decades, she still called John the highlight of her career.

'One, he was terrifically talented. Two, he was a gentleman – at a time when most of them were not. And three, he was divinely spiritual,' she said. 'He probably had a direct line. He was so magnificent as a human being.'

John had cleared months of his calendar to focus on the US, but by August 1997, Logic admitted they'd hit a wall. The only gigs left were in expat enclaves – rooms full of people who already knew and loved him. American radio, especially outside the East Coast, flatly refused to play 'Everybody Jam!'.

The scramble began. Scatman needed reviving – now not just in America, but everywhere else, too.

'We have to come up with a new direction,' Manfred said. 'Away from the Eurobeat.' Tony and Ingo were asked for new demos, but nothing came. The duo had gone their separate ways.

Iceberg, BMG, and John's US team began hunting for new producers. 'We knew we had to reinvent the sound,' says David Helfant, John's US manager, 'but still keep the integrity of what people loved about it.'

Jan introduced John to her husband, Shane Keister, a veteran musician who had worked with Elvis and Paul McCartney.

'John's energy was really neat,' Shane said. 'He was very focused with what he wanted to do.' Shane helped John shape a few early demos and spent a week or two in LA with him, trading ideas. One of them was 'Scat Daddy', a self-deprecating rap about a washed-up star wondering what fame had really meant – the older, wiser cousin of 'Popstar'.

Jan also called her friend Shane Verdi, a young producer she managed. Verdi had been in the band Law & Order and was now producing out of a Manhattan studio.

'I have this very talented guy you could work with,' she said to John, who flew to New York to meet Shane. Over lunch in a deli, Shane found John humble, sharp, and instinctive.

'John told me he wanted more of a street vibe for the next record. He was chill, really smart,' Shane says. 'We went out for dinner, hung out – just a very lovable guy. Two easygoing guys in a studio making good product.'

They cut three or four tracks. 'We're looking for a radio hit,' Jan had told them. Shane thought these demos were some of John's best.

'He was down and dirty on those,' he said. 'More mature. A whole different sound.'

John was just as hyped. 'This kid is an absolute genius,' he told Radio AAHS in a return guest spot later that year. He loved Shane's look, too – tattoos, nose rings, earrings. 'He's created a whole new sound for Scatman,' he announced.

Meanwhile, Iceberg Records explored new directions, too. After the *Buena Vista Social Club* became a sensation in 1996, Manfred sensed a Latin flavor might be the way forward. When a production company asked about a Latin-themed soundtrack for the German film *Love Scenes from Planet Earth*, the timing seemed perfect. The production wanted John on screen and on a new single, with a cover of Pérez Prado's 'Mambo No. 5'.

John agreed to do it and shelved the demos he'd just recorded in New York. He'd already had successful soundtrack side gigs, including co-writing and performing 'Steal the Base' for the movie Major League III, and his Japanese TV ad singles had done well. A Hamburg studio was booked for February 1998 with a new production team.

But first, John closed out 1997 with gigs in Mexico and Eastern Europe. In Mexico City, fellow Eurodance artist Sin with Sebastian watched as John's silhouette and hat appeared before he took the stage, sending the crowd wild. 'I loved it,' Sebastian says. He hadn't felt great about his own performance, but John was kind to him. 'Sebastian,' John said, 'you have a very colorful act!'

Later, as the headliners waited for transport to the airport, Sebastian noticed John had fallen asleep. Judy told him John was sick. 'But when he was on,' Sebastian adds, 'he was wonderful. I never forgot my encounter with him. A very special artist.'

When John reached Estonia, he played to a packed Club Hollywood, followed by a trip to Kaunas in Lithuania. He was driven in a silver limo, past bright yellow posters of himself smiling out over the city. At 55, reporters who had never met him before still latched onto his age.

'If you haven't lost your sensitivity,' John told them, 'it doesn't matter how wrinkled your face is.'

John's set was scaled back to just thirty minutes, with support acts filling out the show. But the audience didn't care, and cheered as balloons fell from the ceiling in a golden haze.

The next night in Vilnius, after another sold-out performance, John kicked off his shoes backstage, thinking it was over. Then there was one more request – an interview for tour sponsor *Respublika* magazine.

He smiled, asked for ten minutes to catch his breath, and said yes. PR rep Vaidas Stackevičius told John he looked tired.

'I'm always tired,' he replied.

In February 1998, Edesio Alejandro and his team had just finished setting up at EcoPark Studio in Hamburg when John walked in.

'A man of great sympathy and modesty,' Edesio said. 'He greeted us all, knew each of our names.'

The label rep asked to hear one of the faster tracks they'd prepared. As Edesio stepped to the console, he glanced at his musicians and shook his head. *No.*

Their eyes widened. *Don't do it*, their faces said.

'I didn't give them time,' Edesio recalled. He hit play on the slow demo.

'You can't explain the annoyance on the face of the label,' he said, 'and the happiness of John.' John started scat-singing along immediately.

'I love it,' he said. And that was that.

'What a thrill,' Edesio said, 'to see how he enjoyed what we had done, with so much love.'

They weren't there to develop demos, though. The real job was 'Scatmambo' – the new single for the soundtrack of *Love Scenes from Planet Earth*. It was now a cover of Pérez Prado's 'Patricia', not 'Mambo No. 5', as originally planned, and John had rare permission to write his own lyrics.

'It was a little difficult for him,' Edesio said, 'because although he was a brutally exceptional pianist, it was difficult for him to sing using the syncopation of Cuban music.'

They worked on it together. Back in his 20s, when asked his ethnicity, John would joke he was 'Puerto Rican by injection.' He'd grown up surrounded by

Latin music, and now, decades later, he was begging Edesio to show him tumbaos – the basic rhythm patterns of Afro-Cuban music.

'Teach me, teach me!' John shouted. Then laughed and cursed 'fuckfuckfuck!' when he got it wrong.

'Little by little, he got into it,' Edesio said, 'until he achieved it. He was really a great jazz musician.'

Manfred dropped in to see how things were going.

'These Cuban cats were dynamite to work with,' John told him later. 'I'd like to work with them more. We understand each other musically.'

What Manfred didn't see – and what John didn't say – was that something else was bothering John. His face was puffier, his upper body slightly swollen. He said nothing. If anyone noticed, they didn't mention it.

Back in LA, the symptoms got worse. He and Judy were, as John put it, 'hoping against hope that it would magically, simply go away.'

Remixes of 'Scatmambo' were commissioned, and Manfred sent early demos around. BMG Ariola Hamburg and Tokyo liked what they heard, and unofficial radio tests came back glowing.

Even better, John had been invited to perform the song live at the German Film Awards in Berlin, broadcast nationwide. A music video was greenlit, with director Kai Sehr pitching a joyful, full-color shoot in a sun-drenched Havana cigar factory. John would sing as dancers joined in, the musical exuberance spilling from room to room and into the streets.

This was it. 'Scatmambo' was set to re-launch Scatman John with a bang in the summer of 1998.

In April, just as excitement for 'Scatmambo' was building in Europe, John and Judy's friend Stacey Heaver – whom they'd met in Amsterdam – came to stay. She was moving to the US, and they'd offered her three months with them: time to find a job, an apartment, and a car. 'Beyond generous,' she said.

She hadn't seen John in months, maybe a year. Exhausted from the sixteen-hour flight, she stepped out of the taxi at John and Judy's place, suitcase and guitar in hand.

What she saw in the doorway stopped her cold.

John.

Every inch of him was swollen with oedema, like someone had pumped him full of wet cement. His face was gone – that's where her eyes landed first. His ears, already big, now looked cartoonish, inflated like balloons. His forehead bulged, stretched taut and red, spiderwebbed with broken capillaries. His eyes, once sharp and quick, had gone watery and sunk into drooping lids. Even his mustache looked like it was struggling to stay afloat in the swelling.

Stacey stared at the purple, puffy impostor. He looked 250 pounds, easy – a man who'd never weighed more than 180. And it wasn't just his face. His arms were thick and mottled beneath a cotton T-shirt, painted in angry purples and reds like storm maps. His chest pushed out with pressure. The skin stretched taut, like it was holding something in.

'I'm s-s-s-sorry Iiiii look like thuh-thuh-this,' he said, catching Stacey's expression as she stepped forward.

'I love you,' she said, and gave him a hug.

His legs were swollen too, with feet and ankles so misshapen they didn't look like they could cross a room.

And they couldn't.

As John paid the driver and shuffled inside, Judy came rushing down the hallway with a cordless phone in her hands.

'John's the new Michelin Man!' she said. John and Judy burst out laughing. Stacey joined in, thinking, *Wow. Humor to distract from reality.*

The swelling had steadily increased for months. John knew he already had serious, irreversible lung disease – something he'd hidden through his entire run as Scatman John. But this was new. The doctors were running test after test, trying to figure out what was going on.

Judy was waiting for a callback from the doctors, she said. Stacey knew Judy: everything was now-time, not tomorrow-time. She wouldn't let up.

Within days, Stacey understood the full picture. John could barely move. Breathing took a huge effort. Getting off the couch was out of the question, so he mostly stayed at the dining table, watching Judy and the dogs in the family room.

Sometimes he made it outside, just for air. Stacey remembered kneeling in the grass, trimming his thick, discolored toenails while he grunted softly. She wondered if it hurt. He was on morphine, he said, and it kept him pain-free. But every movement was slow and heavy, like he was underwater.

Yet John refused pity. That was the rule. He sat there, breathless and ballooned, cracking jokes.

'I'm purple and round, I can't touch the ground,' he'd sing, wheezing through laughter, trying to make Judy smile.

The house bent itself around him. The dining chair became his throne. The TV, his window. His laptop, a tether to whatever passed for normal.

But nothing was normal.

John was drowning in his own circulation, and no one could explain why. Even as his strength gave out, his priority was Judy – he was constantly watching her, worrying for her, trying not to add to the weight she already carried. He was collapsing in slow motion, apologizing the whole way down.

Then Stacey noticed something else. The frequent bursts of air freshener, the constant use of alcohol gel, so that its smell lingered in the air.

Then it hit her.

Judy was drinking again.

34 **TAKE YOUR TIME**

The waiting room lights buzzed above Judy's head. Outside, Sunset Boulevard flickered with smog and late-evening traffic, but in here, time stalled. Judy had been at the hospital nearly ten hours.

Somewhere behind closed doors, John lay on the operating table. There was no scalpel – just a catheter, threaded inch by inch through a vein toward his heart. On a monitor, doctors watched as the tip reached the site of the blockage – a chokehold in his superior vena cava, the massive vein carrying blood from his upper body to his heart. It had nearly strangled him from the inside out.

Then, a tiny balloon inflated inside his chest. The pressure forced the vein open, squeezing blood past the obstruction for the first time in weeks. The swelling had reached a crisis point. Now, at last, the pressure began to ease.

Judy wasn't allowed inside. She sat alone, catastrophizing. It's going well, they said. Minimally invasive.

But what if he doesn't make it?

Finally, the doctor returned. Half the blockage was cleared, he said. The rest would be removed within days. The blood was moving again. And John was alive.

Oh, thank God, Judy thought.

In the middle of the night, Iceberg Records' fax machine hummed awake in Denmark. It spat out a letter from John's attending physician in Los Angeles.

'Mr. Larkin has significant obstructive pulmonary disease,' his doctor wrote, 'but is currently being evaluated for additional medical problems.' Travel, he said, was out of the question – unsafe, high-risk, and against 'his best medical interests' until further evaluation was complete.

The next day, John stirred groggily from the anesthesia. He propped himself up in bed, laptop open, trying to write an email to Manfred. When he learned he wasn't cleared to travel, he begged. Just the music video shoot, he pleaded. Nothing more. The doctor relented, on the condition that John must have oxygen both in the air and on the ground.

John wasn't sure he'd hit send. 'His thinking is a little clouded,' Judy admitted later. She took over, transcribing his message herself.

'Some magic did happen,' John dictated. 'But there is still much work needed to be done. There is a mass at the site of the blockage.'

He told Manfred he'd go ahead with the music video, but couldn't perform 'Scatmambo' at the Film Awards.

'I cannot go to Berlin,' he said. 'This is too much for me. Judy is helping me with this letter … I am too weak.'

More scans were scheduled. But John already looked and felt better. The diagnosis was Superior Vena Cava Syndrome – usually caused by cancer. But none had been found.

'The nightmare is over,' Judy wrote to Manfred. 'And John will be better than ever!'

Stacey greeted John at the door ten days later when he was discharged. She hugged him, feeling muscle on his back instead of bloat.

'You look like a million bucks!' she said.

John smiled. The old John.

His energy began to return. He resumed building his 'Scatland Studio' at home – a project he'd started so he wouldn't need to travel so much for recording. He'd spent thousands on it.

'You've got to see my new studio, man,' he faxed to Ingo Kays. 'It's as state-of-the-art as a home studio can be.'

He laid down tracks with his Sunday quintet, and started writing a new ballad: 'Can You Hear Me', dedicated to 'the children of the world, of all ages.' He floated the idea of recording with Ingo again and invited him over. He mentioned his health, but only briefly.

'I don't want to bore you with the details,' he wrote. 'The last three months have been like the bad dream from hell.'

Stacey, still staying at the house, would sometimes wake at 3 or 4 a.m. to the sound of him playing.

'John was always writing poetry,' she said. 'In the middle of the night, he'd be down there on the piano. It was like *Phantom of the Opera*.'

Soon, he was back at his desk too, tap-tap-tapping on the laptop.

Congratulations. You are a miracle. You have moved into recovery and you are taking action for yourself. You are a brave human being.

He adjusted his glasses – lighter now, both in frame and spirit – and speed-typed an email to Eloise. He'd been pestering her for weeks to attend a stuttering conference. She'd finally agreed.

I hope you are taking time to give yourself a pat on the back, he wrote. *You are confronting some of the worst fears in your life. You will have a wonderful time at the convention. Again. You are a miracle. Don't forget that. Say it to yourself.*

Across the world, Eloise swiveled around in her desk chair, smiling like always when John's name appeared in her inbox. *I'm not a miracle*, she thought. *I'm scared.*

A week later, she tried – and failed – to make it to the British Stammering Association conference. She told John, full of self-blame.

The compliment of giving yourself a pat on the back applies immediately!!!!!!! He replied, hammering out the exclamation marks. *You are looking at your stuttering straight in the eye. You are confronting it. That is what matters. You are in the process of 'owning your stuttering' instead of 'stuttering owning you.'*

'STAY IN TOUCH WITH ME, he added. *This stuttering business is a little too big to handle by yourself. You can do it **for** yourself, but not **by** yourself.'*

When she admitted she was terrified of the phone, John gave her his number. On that first call, he'd stuttered his head off – probably on purpose, she realized later. Feeling brave, she let herself stutter, too, for the first time in years. John jumped on it.

'Ah!' she could hear him grinning down the crackly international line. 'It's so beautiful to hear you stutter.'

That fall, John was scheduled to speak at the Nordic stuttering conference in Denmark. Eloise, feeling better, told him she hoped to be there too, so they could finally talk in person. John would give a keynote and play some jazz.

'I look forward to a wonderful evening,' he wrote to the organizers.

He closed the laptop and wandered into the living room, where Judy was setting out snacks and drinks. The dogs lay by the coffee table, tails thumping when they saw John. Tonight, like many nights during his illness, the house would host an AA meeting. Judy had returned to sobriety after what she called a 'slip.'

'She's only drunk twice since I've known her, and that's a miracle,' John later said. 'Judy is as much an alcoholic as I am an addict. We've developed a sober understanding of each other that is uncanny. It's taken a lot of work for both of us.'

There was another reason to keep the meetings close. John had resisted morphine, an opioid chemically close to heroin. But when the pain became too much, he'd taken it.

'He didn't like that,' his friend Barry Mitchell says. 'He was really upset at first. He felt like people would look at him differently.'

As the swelling eased and his body began to heal, the drug didn't let go. He couldn't stop. He was facing a new version of the same old enemy: medical addiction.

When John's lawyer found out he was about to fly abroad to shoot a music video, he slammed on the brakes. The morphine use had raised red flags. Travel, in his condition, was a liability. Worse, John's business manager warned that flying to Cuba might jeopardize his US passport status.

John's doctor stepped in and also said no, just as the film crew was preparing to leave. Judy intervened. They'd be honest if asked, she said. John's medical addiction wasn't a secret, and he was dealing with it. But it shouldn't be put in writing. BMG and Iceberg were left in the dark.

Manfred was in Japan, fresh from a meeting where everyone had been smiling, clapping, and excited about the video. Now he was told John was grounded.

'John, what is going on?' he pleaded by fax. 'If you're trying to kill your potential hit, you couldn't do a better job.'

Calls went up the ladder to Eckhart Gundel, Managing Director of BMG Ariola Hamburg. There was no path to success if John didn't leave the house, he told Judy. John hadn't been seen in public in nearly a year.

Judy agreed – but as she spoke on the phone, she jotted a note: 'Plan tour w/o killing him.'

Now, there was a hard deadline. *Love Scenes from Planet Earth*, the film 'Scatmambo' was tied to, was scheduled for release in August 1998. The single had to be out by then. With Cuba off the table, location scouts turned to Miami and South America. John's health was so uncertain, they even considered using a body double.

'I realize fully the importance of the video,' John said. 'But I'm grateful we are not filming until August. My body needs that kind of time to heal.'

He had just begun work on new album tracks. A new producer, Kai Matthiesen – known for Mr. President's 1996 hit 'Coco Jamboo' – was on board. The demos were ready. The next step was for John to listen to them.

He never got the chance.

One evening in late June, John clutched his chest, gasping in pain.

'I can't breathe,' he wheezed. '*I can't breathe.*'

Judy ran to the phone. An ambulance rushed him to the ER.

'Acute bronchitis and lung abnormalities,' the notes read. 'Diagnosis unknown.'

Judy and her son Lee sat with the doctor. He was 'leaning toward malignancy,' he told them, though no cancer had been found. John clung to that. Judy clung to that. A bronchoscopy the next day confirmed the same: still no malignancy.

'Yea Team!' Judy wrote to Manfred. 'This is not, however, a 100 percent clean slate.'

John needed an open lung biopsy to be sure – a serious procedure, with at least a month of recovery. The video shoot was now out of the question.

'My doctors want me to build up my strength,' John wrote to Mette Zähringer. 'Will it ever end?'

The success of 'Scatmambo,' he added, mattered just as much to him and Judy as it did to her and Manfred.

'I hope with all my heart that it's salvageable,' he wrote.

Sadly, it wasn't.

BMG considered an animated video to give the single a fighting chance, but it never materialized. 'Scatmambo' was released in the fall of 1998 – without its artist to promote it – and barely made a ripple. Attention now turned to the third Scatman album, which had been in development for over a year. It was the last shot at momentum.

John canceled all personal trips, including the Danish stuttering convention. He asked Mette to help with the cancellations, to ease the load. He apologized to Eloise, knowing she'd be in Denmark, waiting to see him.

I'm not doing so great, he told her. *No answers yet*. She made it to the conference and cheered John up with a Get Well card signed by all the participants.

In mid-July, he went in for the lung biopsy.

'If all goes well, and there is no cancer, he will probably be able to return to work 1st September,' Judy wrote. 'If, on the other hand, they find something … please God, it's treatable.'

They didn't find anything.

It didn't help that John's body was a canvas of old damage. He had 'beached and battered' it, he said, 'until it broke down.' Years of sobriety hadn't erased what came before. He was used to pain and strangeness, so he pushed through, and an album recording session was booked for September in Bremen, Germany.

At first, John bristled. Most of the New York and Cuban demos had been rejected, but he still wanted a Latin studio, with Latin artists represented – so strongly he even tried to back out. But the flights, production team, and studio time were all booked. There was no undoing it.

'Let's do a great album, that's all that counts,' Manfred reassured him. 'Let's get Scatman to the top again. Then we can do experiments, and I will be with you to try other things out.'

John still wasn't entirely sold. 'Are we forgetting that my original audience is older now?' he'd said earlier in the process. His first fans were now in their late teens. He wanted to meet them where they were.

'Take Your Time', the title track, did just that. It was aimed at young men feeling pressure to act macho and rush into love when, John said, the relationship they needed first was with themselves.

'Somehow, I learned at an early age that you're not supposed to have emotions; you're not supposed to show them,' John remembered. 'Men are supposed to be men. Men are supposed to be in full control. But inside, it was a different story.'

He also revisited the slow demo Edesio Alejandro created for him in Cuba, turning it into a song he wanted to call 'Edesio's Dream'. It was renamed 'Dream Again' to sound more commercial and memorable, but John got around it by thanking Edesio in the lyrics.

In August 1998, just before he and Judy left for Germany, John heard that his ex-wife Marcia had died of a brain aneurysm. She had also cleaned up and was sober, and had collapsed while caring for a sick friend. Though they hadn't spoken in years, the news likely weighed on him.

Even with two days' rest after arrival in Bremen, John wasn't at full strength. 'There are still days when my physical pain gets pretty bad,' he told Manfred. He hoped he wouldn't need medication to get through the sessions. Whether he took any, no one knows.

'I never remotely suspected that something was bothering John,' says producer Kai Matthiesen. 'We had fun every day.'

Unlike the first two Scatman albums, everything had been prepped in advance. The tracks were done. All John had to do was show up and sing the lyrics he'd written.

'He had a smoky, distinguishable voice,' Kai's assistant, Billy King, said. The raspiness, he assumed, came from years of smoking.

To Kai and Billy, John – drinking coffee and poring over his laptop notes – seemed like any other artist mid-project. They had no benchmark to compare it to.

But Manfred did. The moment he walked into the studio, he saw it.

'He wasn't really well,' Manfred said. John needed rest breaks more often. 'The sessions weren't long, but the energy wasn't really there.'

John and Judy returned home for a break, and in October they flew back to Germany to finish the album – this time with more color in John's cheeks. He added two more sessions: one in Munich with Tobias Gad to record 'The Chickadee Song', and another with John Ravenhall for a cover of Elton John's 'Sorry Seems to Be the Hardest Word'.

John seemed in better spirits. 'You can sing higher than me!' he shouted at Billy King during a take.

'But you have the sexier voice,' Billy shot back. 'You're a star, and I'm not taking any lame excuses for asking me to bring the key down!' They fell about laughing.

Take Your Time wrapped ahead of schedule, and John returned to LA, demo in hand.

On New Year's Eve, he and Judy threw a party, asking guests to come dressed as celebrities. Judy went as John. John went as himself. They twirled around the living room in their fedoras, dancing to 'Dream Again' on the stereo.

In his home studio, John played nine jazz sets with a rotating crew of musician friends, jamming late into the evening.

At midnight, he and Judy laughed and tossed confetti and balloons in the air.

They had no idea that John's last year of life had begun.

35 I'M FREE

'I didn't think he'd do it,' says film director Peter Nicks. 'It was just a thesis project. It wasn't anything fancy.'

But there was John, sitting in his backyard, holding a conversation entirely in scat with thirteen-year-old Daniel Kremer, who also stuttered. The two were laughing so hard it was nearly impossible to get anything else out of them.

'Gleeful,' Daniel remembers. 'I thought it was the most hilarious thing. He was being completely silly with me.'

They howled, jabbered nonsense, and pointed at everyone.

'I can't get serious, man,' John said as they broke down again. But eventually, he did – at least for a little while.

'The chemistry between John and Danny was just very special,' Pete says.

Daniel first saw John speak at the National Stuttering Project convention in San Diego, as a ten-year-old, staring as John took the stage.

'My eyes were up on the screen for the whole thing,' Daniel said, now sitting beside John. 'I was like, oh God, he's great.'

Producer and director Peter Nicks, whose wife also stuttered, had met John a few years earlier. *Danny and the Scatman* began as his graduate thesis at UC Berkeley – a film tracing two stutterers at different stages of life. One found refuge in music. The other, in film. Most of it had already been shot at Daniel's home in Pittsburgh. Now they were in LA to capture John at home.

In February 1999, John didn't just agree to appear in the documentary – he paid to fly Daniel and his mother from Pittsburgh to Los Angeles so the project could be finished.

'A lot of people who have had the success John had wouldn't do that,' Pete says. John mentioned he'd been ill, but seemed fine, energized by Daniel's presence.

'Dan and I know things about each other that a person who is a non-stutterer may not have experienced,' John said. 'It's almost like a telepathic thing.'

He gave Daniel a tour of the house, showed him his laptop and the Scatman websites, and let him hold his Annie Glenn Award. Then they stepped into the 'Scatland' studio, where John played him 'Can You Hear Me', still a work in progress. Daniel watched, amazed by the microphones, the instruments, the mixing desk where faders moved on their own.

This is in his house? he thought.

During a break, Daniel wandered over to John's brand-new drum kit and started banging away. John rushed in.

'I wanna play with him!' he said, sitting at the piano.

'He was basically following my lead because I wasn't going to keep up with him,' Daniel says. 'He started jamming with me like I was Buddy Rich or something. Even though I was playing those drums terribly, he made me feel like I could do anything.'

When the crew broke for lunch, John and Daniel went for a walk down the street.

'He never liked to be called Scatman in front of me,' Daniel remembers, 'Just John.'

As they walked, John explained that Scatman was like a shield – what most people saw. But if you looked underneath, he said, you would see the heart of someone who stuttered. The heart of John Larkin.

'That's when I realized,' Daniel said later, 'he was my hero.'

They came back to finish filming, and then it was time to go, and let John be interviewed solo.

'I was emotional,' Daniel remembered. 'I didn't want to leave him.' But they promised to stay in touch by email and phone.

Over in Germany, Kai Matthiesen loaded another demo into his DJ set and watched the crowd. This was his litmus test: if people drifted off the dancefloor, something had to change. Several tracks on *Take Your Time* were tweaked this way, tightened before the final master.

Kai presented the album to BMG. The meeting went well, and the lead single, 'Take Your Time', was set for release around May 1999. The album would follow.

'Kai is very gifted,' John said. 'He is able to bring so much out of so little.' It was another dance-centric album, but John was fine with that. 'The album addresses spirituality in dance,' he said. 'Spirituality in movement. It's a beautiful thing for a person to just move, to express themselves.'

John was ready to do his part. His health issues, he told Manfred, were mostly behind him. He gave the go-ahead to start booking TV slots, with one condition.

'Under doctor's orders, my stress levels should be kept at a minimum,' he said. He couldn't do any more live performances. From now on, it had to be full playback – miming from start to finish.

Director Peter Nicks returned with associate producer Ed Wong to film John solo. They recorded him in his home studio, jamming with friends, then prepared for the interview. John sat on his couch, chewing regular gum, nicotine patches hidden under his black turtleneck.

'My life is great,' he said. 'It's a wonderful place to be – because I stutter.'

He talked about everything – from childhood to fame. *What had Scatman done for him?*

'I could look you in the eye,' John said, 'and say hello. Whether I stuttered or not. It brought me to the point of finally feeling equal, that I was finally a person functioning in society.'

But as the interview went on, he got upset. He was 'going fluent' – a maddening phenomenon for many who stutter. He wanted kids to hear his real voice, and this wasn't it. He pointed out that this was rare for him, and that he still stuttered significantly.

'Sometimes it's terrible,' he said. 'As many TV shows as I've done, radio, all that stuff … it still bothers me. But I know, deep inside – I'm free. *I'm free.*'

Asked what his music meant to kids, John said he'd gotten an email just the night before. A young lad had thanked him up and down for giving him direction, a way to go.

But John shook his head.

'I'm not to be praised. I come out of my experience only. That's the greatest thing a person can do – try to help someone else. See, I don't want you to misunderstand me when I tell you I'm a very selfish person,' John said. 'When I discovered how self-involved I was, I realized how much I was cut off from the rest of the world.'

He paused.

'Even if I don't feel it in the moment, when I help someone else, I know I'm doing the right thing. Sometimes I help. Sometimes I don't. Sometimes I want to be left alone.'

He'd said something similar back in '96 – that sometimes he did it despite himself. 'I don't want to wear the damned scat-hat for one second more. I'm sick of this shit and I hate everyone! Then the real me kicks in,' he said.

When that happened, he talked to his inner child.

'There's a child inside, and as an adult, you've got to talk to it,' John said. '"I don't want to anymore!" the angry child says. "C'mon, Paul," I say – Paul is my middle name – "we're doing this to be good to ourselves."'

John laughed, joked, scat-sang, and did indeed put the hat on for a second, smiling, practicing what he preached. He looked straight into the camera.

'Danny, I know what you're going through, man,' he said. 'Hang in there, man, because I understand you. Totally.'

Cancer. There was that word again.

It had been on his medical team's lips for a year. They suspected it, John's doctor told him. They just couldn't find it. Tumor markers in his blood now confirmed something was there, even if they hadn't nailed it on a slide. Yet another biopsy had come back inconclusive.

'They're telling me I have cancer,' an incredulous John told Ingo Kays over the phone. Still not quite believing it, he began chemotherapy. He would beat it, he said. He was ready to fight.

In the meantime, he kept working, finalizing plans for the Scatland Foundation, and answering fan mail. The hits had stopped in '96, but the letters hadn't. Through fan websites, kids were still writing, asking where they could find his music now that it was almost gone from store shelves. John wrote to Manfred asking if BMG could fulfill the orders.

'I feel an obligation to them, and as you know, they have certainly enhanced our lives,' John said, noting that the queries numbered in the hundreds. 'But I want to take care of them.'

The *Take Your Time* track list and artwork came in, and John approved it. Then, when asked for his dedication text, he made an unusual request.

'I'm being sincere about this, Mette,' he told her while Manfred was away on business. He wanted to dedicate the album to his golden retriever, Winston, who, John said, had taught him more about being human than any person ever had.

When Manfred returned, he shared his concern that John's audience might think John had lost faith in humanity.

John offered another dedication instead: to Manfred, Mette, and their children: Oliver, Felix, and Natascha, writing that Manfred had 'a belief in me that sometimes ran deeper than my belief in myself.'

Manfred, although flattered, pushed back on this, too.

'My medal will be good sales figures,' he said. 'You know me.'

Just before starting university that summer, Eloise received a package from Japan. Inside was *Take Your Time*.

She was showing it to her friend Jonathan when they decided, on a whim, to call John and tell him what they thought. Eloise leaned against the phone box while Jonathan fed pound coins into the slot.

John answered, sounding bright and chipper.

What Eloise couldn't see was that, not long before, he'd shaved off all his hair. It had started falling out after the chemo, so he'd invited some friends over one evening and then laughed and sang as the razor buzzed and his dogs sniffed at clumps of dark hair falling to the floor. It hadn't even had the chance to go grey. Now bald, John joked he could finally do his throat chants properly, like a monk.

'We like your new album,' Eloise told him, then handed the phone to Jonathan. She watched as his knees buckled. She could hear loud scat-singing coming through the receiver.

'He scat-sang for me!' Jonathan laughed, then passed the phone back.

'My album's out?' John asked Eloise, suddenly serious. He didn't seem to know it had shipped.

The accompanying single – 'Take Your Time' – had been released but struggled to gain radio play. Without promotion, and with no one in Europe knowing what John even looked like anymore, BMG chose not to invest further. The album was re-licensed to another label.   John didn't seem to mind. Quite the opposite. His tone turned strange and reflective.

'Whatever God wants is fine by me,' he told Eloise. 'I've had the very best life. I have tasted beauty.' He said this cheerfully, like a cosmic joke only he understood.

His tumor markers had recently dropped. It looked like treatment might be working.   But he never mentioned any of this. As she hung up, Eloise chalked it up to John being John.

Days later, John and Judy got the news.

We're sorry, the doctors said.

They'd found it: small cell lung cancer. Smoker's cancer. Fast-growing and aggressive, it often ducked scans, masked symptoms, and hid until it was everywhere it shouldn't be.

By the time it showed itself in John, it had already reached his brain.

36 CAN YOU HEAR ME?

It is a golden Sunday afternoon in 1970s California, warm and wide open. John is hiking with his drummer friend Chuck Glave and Joe Celia, who plays bass. They are somewhere up near Mount Wilson, taking a break before their jam session at a little bar tucked behind another bar.

As they head down the trail, someone spots it: a fallen tree, stretched out in a gully like a broken instrument. They climb down for a closer look.

And then they start to play.

Joe takes the roots and the trunk. Chuck grabs some sticks and hits the middle section, finding bounce and tone in the bark. John goes for the high branches – brittle, thin, sun-dried limbs that sound tuneful if you tap them just right. The tree becomes a kit. They laugh, beating out a rhythm in the early evening light.

Eventually, Chuck glances up and says, 'We gotta go to work.'

They haul themselves out of the ravine, still holding the sticks they'd been drumming with. At the top, they toss them back down toward the tree, thanking it for the experience.

Then it's into the cars, windows down, dust on their clothes, sweat on their foreheads, straight to the bar's gate.

Two decades later, the dappled early morning light catches John's bare scalp as he leans in, eyes closed, nose deep in the petals, breathing them in.

Behind him, Gladys watches.

Most mornings, they're up by five. John doesn't sleep much these days.

'Let's go for a walk,' he says, and they do – around the block, sometimes up the nature trail beside the house if he's feeling strong enough, where he loves to hear the wind move through the trees.

Gladys's mother, Maria, had been John and Judy's housekeeper for years, but now Gladys has moved in to help care for John.

'He was more than a boss to me,' she says. 'He never treated me like a worker. More like family.' They talk. John worries that Judy will be left alone. Worries what will become of the Scatland Foundation.

He stops and smells every flower, wondering out loud if this walk will be his last. Gladys smiles and tells him not to worry. They can stay as long as he wants.

When the doctors delivered the final blow – *There's nothing more we can do* – something in John gave way.

'I watched a very joyful, playful, wonderful man become frightened,' Judy said. John locked himself in a room for hours. Behind the closed door came the sounds of guttural sobbing. Anyone who dared to knock was met with the same response: *Go away.*

But Gladys wouldn't leave. She stood outside his door.

'It's okay,' she would say gently. 'I'm here. I'll be outside.'

'Go home to your family,' John snapped through tears. 'I don't need you here.' But Gladys stayed. She knew it was the anger talking. She'd worked with seniors and recognized this stage of grief.

John didn't want anyone to know. Didn't want to see his friends.

'The house was quiet, for a while,' Gladys remembers.

He was supposed to be promoting *Take Your Time*, but instead, there was silence. Napster, the MP3 sharing platform, had just arrived, and anyone who really wanted the album was downloading it for free anyway. It nearly disappeared without a trace.

'I was determined to keep him at home,' Judy said, 'and not put him in one of those weird hospitals where they leave you out on a gurney in the hall for five hours.'

John's stepson, Lee, was staying at the house. One day, he found John sitting alone in the bedroom.

'He started crying,' Lee remembers. 'He just looked at me and said, *I don't want to die*. I don't know what the hell I said to that.'

After the anger passed, John did what he'd spent years training himself to do: adapt. Live in the moment. Let it go.

At first, he didn't want anyone to see him sick. But the community came back. Friends returned. AA meetings resumed in the living room. He turned again to the principles that had carried him this far: *Let go, let God, let good*, as the old AA saying went.

Sitting at his laptop, he opened his address book and clicked on Eloise's name. It had only been a few weeks since her payphone call, so he started with a joke:

'Hey there – remember me?'

But then came the real reason he was writing.

'It is now my turn to thank you for touching **my** life,' he wrote. 'Watching you grow up in front of us all has been such a wonderful experience. To see how far you've come in such a short time is nothing short of a miracle.'

'We will both be here for the rest of our lives,' he said. 'So let us never say "goodbye", but only "to be continued." I love you. John.'

Eloise, on summer holiday, sat reading the message. Her heart began to race. *Oh no.*

It was rare for John to write out of the blue. The tone made her feel sick.

She'd assumed he was busy with the third album and hadn't wanted to disturb him, knowing it was a high-stress time. She picked up the phone and dialed his number from memory.

No answer.

She tried again. And again. Days passed, then weeks. Still nothing.

Is something wrong? She had written back. *Are you okay?*

There was no reply.

While he still can, John sits at the mixing desk in his home studio, a couple of friends at his side, trying to finish another take of 'Can You Hear Me?'. He starts singing to the guide track, but his voice sounds thick and hoarse.

Pardon me, can we talk? Can I have just a moment of your time … I'm singing this song for you … Sometimes it's hard to talk, so let me sing it in rhyme …

Then, he forgets the lyrics. Misses others. Comes in too early or too late, his impeccable timing gone. Halfway through, he stops. The track keeps going for two full minutes without him.

Cut the mic, someone says.

It was the last thing he ever recorded.

By September 1999, increasingly frantic faxes were arriving from the Iceberg office. Manfred and Mette had been told John was very ill – 'not very mobile' – but little else. Invitations for promotional gigs were still coming in, and Manfred didn't know what to say.

Judy didn't want to accept the truth yet. She refused to give up. She searched for alternative treatments, grasping at even the smallest chance.

'Please let me hear from you, if everything is OK,' Manfred wrote. 'You are getting me all worried.'

In early October 1999, as soon as her dorm room phone was connected, Eloise dialed John's number again. It was her first month at university, and she felt anxious and alone. Her new friends were kind, but the social, fast-talking world of campus life was overwhelming. She was back to hiding her stutter.

The international dial tone beeped. She looked forward to hearing John's warm, reassuring voice – the voice that always told her everything was going to be all right.

John didn't pick up. But Gladys did.

'Hey, Gladdy. Can I talk to John, please?'

Gladys seemed awkward. There was a pause and a shuffling noise as the phone was handed over to someone else.

Judy came on the line. Eloise had never spoken to her before, but explained why she was calling. Judy knew who she was, and had bad news.

'He's dying, honey,' she said.

Stunned, Eloise asked if she could come visit.

'If you can, come soon,' Judy said. 'He doesn't have long left … please don't be disappointed if he doesn't respond. He's slipping. He's stopped recognizing people.'

Eloise hung up, a decision already half-formed. Her first student loan payment had just landed in her bank account. It would just about cover a flight to Los Angeles.

Forty-eight hours later, she had abandoned her lectures and was on the plane.

37 WHATEVER GOD WANTS

Fryman Place sat at the corner of Ventura Boulevard and Laurel Canyon Drive, in an enviable spot across from Wilacre Park. *Close to everything, but away from everything*, John used to say.

It was a bright, hot October morning when a cab disgorged a jet-lagged Eloise onto the driveway. Gladys was waiting for her – smiling, but with sadness.

'Mr. John is up,' she said, letting Eloise walk ahead of her into the house.

Eloise entered the hall and peered around the doorway.

There he was.

She had imagined, many times, what it would be like when they finally met. Hugs. Laughter. Not like this.

John was sitting upright on the edge of a makeshift bed in his downstairs office. He was bald. His mustache had greyed. His white T-shirt and sweatpants hung loose on his thinner frame. He was motionless, silently staring into space.

Eloise stepped forward. He looked up.

Please let him know it's me, she thought, knowing her heart would break if he didn't.

She needn't have worried.

John's eyes widened.

'Oh my God,' he said. '*Oh my God!*'

'John …,' she began, her voice breaking.

'It's you! It's you!' he said, and held out both his hands. She took them, and he guided her down to sit next to him on the edge of the bed. She began explaining about the phone call, the last-minute flight.

'Judy told you?' he asked. Eloise nodded, already blinking back tears. John looked so different. So diminished. But his eyes were sharp and bright, staring into hers. Nobody had ever looked at her like that before. He knew everything. He saw everything.

'Ahhhh …,' he sighed, and squeezed her hands. *Typical*, she thought. *Comforting me on his deathbed.*

'I love you, honey,' he said, gently.

She told him she loved him too, and managed to croak out a thank you. She can't remember if she said it all out loud or not. *Thank you. Thank you for saving my life.*

Judy poked her head around the door and looked at the pair of them sitting on the bed. She smiled and nodded at Eloise, and then disappeared again.

'I wanna … show you … something,' John huffed, pushing himself to his feet. He shuffled towards another door and held it open.

His studio.

Eloise followed him in, awed by the sound desk, the tangled wires, towers of tapes and CDs, shelves of trophies and memorabilia, ending with the glossy, black, beautiful baby grand.

John eased himself onto the piano bench, facing outward, breathing heavily. He made a sweeping motion at the wall with his hand, adorned with Platinum and Gold awards.

Eloise felt a hole where happiness should be. Normally, she'd be thrilled to see all this, but it was too cruel to see the smiling man on the CD covers looking down at the fragile version of him stooped below.

'This is where I record … Scatman,' he said, and then he began to fade. Those dozen steps had taken all his strength.

He leaned forward, groaning, cradling his head. Judy told her that John had lesions in his brain, that the spreading cancer was causing blinding headaches. Eloise hovered, afraid to touch him. *Are you all right?* She asked, knowing he wasn't.

John didn't reply and kept his head down, softly yowling in a way that made Eloise wince. Gladys came in. Perhaps it would be best if Mr. John had a nap now, she said. He needed more morphine.

Over takeout lunch while John slept, Judy told Eloise about everything they'd tried – and everything that had failed – to stop the cancer. When chemo didn't work, they'd chased every avenue: alternative medicine, Chinese herbs, even a clinic across the border in Mexico, offering unproven treatments banned in the US.

John had accepted it before Judy did. He didn't want any more interventions. They'd argued. She couldn't let go.

She lost weight. Chain-smoked. Friends worried she wasn't taking care of herself. But now, at least, she'd let it in.

Before things got worse, Daniel Kremer had called.

'I remember him getting on the phone and this really depleted voice saying, *Hi Danny*,' he said. 'Hearing that, I knew. He was not long for this world.'

Manfred had spoken to John too, via video call. John sat propped in a chair, pale and worn. Nobody said it out loud. They didn't need to. John wasn't coming back.

The public still had no idea. Judy and Iceberg considered releasing a statement – something respectful – but hadn't yet. To do so would make it real.

AA meetings were still being held at the house. Weeks later, when John could no longer walk, one of his friends – a big, strong Ethiopian man – would go into John's bedroom, scoop him up in his arms, and carry him out. But today, the house was quiet.

Eloise was struck by Judy's kindness, even with everything she was dealing with. She loaned Eloise a cardigan when she misjudged the cool LA evenings. She kept asking – *Are you all right?* After Eloise assured her she was, Judy got up and went to check on John. A few minutes later, she returned holding a CD-R.

'John wants you to have this,' she said.

Eloise took it. 'Can You Hear Me?', it read. It was his last song, Judy told her, recorded in fragments as he grew weaker.

The next afternoon, John was sitting hunched over in the living room. Earlier, he had been stretched out on his oversized, cream leather sofa, looking so peacefully asleep, Eloise found herself checking he was still breathing. Then he started dreaming, his feet kicking outward. A nightmare. He woke with a start as his eyes flew open and found hers.

'Did I die?' he asked, frightened.

No, she told him. *No, John, you're still right here.*

Now Gladys had helped him up into his preferred stance: leaning forward, one hand supporting his chin like a weary version of Rodin's *The Thinker*. Eloise went to sit next to him on the couch. Judy put on some VHS tapes of Scatman appearances for them to watch together.

The static cleared, and one of his music videos danced across the screen. John glanced up at the TV every now and again. Sometimes there was recognition in his eyes, sometimes not.

Judy stood and watched too, her cigarette smoke winding through a late afternoon sunbeam as the fuzzy footage rolled. John being interviewed by MTV. John preparing for his world tour. John being told not to look into the camera lens when talking to 'the kids' but doing it anyway.

Beside Eloise, John occasionally groaned with pain. When one episode lasted longer than usual, she patted his spare hand. He locked his fingers with hers. The strength in his grip surprised her; those piano-playing muscles the only thing not wasting away.

On screen, John and Judy walk down a red carpet in Germany in 1996, waving as they pass through screaming crowds of fans at the Echo Awards.

Inside the theater, the camera finds John, sitting with Ingo, Tony and Manfred, the four of them in suits, grinning like schoolboys. John is up for the Single of the

Year award. The presenter appears, and announces what everybody already knows. Scatman John has won.

Applause thunders and cameras flash. Here is John, getting up, accepting back-pats, making his way to the stage. Beaming, he turns around and makes a dampening motion with his hands, as if he doesn't think there should be so much fuss. He strides up the steps, kisses the presenter on each cheek and takes the award. Holding it tightly, he approaches the podium.

On the couch, John says to nobody in particular, 'That's me.'

Eloise feels his hand squeeze hers. She doesn't answer. She is intently watching the screen.

The clapping dies down, and suddenly the theater is quiet.

John stands behind the microphone, gazing out at the thousands of faces before him. The camera is close on him now. He swallows and pauses for a moment, glancing again at the waiting crowd.

Then, a little voice inside his head says:

It's okay, Johnny. Just go ahead and stutter.

John smiles, takes a breath, and begins to speak.

EPILOGUE

The Pacific Ocean churned beneath the boat as it cut through choppy waters off Catalina Island. A jazz trio played on deck while Judy stood at the rail, holding the bag against her chest, eyes closed against the salt spray, steadying herself.

She was ready.

The ashes caught the wind, scattering over the water in a fine, grey mist. The music followed, rising with the waves, folding into the open sea.

John died on 3 December 1999, surrounded by his friends, his family, and his animals. He was 57. Judy kept her promise – he never went to a hospital.

'John wouldn't have wanted a memorial,' she told a standing-room-only crowd days later. 'He would have wanted to get on with the music.'

And that's what they did. Jazz, of course. Straight ahead.

News of John's death spread so fast across the early internet that the traffic crashed the servers hosting his website. For one last time, John was a global headline – the man who told the world he had turned his greatest problem into his greatest gift.

A year later, in 2000, Judy moved. 'It's a big house for me, with too many memories,' she said, and bought a new house a few miles from the one they had shared. She was lost without John – everyone could see it – but she found a way to carry on. In 2001, with Manfred, she orchestrated the release of *Listen to the Scatman*: a collection of John performing jazz standards.

'A very fitting tribute to my baby,' she said. And it was. Afterwards, she tried to move on, but part of her never did.

'Sleep tight, my prince, and wait for me,' she said at his memorial. She never remarried. Judy died in January 2023, at the age of 83.

Today, Scatman John's music has reached over half a billion streams. Unlike many of his '90s contemporaries, John – and his message – never faded. Passed from one generation to the next, he endures as listeners discover the truth hiding beneath the kitsch.

You can call out from Scatman's World anywhere now: in remixes, cartoons, memes, TikTok. Everyone from the Black Eyed Peas to Alan Walker has sampled him. In 2019, Lou Bega released 'Scatman & Hatman' as a tribute. The requests – for TV, film, ads, and covers – never stop.

'More now than it's ever been,' Manfred tells me, tapping ash from his cigar. We're sitting in the Iceberg office in Silkeborg, Denmark, still going strong as one of the best-known independents in Scandinavia. Manfred, now in his 70s, and his wife Mette still run the label.

'We turn down 80 percent of them,' he adds. 'We don't want to water it down.'

I watch the smoke curl toward the ceiling, past John's framed CD awards. Thirty-nine in total: seventeen Gold, twenty-two Platinum. Still Iceberg's biggest success. And some of their fondest memories.

I ask Manfred to sum up the Scatman years.

'Phenomenal,' he says.

From Denmark, I head to Los Angeles, to the San Fernando Valley, where John and Judy lived.

'You can do anything if you put your mind to it. It doesn't matter what stifles you – stuttering, whatever it may be,' Christena Rich-Newman tells me when I ask what John's music means to the next generation. 'Those are the messages I want my son to hear. And I want him to tell someone else, too. Because we're not in this world alone.'

I'm sitting with Judy's son – John's stepson – Lee Newman, and his wife, Christena, watching their 11-year-old, Heston, strum effortlessly on his guitar. He plays like it's second nature. I ask what he thinks of his famous step-grandfather.

'He's pretty cool,' he says. Then, without being asked, he picks up a kazoo and starts buzzing 'Scatman.'

They live in Judy's old house – the same place where they cared for her in her final days, just as she had cared for John. His grand piano still sits in the center of the room.

I stare at it for a long time. Then I walk over and touch the keys.

Lee and Christena understand that coming from a famous family doesn't mean inheriting its pressure. Judy knew that all too well. So instead of repeating the cycle, they break it – honoring the Jimmy McHugh songbook by singing it together, as a family.

Eighty miles east of LA, John's older brother, Billy, greets me with a bear hug. He's 83 now, and though he and John were different in temperament, he shares the same broad smile, the same impish humor.

His son David is there too with his daughters, Jillian and Sarah.

'I've always felt very connected to him,' Jillian says. She and her sister didn't grow up knowing their Great-Uncle John, but they danced to his music as kids, and they still have his old white spinet piano, the one he played before he bought the grand. Billy's other son, Steve, isn't there, but he knows I am.

'Music has always been the binding force of the Larkin family,' he writes to me afterward. I hear many tales of John at family gatherings: brilliant at the piano, yet struggling to get a word out.

Today, the stuttering community has moved closer to John's philosophy, where feelings are the focus, and self-help is central. 'I remember John as a person who got it,' says stuttering advocate and friend Anita Blom. 'A person who made that shift – it's okay to stutter. It's okay to be me. It's okay not to be perfect, not to fit in one box,' she says. 'We need him back', she adds. 'We need to play his songs.'

The National Stuttering Association echoes that sentiment. "With love and compassion, John shared his story in the hopes of inspiring others who face the challenges of stuttering," say past Executive Director Annie Bradberry and current Executive Director Tammy Flores-Romano. "Ahead of his time, he understood the profound importance of self-acceptance. Through his music, he touched generations, shedding light on the experience of stuttering and offering a voice to those who needed it most."

Modern therapy now begins with the individual. No more one-size-fits-all. It's about what you want, not just how you sound.

'Our philosophy is, it has to be okay to stutter,' says Heather Grossman of the American Institute for Stuttering. 'You have to give yourself full permission to be who you are. And if that includes stuttering, then you have to give yourself permission to stutter.'

She still plays 'Scatman (Ski-Ba-Bop-Ba-Dop-Bop)' for clients, asking if they knew it was about stuttering. 'John was just so honest, vulnerable, open, and accessible,' she says.

'Scatman John was an inspiration to young people who stutter for sure' says Jane Fraser, President of the Stuttering Foundation. 'The fact that he was open about it encouraged others to also be open.' After John died, work on the Scatland Foundation stopped. It was too painful for Judy to keep it going, so the funds were donated to stuttering organizations around the world.

Yet the people John helped – in AA meetings, at conferences, through emails, behind closed doors – became their own ripple effect.

Which is how I end up in East Los Angeles on a bright spring morning, trying not to cry.

It was a cool, clear day in El Sereno, the air still beneath a pale blue sky. I walked past the tall fences of All Saints Catholic School, now closed, and crossed the street towards the church.

As I climbed the stairs, I could hear a deep, solemn voice through the open door. Mass was in session. I didn't go in.

I paused in the vestibule, thinking about the little boy who would become the man who changed my life. A wad of leaflets caught my eye. I plucked one from the stack and held it up to the daylight. It was about the prevention of child abuse.

Some things had changed, after all.

It was March 2023. Almost twenty-four years had passed since my first visit to Los Angeles, when I had walked through John's door as a shy teenager. Back then, neither of us could have known that I would one day write his biography.

I am Eloise, the girl he took under his wing.

And I am the author of this book. Eloise is my middle name.

Judy and I kept in touch for years after John died. We often talked about his remarkable life and how it deserved to be more widely known. But then Judy got sick.

When she died, it was a trigger. I knew if I didn't act soon, John's story would be lost forever – and the people who remembered him would be gone.

But there was a problem. I had gone back to hiding my stutter. It was just too damn hard not to. My stutter is subtle, but its weight never leaves me. Society still loves – and rewards – smooth talkers. Stuttering is still misunderstood, still fair game for mockery, still rarely met with patience or grace.

John used to say that hiding your true self is like trying to hold a beach ball underwater. You can't keep it down forever. Eventually, it rises.

When I began researching John's life, I found a preface to the autobiography he never finished. 'This is a book about the life of a stutterer, written by a stutterer, for a world largely uninformed on the subject,' he wrote. He believed a reader should *feel* what it's like to stutter, not just intellectually understand it. He believed only a stutterer could write such a book.

When I read that, I felt the beach ball rise.

It had to be me.

Okay, John. I thought.

He reached across three decades and nudged me out of my comfort zone again. Because if I wanted to do him justice, I knew what I had to do. I had to pick up the phone. I had to schedule interviews. In short, I had to do everything I hated – everything I'd been avoiding for years. I had to talk to hundreds of strangers.

As he had in life, John made it easier. The people I interviewed were already used to talking to someone with a speech difference. What struck me most was that so many either forgot or didn't pay much attention to John's stutter. They remembered his music, his humor, his philosophy. His humanity.

How I wish I could go back and tell him: the thing that haunted you was such a small part of who you really were.

Interview by interview, stuttering shrank back to its proper perspective – in his life, and in mine. The story – his story – took its rightful place at the center.

John's life wasn't easy. He said himself, he was no saint.   But he showed me that vulnerability isn't weakness. That kindness isn't naïve. That it's never too late to become who you were meant to be.

His greatest legacy wasn't music. It was what he gave away, again and again: hope.

Hope for awkward kids like me.

Hope for the late bloomers and the long shots.

Hope for those who've been laughed at more than listened to.

Hope for anyone who believed they had to hide who they are just to survive.

He gave that truth to me.

And now it's yours.

Because if the Scatman can do it –

So can you.

RESOURCES AND SUPPORT

A portion of the profits from this book will go toward re-establishing the Scatland Foundation. To learn more or support directly, visit scatlandfoundation.com.

Stuttering Support

The American Institute for Stuttering (USA) – https://www.stutteringtreatment.org/
British Stammering Association / STAMMA (UK) – https://stamma.org
Friends: The National Association of Young People Who Stutter (USA) – https://friendswhostutter.org
The International Stuttering Association (ISA) (Worldwide) – https://www.isastutter.org/
National Stuttering Association (USA) – https://westutter.org
Stamily (Worldwide) – https://stamily.org
The Stuttering Foundation (USA) – https://stutteringhelp.org

Addiction and Recovery Support

Alcoholics Anonymous (Worldwide) – https://www.aa.org
Al-Anon (family and friend) groups – https://al-anon.org
Narcotics Anonymous (Worldwide) – https://na.org
SMART Recovery – https://smartrecovery.org
Musicares (formerly Musician's Assistance Program) – https://www.musicares.org/

ACKNOWLEDGEMENTS

I'm immensely grateful to the many people who helped bring this book to fruition. My first thanks go to my editor, Michael Tan, whose stellar insight, patience, and guidance made the process both rewarding and meaningful. From the start, Michael understood this was not just a book about a '90s pop star, but about disability, difference, and the power of authenticity.

My heartfelt thanks to my literary agent, Rita Rosenkranz, for her razor-sharp instincts, professionalism, and encouragement. She knew this book would find its place, and it's been a pleasure to work with her ever since.

Thanks also to the broader team at Bloomsbury – Kristin Susser, Linda Kessler, and Sandra Creaser – whose hard work behind the scenes has not gone unnoticed. Special thanks to my publicist, Meghan McDonagh, and to Sally Rinehart, who designed the wonderful cover.

The Scatman phenomenon happened at the cusp of the modern internet era, so much of John's life wasn't online but instead buried in the analog world of fuzzy VHS tapes, CDs, cassettes, magazines, DATs, newspapers, and yellowing faxes in boxes scattered across America and Europe. My most important source, in the end, was living memory. Pulling together the disparate threads of the jazz, Eurodance, recovery, and stuttering communities would have been impossible without the generosity of so many people who trusted me with their time, their memories, and their love for John.

John's stepson, Lee Newman, was the backbone of this project. He generously drove me all over Los Angeles, set up interviews, and let me spend many hours digging through his mother's and stepfather's archives and storage. He gave me access to material that made this book possible. I'm hugely grateful to Lee, his wife Christena, and their son Heston for their unwavering support and patience. Thank you so much, and for letting me cover your living room in Scatman memorabilia more times than was probably reasonable.

Manfred and Mette Zähringer not only opened their Iceberg Records archive, but also their home, never tiring of my countless questions, emails, and calls. Manfred told stories like they'd happened yesterday, not decades ago, and together they brought the Scatman years vividly back to life with warmth and humor. Thank you both – your enthusiasm, hospitality, and belief in this strange little project from the beginning mean a great deal to me. My thanks also to the wider Iceberg Records team – Frida Malmø, Anna Moland, Alice Sørensen, and Magnus Vad – for helping me at every turn, and letting me gatecrash your office and ask endless favors.

John once called Ingo Kays and Tony Catania the "architects of Scatman," and both were instrumental in shaping this book. They gave many hours of their time and shared their insights freely, answering questions down to the fan–nerd level. Tony and his wife Ilona were among my first interviewees, and their immediate enthusiasm made clear how deeply John's story mattered to them. Ingo answered my barrage of questions with patience, humor, and grace, and introduced me to Iris Riemann, whose vivid recollections of the Bottrop days helped bring the story to life. I'm indebted to both of John's "magicians" for their openness, support, and brilliant musical minds.

Had he lived, John would be in his eighties. Many who knew him are no longer with us, and some sadly passed before this book was finished. The most heartbreaking loss was his sister-in-law, Sharon Larkin. Alongside her husband, John's older brother Billy, she welcomed me like family and shared memories of "Johnny" with honesty and care. I am deeply grateful to you both. My warmest thanks also to the wider Larkin family – David, Jillian, Sarah, and Steven – for your stories, your music, and your belief that John deserved to be understood, not just remembered.

The family of John's first wife, Marcia, were also incredibly helpful. My thanks to Shelley Gilman and Daniel Hamel (aka Skornbread) for sharing their memories of their mother and John with me.

Thank you to those who knew both John and Judy together: Judy's cousin Mike Metzger; her brother Jimmy McHugh, who let me dig through his impressive photo archive; John and Judy's business manager Michael Schur and his wife Laurie; and Gladys Navas, who was just as kind and patient with me in 2023 as she was in 1999. My thanks also to Gary, Jackie, and Marc Hewitt, who have been as enthusiastic as I am about sharing the "real" John with the world. And to Sabrina Braham, David Glasband, Marci Herrara, Darryl Jacobs, Josh Jacobs, Tony Miali, Liz Miller, Barry Mitchell, Leslie Page, Mimi Smith, and the late Chuck Wert – some of whom knew John in school and reached back more than fifty years to share their memories.

I'm lucky to count many of John and Judy's friends as my own. One of the unexpected gifts of researching this book was reconnecting with old friends and finding new ones through shared memories of John. I finally met some in person, including George Rivera and his wife Gloria – thank you for your friendship and for the love you've always shown when speaking about John and Bobby. I hadn't met Stacey Heaver before starting this project, but I'm glad I did – her support, enthusiasm, and generosity meant a great deal. I'm also hugely grateful to D. Jennings, who made my L.A. trips fun, looked out for me, and introduced me to Gregg Pincus, who was also very helpful.

Spending time with musicians and jazz cats (and hearing them play) was one of the great joys of writing this book. Even over the phone, I found myself saying "Hey man" like John. Good things rub off. Big thanks to Gus Angelo, Andrea Black, Rusty Crutcher, Mike Del Ferro, Jimmy Espinoza, Chuck Glave, Rashidii Graffiti, Bob Harrison, Jon Hartmann, Steve Larrance, Carli Muñoz, John Morrell, Sam Provenzano, Steve Rawlins, Mayo Tiana, Joe Whiteman, and Scott Woodard. Special thanks to Joe Celia for marking my homework, to Duke McVinnie for rescuing some of John's older recordings, and to Sam Phipps for his generous encouragement. A heartfelt thank you to the late Edesio Alejandro, who never mentioned his cancer but instead gave me hours of enthusiastic help. Light to your soul.

It's a testament to John's legacy that everyone who interviewed, worked, or performed with him remembered those times with such warmth. My thanks to Axel Alexander, Hans Christian Andersen, Philip Cacayorin, Karl Garderer, Shane Keister, Billy King, Nanou Lamblin, Peter and Cindy Lorimer, Kai Matthiesen, Sabine Nagel-Heyer, Janine Ramond, Sebastian Roth (aka Sin with Sebastian), and to Michael Totten and Shane Verdi for their studio stories. Thanks also to John's US managers, Dave Helfant and Jan Roeg; his tour manager, Ulrik Hinsch; and the three Steves of the Scatman touring band: Steve Brzezicki, Steve Hamilton, and Steve Williams. To those who brought his music to life on screen – Gregor Schnitzler and Zowie Broach – and to Laura Hagger, who lived many a kid's dream by appearing in a Scatman video – thank you.

I'm incredibly grateful to the worldwide stuttering community – past, present, and emerging – for the courage and solidarity you show one another, and that you have always shown me. You saved my life, and this book is as much yours as it is mine.

I'm especially indebted to my dear friend Anita Blom, who met me – seventeen and terrified – at my first stuttering conference (where we'd turned up to jam with John) and has kept me talking ever since. My deep thanks also go to Steff Lebsack and Heather Najman for their unwavering encouragement and for reading the manuscript with the insight of their expertise.

A big hug to Annie Bradberry, who was with John right up until the end; and to Nora O'Connor for sharing your friendship with him and being so generous and encouraging; and to Heather Grossman at the American Institute for Stuttering, for being so enthusiastic and supportive and for keeping John's message alive. I'm grateful as well to Gail Wilson Lew, who knew John before he was famous and witnessed his transformation first-hand, and to my dear friend Konrad Schaefers, whom I know would have loved to see this story finally told.

My thanks to Tammy Flores-Romano and the team at the National Stuttering Association for all the tireless and brilliant work you do; to Caryn Herring, the late Lee Caggiano, and everyone at FRIENDS, where the kids continue to uplift and inspire the adults; and to my many friends in Stamily. To the fellow authors in the stuttering community I've been lucky enough to meet or talk with during this process: Patrick Campbell, Dori Holte, Hanan Hurwitz, Daniele Rossi, Sam Simpson, and Steven de Jong – thank you for lighting the way, keeping stuttering in the public eye, and helping to destigmatize it one sentence at a time. Special thanks to Jonty Claypole, John Hendrickson, Katherine Preston and Geoff Spink, who all generously read the manuscript and offered to endorse it, for which I am incredibly grateful.

Thank you to the American Speech-Language-Hearing Association (ASHA); Jane Fraser of the Stuttering Foundation; Ulrike Genglawski and the team at BV Stottern & Selbsthilfe; Arne Hope for the translation help; the International Stuttering Association; Judy Kuster; Nina G, the stuttering comedian who uses Scatman as her walk-up music; Jane Powell and the team at STAMMA (the British Stammering Association), Jeff Shames, Michael Sugarman, and all those who understand that the stutter and the scat were, at heart, the same thing.

I'm grateful to Satoru Hanazono for a joyful day of sushi and Scatman in Tokyo, and for helping me navigate archives for an afternoon of nostalgia. Thanks also to Masuhiko Kawasaki and Kazue Shinji for their friendship and hospitality, and to Shinji Ito, who kindly shared his correspondence with John after so many years. My thanks also to Daniel Kremer, who shares a kinship as another kid mentored by John, and to Peter Nicks, who captured that connection on film and generously shared his time – and his archives – to help tell this story.

My thanks to the people, organizations, and institutions that supported my research, including the El Sereno Historical Society, the Getty Center Library, the Jazzinstitut Darmstadt, the Los Angeles Public Library, the Menifee Public Library, the National Diet Library in Tokyo, Reid's Palace Hotel in Madeira, and several archival libraries. Thank you to Sierre Monk and the Thelonious Monk estate for permission to use the epigraph quote, and to Iceberg Music Publishing, EMI Music Publishing, Tony Catania Music Edition, Edition Scales, and Edition K-Tracks Publishing for permission to use Scatman John lyrics.

My gratitude also to those who, while not formally interviewed, still gave their time and efforts to help – especially Jeff Chi (who wrote a fabulous graphic novel about John); Allen Harris, who helped me digitize all the DATs, John Lasonio, who dug into his own archives, Vaidas Stackevičius, for his memories and photos of John's time in Lithuania; and Karen Walsh, my first beta reader.

To my fellow Scatman fans – thank you for carrying the torch of John's music and message. Special thanks to Jonathan Dolan, who has shared my enthusiasm for over thirty years and whose unmatched support means everything, and to Josh Phillips for his friendship and encouragement. Thank you to Charles Alpert, Tony Bernardo, Nic Christensen, Alex King, Allan Larsen, Vivian Lajoie, John Neace, Cristian and Mai Saavedra, Seia Tanabe and Elson Trinidad – and all the other "kids of all ages" out there.

I'm grateful to my family – my dad, John; his partner, Gillian; my sister, Sam; and her husband, Stuart – who all deserve a medal for tolerating years of Scatman obsession from me without complaint. My nephews, Tommy, Dougie, and Bobby, have already proven their superior music taste by liking Scatman as much as their auntie Gina.

When you tell your boyfriend you're taking a year off to write a book about a weird '90s pop star (which turned into two), some alarm would be understandable. But my partner, Graham Hoyland, completely understood the complicated catharsis I needed to go through to write this book, and gave me nothing but love, encouragement, and endless coffee. You have all my love and thanks – I couldn't have done this without you.

Thank you to my most enthusiastic supporter and friend, the late Judy Larkin, for your trust, your notes, your warmth, generosity, humor, and unwavering belief that John's full story deserved to be told. I hope this honors the love and life you shared.

And finally, there is you, John. You not only changed the way I saw the world, but the way I saw myself. Even now, you reach across time and give me the courage to speak. You refused to let my light go out, and it's an honor and a privilege to do the same for you. Thank you.

AUTHOR'S NOTE

This is a true story, a work of non-fiction, based on factual events, people, and places. John Larkin began his unfinished memoir, *To Truly Hear Me: My Stutter and I*, around 1990, but it was partially lost when his laptop was wiped in 1998. In 2011, Judy Larkin and I salvaged what remained. One of the many ironies in John's life is that he never got around to writing about his time as Scatman John – he was too busy *being* Scatman John.

John intended to disclose the difficult topics you'll read about here, including his experiences as an abuse survivor and his struggles with sexual identity. To protect the privacy of some individuals, John changed names and altered identifying details, and so have I.

Due to extensive periods of alcohol and drug abuse, John admitted to losing not just weeks but months of his life. His memories of events – and the order in which they occurred – were sometimes inconsistent. I've strived for accuracy and have attempted, wherever possible, to corroborate his recollections through multiple interviews and sources listed at the end of the book.

In 2011, Judy Larkin provided me with access to John Larkin's unpublished, incomplete autobiography. During the research for this book, John's stepson, Lee Newman, also generously shared more of John and Judy's private scrapbooks, notes, and other documents. Some of these materials are missing full publication information. In the following notes, all references to John's unpublished memoir are marked (JPL), and references to incompletely sourced private materials and clippings are marked (NPN) – *No Publication Named*.

Many sources were in languages other than English. Translations were made with attention to nuance, but some idiomatic meanings may have been altered in the process.

All interviews were conducted by the author, except where otherwise specified. To preserve the anonymity of those in Alcoholics Anonymous or similar programs, some sources are cited without identifying details. Historical events are described based on commonly available sources, unless otherwise cited.

NOTES

Introduction

1 ['If I c-c-can.']: typical stage banter during live performances: audio recording, Fiesta of World Dance Music, Spain, 1995.
2 [couldn't get a word out,]: *VIVA Jam* special interview, 1996.
2 [made it even better.]: 'The story behind Jason's favorite song makes it even better', *New Heights* podcast, short from Episode 97, Aug. 2024, https://www.youtube.com/watch?v=3UYptoGIrxk.
2 [half a billion times.]: As of May 2025, combined YouTube and Spotify plays exceed 600 million.
2 [Ed Sheeran, Kendrick Lamar.]: 'Famous People Who Stutter', retrieved from The Stuttering Foundation, May 2025, https://www.stutteringhelp.org/famouspeople.

Prologue

5 ['USA A-Bomb and H-Bomb Arsenal Growing Rapidly']: *Los Angeles Daily News*, 31 July 1954.
5 ['Record Wave of Heat Continues Across Nation']: *The San Bernardino County Sun*, 14 July 1954.
5 ['Eisenhower Raps Split of Viet-Nam']: *Los Angeles Times*, 22 July 1954.
6 [back to his seat.]: 'Current Events' story drawn from JPL and interviews, including *Danny and the Scatman* documentary, 1999.

Chapter 1

9 [radiators frozen solid.]: Scott Harrison, 'From the archives: In 1949, Angelenos get a rare taste of snow at home', *Los Angeles Times*, 21 Feb. 2019.
9 [Academy Awards,]: 'The 21st Academy Awards | 1949', Academy of Motion Picture Arts and Sciences, accessed 1 May 2025, https://www.oscars.org/oscars/ceremonies/1949.
9 [Harry Truman was inaugurated.]: Harry S. Truman, 'Inaugural Address', 20 Jan. 1949, Harry S. Truman Library & Museum, accessed 1 May 2025, https://www.trumanlibrary.gov/library/public-papers/19/inaugural-address.
9 [opening night.]: 'Birdland (New York jazz club),' Wikipedia, last modified Apr. 2024, https://en.wikipedia.org/wiki/Birdland_(New_York_jazz_club).
9 [Stanley Hospital in El Monte.]: California Department of Public Health. *Certificate of Live Birth for John Paul Larkin*, 13 Mar. 1942. Los Angeles County. Copy in author's possession, also JPL.
9 [shortly after they were married.]: JPL.

9	['didn't want any of that Junior business.']: Undated newspaper clipping, 'Our Youngest Generation', Larkin Family Archive.
10	[Million Dollar Theatre]: JPL.
10	[Billie Holiday and Artie Shaw once performed.]: 'Million Dollar Theatre', Los Angeles Conservancy, accessed 1 May 2025, https://www.laconservancy.org/learn/historic-places/million-dollar-theatre.
10	[denouncing it as 'Negroid' music.]: J. J. Gould, 'Josef Skvorecky on the Nazis' Control-Freak Hatred of Jazz', *The Atlantic*, 3 Jan. 2012, accessed 1 May 2025, https://www.theatlantic.com/entertainment/archive/2012/01/josef-skvorecky-nazis-jazz/250837/.
10	[In the USA, however, it thrived.]: 'Million Dollar Theatre', Los Angeles Theatres, accessed 10 May 2025, https://losangelestheatres.blogspot.com/2018/02/million-dollar-theatre.html.
10	[two-bedroom home in El Sereno.]: JPL.
10	[Brahms' *Lullaby*.]: Interview with Billy Larkin, 10 Apr. 2023.
10	[language of words.]: 'Scatman John RARE CBS Interview Unaired Footage + Aired News Clip' CBS News, 1996, YouTube video, 5 Feb. 2016, https://www.youtube.com/watch?v=bE1CPiN3i8Q.
10	[speech differences: stuttering.]: 'What Is Stammering?' STAMMA	British Stammering Association, accessed 1 May 2025, https://stamma.org/about-stammering/stammering-facts/what-is-stammering.
10	[early shock]: 'Stress & Stuttering', Stuttering Foundation, accessed 1 May 2025, https://www.stutteringhelp.org/stress-stuttering.
11	[had caused his stutter.]: Both possible inciting event stories, JPL.
11	[isn't psychological, but neurological.]: Lydia Denworth, 'The Stuttering Mind', *Scientific American*, 1 Aug. 2021, https://lydiadenworth.com/articles/the-stuttering-mind/.
11	['the ever-present saboteur.']: 'Press News: Scatman John', BMG Ariola Hamburg GMBH press release, Jan. 1995.
11	[would laugh.]: Interview with Billy Larkin, 10 Apr. 2023.
12	[It would be his secret.]: Boyhood creek, weather, and The Thing, JPL.

Chapter 2

13	['Take a deep breath.']: Conversation with the author, also NPN undated 1997 article titled 'Respect Yourself!'
13	[Sinsinawa Dominican Sisters,]: *All Saints Catholic Church*, LA Catholics, https://lacatholics.org/venue/all-saints-catholic-church/.
13	[willpower alone.]: Joshua St. Pierre, '"Satan is Holding Your Tongue Back": Stuttering as a Moral Failure', *African Journal of Disability* 10 (2021): 1–7.
13	[try harder.]: 'Stuttering: The Role of the Classroom Teacher', Minnesota State University, Mankato, Center for Communication Sciences and Disorders, accessed 10 May 2025, https://ahn.mnsu.edu/services-and-centers/center-for-communication-sciences-and-disorders/services/stuttering/speech-and-language-disorders/support-for-teachers/stuttering-the-role-of-the-classroom-teacher.
13	[punishing it.]: Starkweather, C. Woodruff, ed. *Conditioning in Stuttering Therapy: Applications and Limitations.* Publication No. 7. Memphis, TN: Speech Foundation of America, 1970. https://files.eric.ed.gov/fulltext/ED081139.pdf.
13	[made sure he knew it.]: Memories of All Saints, JPL.
14	[Bobby Rivera,]: John and Bobby's friendship: Interview with George and Gloria Rivera, 24 Apr. 2023.
14	[talk to my brother that way again.]: Interview with Billy Larkin, 29 Apr. 2024.

15 [He would carry it as fuel.]: Bullying walking home from school: JPL and several interviews, including CBS Interview, 1996, and *Danny and the Scatman*, 1999.
15 [*Not good enough.*]: Konrad Schäfers, Jutta vom Hofe, Claudia Mende, Erhard Hennen interview with Scatman John for the BVSS (Die Bundesvereinigung Stottern & Selbsthilfe), Nov. 1995.
15 [nothing wrong with you.]: John Larkin's keynote speech, National Stuttering Association convention, July 1995.
15 ['What's wrong with this child?']: Ira Zimmerman, 'The Stutter and the Scat Is the Same Thing', *Advance for Speech-Language Pathologists and Audiologists*, 20 Nov. 1995, https://ahn.mnsu.edu/services-and-centers/center-for-communication-sciences-and-disorders/services/stuttering/information-about-stuttering/fun-information/famous-people-who-stutter/interview-with-scatman-john-larkin/.
16 [Everything began with 'if only'.]: Communion and sitting in class: JPL.

Chapter 3

17 [smoke the year before.]: Teenage smoking: JPL and interview with Billy Larkin, 10 Apr. 2023.
17 [mask the smell.]: Stealing cigarettes, chewing leaves: Interview with Tony Miali, 15 Sept. 2023.
17 [confusion and longing.]: Fights, burdened and father's affection from JPL and undated documents from the John and Judy Larkin archive.
18 [grow out of it.]: 'What Is Stuttering?' National Stuttering Association, WeStutter.org, accessed 1 May 2025, https://www.westutter.org/post/what-is-stuttering.
18 [eating him alive.]: Therapy quotes from unreleased footage, Danny and the Scatman documentary, 1999.
18 [a language he had never spoken but at once understood.]: Imitating Brubeck: undated document in John and Judy Larkin archive, also *VIVA Jam* special, 1996.
18 [see through it.]: Coffee table story: JPL, also *VIVA Jam* documentary special, 1996.
18 [emotion without uttering a word.]: Louis Armstrong uplifting John: Radio AAHs interview, 29 Mar. 1997, also *The Making of Everybody Jam!* documentary 1996.
18 [he had to learn to play]: John discovering Ella Fitzgerald: email from Judy Larkin to the author, 23 June 2011.
19 [*There's something in here for me.*]: Untitled interview, YouTube, from 1996, https://www.youtube.com/watch?v=aUOKLCktb4g.
19 [mother and father, too.]: JPL, also interview with Billy and Sharon Larkin, 27 Mar. 2023.
19 [sing fluently.]: Catherine Y. Wan and Gottfried Schlaug, 'The Therapeutic Effects of Singing in Neurological Disorders', *Music Perception* 27, no. 4 (2010): 287–95, https://www.ncbi.nlm.nih.gov/pmc/articles/PMC2996848/.
19 [to hear the difference.]: Telephone interview with Chuck Wert, 5 Apr. 2023.
19 [but he never did]: John's relationship with Johnny Peverada: JPL.
19 [parakeets.]: Interview with Billy Larkin, 10 Apr. 2023.
19 [animals or children.]: Ilia U. Rasskazov and Natalia M. Rasskazova, 'Why Do So Many Stutterers Fail to Stutter When Alone and How Can This Phenomenon Be Used In Treatment?' paper presented at the International Stuttering Awareness Day Online Conference, Oct. 2007, https://web.mnsu.edu/comdis/isad10/papers/rasskazov10.html.
20 [*who wants to help you.*]: John's relationship with Mr. Lofgren: JPL.
20 [into his circle, and him into mine.]: Interview with Billy Larkin, 27 Mar. 2023.
21 [been kicked out.]: John kicked out of school: JPL.

Chapter 4

22 [Especially the girls.]: John entering Woodrow Wilson High: JPL, Larkin Family Archive photo, and telephone interview with Sabrina Braham, 26 July 2023.
22 [lit up his confidence.]: Friendship with Paul Ackerman, drinking: JPL, also Danny and the Scatman documentary, 1999.
23 [*fucked up inside*.]: Sexuality and attention from girls: JPL.
23 [not paying attention.]: Comment by Janet Francisco on Classmates.com, 2023, retrieved 1 May 2025, https://www.classmates.com/conversations/school/woodrow-wilson-high-school.
23 [separate world.]: Telephone interview with Sabrina Braham, 26 July 2023.
23 [*watch this*.]: *VIVA Jam* documentary special, 1996.
23 ['Let me finish.']: Telephone interview with Tony Miali, 15 Sept. 2023.
23 [got up and walked out.]: Interview with George and Gloria Rivera, 24 Apr. 2023.
24 [my favourite drugs.]: Depression, girls and cigarettes: JPL.
24 [drove him home.]: Police questioning: Telephone interview with Tony Miali, 15 Sept. 2023.
25 [someone else.]: Relationship with Anne: JPL.
25 [he was glad.]: John playing football: JPL, also interview with George and Gloria Rivera, 24 Apr. 2023.
26 [preferred her over him.]: Volkswagen, cars, relationship with Sharon: Interview with Billy and Sharon Larkin, 10 Apr. 2023.
26 [clipping trash cans]: Interview with George and Gloria Rivera, 24 Apr. 2023.
27 [like a vine from the inside of me, out.]: Destroying the music room, kicked out again: JPL, also interview with Billy and Sharon Larkin, 27 Mar. 2023.
27 ['new Larkin' on campus,]: Getting into the fraternity, drinking more: JPL, Interview with Billy and Sharon Larkin, 10 Apr. 2023, *East Los Angeles College Campus News*, 2 Nov. 1960.
27 [charged with attempted murder.]: 'Three Men Arrested By Local Police Charged With Attempted Homicide', *South Pasadena Review*, 31 Jan. 1961, 'Guilty Pleas Entered in Party Fight', *Pasadena Independent*, 31 Jan. 1961.

Chapter 5

28 [wrong house number]: 'Guilty Pleas Entered in Party Fight', *Pasadena Independent*, 31 Jan. 1961, interview with Billy and Sharon Larkin, 10 Apr. 2023.
28 [return to college.]: Time in jail, release: 'Guilty Pleas Entered in Party Fight', *Pasadena Independent*, 31 Jan. 1961, interview with Billy and Sharon Larkin, 10 Apr. 2023.
29 [one of the most beautiful moments]: Choir song fest: JPL.
29 [They played everything,]: Johnny Larkin performances: *East Los Angeles College Campus News*, 15 Mar. 1961, 'Quartet Due at Noon Hoop', 8 May 1963, also 11 Mar. 1964, 6 May 1964.
29 [began playing together.]: Friendship with Jimmy: Interview with Jimmy Espinoza, 6 Apr. 2024.
29 [John played piano while Gus blew his cornet.]: John practising, coffee houses, playing with Gus: Interview with Gus Angelo, 22 Aug. 2023.
29 [The crowd loved it.]: Geert Desmet, 'I Bring Out the Child', *Het Nieuwsblad*, 2 Aug. 1995.
29 [influenced his melodic jazz phrasing.]: Undated document circa 1991, John and Judy Larkin Archive.
29 ['they're real close,']: Undated Scatman John interview, YouTube, https://www.youtube.com/watch?v=aUOKLCktb4g.
29 ['scatting']: 'Scat Singing,' Wikipedia, last modified 25 Apr. 2024, https://en.wikipedia.org/wiki/Scat_singing.

29 [ad-lib for half an hour on one tune,]: Telephone interview with Gus Angelo, 22 Aug. 2023.
30 [piano would never be the same again.]: Interview with George and Gloria Rivera, 24 Apr. 2023.
30 [conditioning his fingers for speed.]: Interview with George and Gloria Rivera, 24 Apr. 2023.
30 ['The Norsemen']: Forming of the band: JPL, telephone interview with Gus Angelo, 5 Sept. 2023.
30 [People would drop their drinks]: Norsemen performances, telephone interviews with Gus Angelo, 22 Aug. 2023 and 5 Sept. 2023.
30 [playing commercial jazz.]: Robin Paul headlining: JPL, telephone interview with Gus Angelo, 22 Aug. 2023.
31 [the fuse that triggered it.]: Pilot approaching John: JPL.
31 [we realized it was restricted.]: Telephone interview with Gus Angelo, 22 Aug. 2023.
31 [His kid was wounded.]: John's pain, returning home: JPL.
31 [His stuttering became worse.]: Telephone interview with Gus Angelo, 5 Sept. 2023.
31 ['The wound of my childhood was now festering,']: troubled, sleeping in car: JPL.
31 [what was troubling him.]: Interview with Billy and Sharon Larkin, 10 Apr. 2023.
32 [recommended John.]: JPL, also email from Mayo Tiana to the author, 10 Apr. 2023.
32 [Mayo says]: Email from Mayo Tiana to the author, 10 Apr. 2023, interview with Jimmy Espinoza, 6 Apr. 2024.
32 [he felt it, then he got it.]: Interview with Jimmy Espinoza, 6 Apr. 2024.
32 [that's where he was headed.]: JPL, email from Mayo Tiana to the author, 10 Apr. 2023.
32 [I just couldn't.] Had nothing he could believe in: JPL.

Chapter 6

33 [family wanted no part of.]: John's estrangement from his family: Interview with Billy and Sharon Larkin, 10 Apr. 2023, being in East LA: JPL.
33 [lived with Clarence,]: John living in East LA: JPL.
33 [make a career as a jazz musician work.]: John taking Benzedrine, menial jobs, gigs at Marty's: JPL.
34 [knocking him flat.]: Fights breaking out, bass smashing: Telephone interview with Chuck Glave, 8 Apr. 2024.
34 [Jazz KNOB]: JPL, also Don Page, 'Outlook for FM Fans', *The Los Angeles Times*, 18 Aug. 1957.
34 [early hours of the morning.]: John's setlist, relationship with Maria: JPL, also an undated document circa 1991 from the John and Judy Larkin Archive.
34 [They got away with it.]: Jimmy's mustache peeling off: Interview with Jimmy Espinoza, 6 Apr. 2024.
34 [their friendship took root.]: Freddie Gruber's history: JPL, also Bill Milkowski, 'Freddie Gruber: None of a Kind', *JazzTimes*, Nov. 2004; Ian Wallace, 'Freddie Gruber: A Passion for Teaching', *Modern Drummer*, Jan. 1996.
35 ['They were still together and happy.'] Clarence's relationship: JPL.
35 [wanted to be destructive.] Beverly Bowl gig, meeting Al Surratt: JPL.
35 ['I was so naive and trusting.']: Relationship with Paula: JPL.
35 ['He didn't judge.']: Telephone interview with Gus Angelo, 22 Aug. 2023.
36 ['my idols.']: Moving in with Tony and Freddie: JPL.
36 [New York.]: Wishing he'd been born in New York: Radio AAHS Hollywood interview, 29 Mar. 1997.
36 [He was such a spiritual human being, man.]: Wishing he'd been born in New York: Radio AAHS Hollywood interview, 29 Mar. 1997.

37 [wanted to punch Freddie many times, but never did.]: John trying heroin, Freddie using heroin: JPL.
37 [married doctor who paid her for sex.]: Relationship with Connie: JPL.
37 [Groove-Fuss.]: Kapu Kai Group, *The Daily Report*, 17 Oct. 1966.
37 [left and never went back.] Slapped by Connie: JPL.
38 [completely transformed man.]: Meeting Stanley Crouch, learning about LSD: JPL.

Chapter 7

39 [worked for Jimmy as a song plugger.]: Alyn Shipton, *I Feel a Song Coming On: The Life of Jimmy McHugh* (Urbana: University of Illinois Press, 2009); Judy McHugh conversation with the author circa 2013, Interview with Lee Newman, 11 Apr. 2024.
39 [regularly came to visit.]: Interview with Lee Newman, 11 Apr. 2024, Alyn Shipton, *I Feel a Song Coming On: The Life of Jimmy McHugh* (Urbana: University of Illinois Press, 2009).
39 [allure of straight-ahead Jazz.]: Interview with Lee Newman, 11 Apr. 2024.
39 [like Judy herself.]: Judy's idols: Undated handwritten note from the John and Judy Larkin Archive.
39 [socialize with the cast and crew.]: Interview with Lee Newman, 11 Apr. 2024, also Judy McHugh conversations with the author circa 2011.
40 [every hippie ritual, phrase, and behaviour,]: JPL.
40 [scribble on CDs thirty years later.]: Dedication on a CD in the author's possession.
40 [made political cracks in tuxedos the next]: *Laugh-In* background: Marc Freeman, "'Laugh-In' at 50: How the Comedy Helped Elect Nixon and Set the Stage for "SNL", *The Hollywood Reporter*, 22 Jan. 2018.
40 [put the pieces of his past back together.]: JPL.
40 [when he called home.]: Interview with Billy Larkin, 29 Apr. 2024.
40 [admit how messed up he really was.]: JPL.
40 [looming specter of war.]: Realizing others held the same opinions: Undated typed note by John Larkin, John and Judy Larkin Archive.
41 [language wouldn't, couldn't touch the sides.]: Acid trip: JPL.
41 [To stand for …]: 'Happy Birthday' Lyrics: JPL, also undated handwritten lyrics, Larkin Family Archive.
41 [whatever I could experience chemically.]: JPL.
41 [even fluent people recognize.]: 'Stuttering and Drugs', Minnesota State University, Mankato, Center for Communication Sciences and Disorders, accessed 11 May 2025, https://ahn.mnsu.edu/services-and-centers/center-for-communication-sciences-and-disorders/services/stuttering/information-about-stuttering/serious-information/types-of-fluency-disorders/stuttering-and-drugs/.
41 [clung to them like a lifeline.]: Undated typed notes by John Larkin, John and Judy Larkin Archive.
43 [protest the Vietnam War.]: '1967 Century City Anti-Vietnam War March', Wikipedia, last modified Feb. 2023, https://en.wikipedia.org/wiki/1967_Century_City_anti-Vietnam_War_march.
43 [just over the age limit.]: John's pacifism, missing the draft: JPL; 'Vietnam Lotteries', Selective Service System, accessed 12 May 2025, https://www.sss.gov/history-and-records/vietnam-lotteries/.
43 ['If you've got the dough, you don't have to go,']: Lee Lescaze, 'At War With The Draft Board', *The Washington Post*, 11 June 1978, https://www.washingtonpost.com/archive/entertainment/books/1978/06/11/at-war-with-the-draft-board/6daa5799-4cf9-43e2-b4d1-2eae88ca1311/.

43   [Methamphetamine could keep a person unnaturally awake and wired for days.]: 'The Nazi Death Machine: Hitler's Drugged Soldiers', *Der Spiegel*, accessed 12 May 2025, https://www.spiegel.de/international/the-nazi-death-machine-hitler-s-drugged-soldiers-a-354606.html.

43   [It wouldn't be regulated until 1970,]: 'Controlled Substances Act', DEA.gov, accessed 12 May 2025, https://www.dea.gov/drug-information/csa.

43   [Prolonged use triggered paranoia, aggression, and psychosis.]: 'Methamphetamine', Wikipedia, last modified 10 May 2025, https://en.wikipedia.org/wiki/Methamphetamine.

44   [memory remained blank for weeks afterwards.]: John's meth binge, visiting parents: JPL.

44   [all the way across the country.]: Nancy's concern, road trip: JPL.

44   [favorites to play live.]: John performed 'Route 66' on tour in 1996 (https://www.setlist.fm/setlist/scatman-john/1996) in Yokohoma, Japan, 4 Sept. 1995 (https://www.youtube.com/watch?v=vv-OwPTJcTc) and on Portuguese TV show Zona+ Mais, 5 June 1995 (https://www.youtube.com/watch?v=BVldCAPbfq4).

44   [*Hair* was coming to the Royal Alex Theatre for its Canadian debut.]: 'Northward Hair Ready for Rehearsals', *RPM Weekly*, 13 Dec. 1969, p. 2.

44   [Toronto's main music hall.]: Audition location and dates: Vintage Toronto, Facebook photo post, 29 Dec. 2019, https://www.facebook.com/VintageToronto/photos/the-toronto-production-of-the-original-rock-musical-hair-played-at-the-royal-ale/2900969989972966/.

44   [rebellion, charisma – the real thing.]: Emma John, 'How We Made Hair', *The Guardian*, 26 Feb. 2019.

45   [he almost certainly had a part]: 'Eleanor Rigby' performance at the audition: JPL.

45   [forced to watch.]: Bad acid trip: JPL.

Chapter 8

46   [*One, two, three, four.*]: Playing outside, counting on fingers: JPL.

46   [liquor store and back.]: Interview with Billy and Sharon Larkin, 10 Apr. 2023.

47   [On top of that, he stuttered.]: Experience of The Thing: JPL.

47   [*Wipe out a kid, why don't we?*]: Ira Zimmerman, 'Interview with Scatman John Larkin', *Advance for Speech Pathologists and Audiologists Magazine*, 20 Nov. 1995, https://ahn.mnsu.edu/services-and-centers/center-for-communication-sciences-and-disorders/services/stuttering/information-about-stuttering/fun-information/famous-people-who-stutter/interview-with-scatman-john-larkin/.

47   [*Who am I, really?*]: John's breakdown, bisexual admission: JPL.

Chapter 9

48   ['As if it had been together.']: Turning down the role in *Hair*, breakup with Nancy: JPL.

48   [would stay with him for years.]: John wrote out lyrics from the song, found in undated memoir notes by John Larkin, John and Judy Larkin Archive.

50   [As long as he could play, he kept going.]: Jazz on the gig story: telephone interview with Joe Celia, 12 Sept. 2024, email from Joe Celia to the author, 11 Sept. 2024.

50   [the next day be broke again.]: telephone interview with Gus Angelo, 22 Aug. 2023.

50   [We almost jumped through the phone,]: Earning enough to pay the bills: Telephone interview with Joe Celia, 12 Sept. 2024.

50   [teaching me how to use it.]: John's kindness: Telephone interview with Mimi Smith, 18 Sept. 2024.

50 [gave more than most people could in three lifetimes.]: Telephone interview with Sam Provenzano, 24 Feb. 2024.
50 [So just dig it and *play*.]: John's encouragement: Telephone interview with Joe Celia, 12 Sept. 2024, email from Joe Celia to the author, 18 Nov. 2024.
50 [yes right away.]: Joining Stax: JPL.
51 [promote its artists in TV and film.]: Allyson McCabe, 'Wattstax drew 100,000 people – this 1972 concert was about much more than music', NPR, updated 2 Mar. 2023, https://www.npr.org/2023/03/02/1158876105/wattstax-drew-100-000-people-this-1972-concert-was-about-much-more-than-music.
51 [Sure enough, it all fell apart.]: Touring with Luther Ingram, Marshall Hooks: JPL.
51 ['He got into using harder stuff.']: Interview with Joe Celia, 12 Sept. 2024.
52 [It wasn't a mess he wanted to untangle. Not yet.]: Connection with Eric: JPL.
52 ['I've quit playing music,' he announced.]: Decision to move home: JPL.

Chapter 10

53 [A straight job was what he needed.]: Return home, lecture from Bill: JPL.
53 [Americans with Disabilities Act offered any protection.]: 'The Americans with Disabilities Act: How it relates to stuttering', American Institute for Stuttering, accessed 12 May 2025, https://www.stutteringtreatment.org/blog/the-americans-with-disabilities-act-what-it-means-to-people-who-stutter.
54 [He felt trapped.]: Home atmosphere, laundry job: JPL.
54 [where Billy worked.]: Getting John a job, John being fired: Interview with Billy and Sharon Larkin, 10 Apr. 2023.
54 [wild creature on the couch that was Uncle Johnny.]: Email from Steve Larkin to the author, 27 May 2023.
54 ['Sometimes hard to follow.']: Interview with David, Billy, and Sharon Larkin, 27 Mar. 2023.
54 ['I know it wasn't really him.']: Interview with Billy Larkin, 29 Apr. 2024.
54 [John on vocals with his Wurlitzer keyboard.]: Origin of Fred: JPL.
55 [One fan even knitted them a banner.]: Telephone interview with Duke McVinnie, 30 Mar. 2024.
55 [We dug what we were doing.]: JPL.
55 [his voice produced a strange resonance.]: Zan Stewart, 'Pianist Has Found Right Voicings', *Los Angeles Times*, 21 Dec. 1990.
55 [honed both his control and speed.]: Discovering chord singing: Konrad Schäfers, Jutta vom Hofe, Claudia Mende, Erhard Hennen interview with John Larkin for the BVSS (Bundesvereinigung Stottern & Selbsthilfe), 1 Nov. 1995.
56 [help to work those ten-to-fourteen-hour days.]: Return to drinking, pot, performing: JPL.
56 [to smooth things over.]: Playing at Gus's wedding, telephone interview with Gus Angelo, 22 Aug. 2023.
56 [wasn't wrapped together too well,' John said.]: JPL.
56 [a wonderful something about him.]: Interview with Gary, Jackie and Marc Hewitt, 26 Jan. 2024.
56 [playing straight-ahead jazz.]: JPL.
57 [we kept going.]: John throwing the Wurlitzer: Telephone interview with Duke McVinnie, 30 Mar. 2024.
57 ['Marcia was the lady's name – and this was the beginning.']: Playing at the Winery, meeting Marcia: JPL.

Chapter 11

58 [powerful psychedelic trips.]: The night of the paints: JPL, description of the room, telephone interview with Damien Hamel, 14 Apr. 2023.
58 [volatile and confrontational.]: Marcia's background and previous husbands: Facebook Messenger chat between Shelley Gilman and the author, Apr. 2023.
59 [a few bottles of wine a night.]: John playing at the Winery: JPL.
59 [Two Dollar Turkey.]: John's band and performance names: Interview with Gary, Jackie, and Marc Hewitt, 26 Jan. 2024.
59 [He proposed.]: Arguments with Marcia, wrist-cutting, oven incident: JPL.
59 [24 June 1979,]: Marriage date confirmed by Los Angeles County Registrar-Recorder/County Clerk with the author, Apr. 2023.
60 [get very bad indeed.]: Wedding details: Facebook Messenger chat between Shelley Gilman and the author, Apr. 2023; Interview with Billy and Sharon Larkin, 27 Mar. 2024.
60 [rather than a new stepfather.]: Facebook Messenger chat between Shelley Gilman and the author, Apr. 2023.
60 [insanely gifted as a jazz pianist.]: Telephone interview with Damien Hamel, 14 Apr. 2023.
60 [dopamine activity in the brain.]: 'Thioridazine Hydrochloride – Drug Information', Drugs.com, accessed 12 May 2025, https://www.drugs.com/monograph/thioridazine.html.
61 [his life was about to go up in flames.]: PCP violence, rage, John's self-hatred: JPL.
62 [The chemicals and booze had to stop.] Drink-driving, arrests, decision to stop: JPL.

Chapter 12

64 [But he wasn't ready to listen. Not yet.]: Junkie's Credo, pot only policy, selling, trip to Seattle: JPL.
64 [a new hustle: dealing cocaine.]: Junkie's Credo, pot only policy, selling, trip to Seattle: JPL.
64 [cocaine had come roaring back.]: 'Cocaine in the United States', Wikipedia, last modified Feb. 2025, https://en.wikipedia.org/wiki/Cocaine_in_the_United_States.
64 [easy to find, and easy to sell.]: 'Cocaine boom', Wikipedia, last modified Mar. 2025, https://en.wikipedia.org/wiki/Cocaine_boom.
65 [*I knew I couldn't drink.*]: Peeing in the cruise ship cabin: JPL.
65 [Crazy passionate.]: Interview with Carli Muñoz, 5 Feb. 2024.
66 [first known commercial recordings of John's playing.]: *Animal Sounds* sessions: Telephone Interview with Sam Phipps, 22 Apr. 2023, 'Sam Phipps – *Animal Sounds*', Discogs, accessed 3 May 2025, https://www.discogs.com/master/885673-Sam-Phipps-Animal-Sounds.
66 [John Hartman to fill in for him]: Interview with John Hartman, 4 Apr. 2023.
66 [sell on the side.]: Decision to sell coke: JPL.
66 [stretch the product and the profits.]: Common cocaine cutting agents: Claire Cole, Lisa Jones, Jim Mcveigh, Andrew Kicman, Qutub Syed, and Mark Bellis, *CUT: A Guide to Adulterants, Bulking Agents and Other Contaminants Found in Illicit Drugs* (Albany, NY: New York State Department of Health, 2012). https://www.health.ny.gov/diseases/aids/consumers/prevention/oduh/docs/cut.pdf.
66 [over five thousand dollars in profit.]: Coke dealing profits: JPL.
66 [somehow still able to play.]: #4 category of Codeine: 'Acetaminophen and Codeine', MedlinePlus, last modified Oct. 15, 2023, https://medlineplus.gov/druginfo/meds/a601005.html.
67 [I never heard from him again.]: KPFK radio story: Telephone Interview with Sam Phipps, 22 Apr. 2023, Discogs. 'Sam Phipps – *Animal Sounds*', accessed May 3, 2025, https://www.discogs.com/master/885673-Sam-Phipps-Animal-Sounds.

67 [creaking shut.]: Shadier drug customers: JPL.
67 [coke carried serious penalties.]: 'The Drug War, Mass Incarceration and Race', Drug Policy Alliance, June 2015.
67 [funding for drug enforcement had doubled.]: 'War on Drugs', Wikipedia, last modified 13 May 2025, https://en.wikipedia.org/wiki/War_on_drugs.
67 [we were having a splendid time,' John remembered.]: Dipping into the coke, parties: JPL.
68 [one of many friends John would never see again.]: John's coke binge, hanging up a gig: JPL.
69 [gig from sinking]: Telephone interview with Rusty Crutcher, 24 Jun. 2025.
69 [was closer than he realized.]: Cruise ship gig, cycle trip: JPL.
69 [John wasn't breathing.]: John and Marcia's coke binge, speedball overdose: JPL.

Chapter 13

70 [*Press. Breathe.*]: John and Marcia not breathing, receiving CPR: JPL, undated *Entrevue* magazine interview clipping, circa 1995.
71 [nothing would come out.]: Judy's car accident, marriage: Interview with Lee Newman, 11 Apr. 2024; Joe Harnell and Ira Skutch, *Counterpoint: The Journey of a Music Man* (Philadelphia: Xlibris, 2000).
71 [the desensitizing nature of heavy-duty drugs.]: John and Marcia's resuscitation, continuing drug use: JPL.
71 [police couldn't always tell where it was coming from.]: Jazz bouncing around the canyon: Telephone interview with Joe Celia, 12 Sept. 2024.
72 ['I *love* your piano,' John said.]: John in Central Sound studios: Email from Michael Totten to the author, 17 Feb. 2024.
72 [It had never been that loud.]: Interview with Philip Cacayorin, 19 Apr. 2023.
72 [used together and played together.]: JPL.
72 [how he said it was irrelevant.]: Telephone interview with Bob Harrison, 8 Sept. 2023.
72 [That's the first thing I noticed.]: Interview with Philip Cacayorin, 19 Apr. 2023.
72 [Neumann U87 mic and nothing else.]: Email from Michael Totten to the author, 17 Feb. 2024.
73 [They found John meditating under the piano.]: Joe asking for money, John meditating under the piano: Interview with Philip Cacayorin, 19 Apr. 2023.
73 [The 2-inch, 24-track tape rolled,]: Email from Michael Totten to the author, 17 Feb. 2024.
73 [He trails off, overcome.]: Telephone Interview with Bob Harrison, 8 Sept. 2023.
73 ['so perfectly executed that it's hard to believe it's real.']: Tony Bernardo, 'John Larkin "John Larkin LP"', BassDress Blog, 24 Nov. 2011, https://bassdress.com/blog/2011/11/24/john-larkin-john-larkin-lp/.
73 [overdub some vocals a few weeks later.]: John mumbling at the piano, Joe Farrell's breaks, rest of recording: emails from Michael Totten to the author, 17 Feb. 2024 and 19 Feb. 2024.
74 [The songs, tracks, and mixes were beautiful.]: Emails from Michael Totten to the author, 17 Feb. 2024 and 19 Feb. 2024.
74 ['My Funny Valentine'.]: Takes that didn't make the John Larkin LP appeared on an unofficial bootleg recording: 'Clark Woodard & Joe Farrell', in 2005.
74 [hiss of the tape machine]: Some imagery adapted from Tony Bernardo, 'John Larkin "John Larkin LP"', BassDress Blog, 24 Nov. 2011, https://bassdress.com/ blog/2011/11/24/john-larkin-john-larkin-lp/.
74 [too angry for reissue,]: Email from Judy Larkin to Iceberg Records, 17 Oct. 2000.
74 [But she was right.]: Yosemite vacation, everything ending: JPL.

Chapter 14

76   [it was all familiar.]: Sheri's suicide attempt: JPL, telephone interview with Damien Hamel, 14 Apr. 2023.
76   [how he'd ended up there.]: Daily heroin, John waking up in hospital: Email from Tony Miali to the author, 14 Sept. 2023.
77   [He had saved her life.] John on methadone, cleaning up, death of Joe Farrell: JPL.
77   [back into old habits at least once.]: 'Treatment and Recovery', *Drugs, Brains, and Behavior: The Science of Addiction*, National Institute on Drug Abuse, July 2020, https://nida.nih.gov/publications/drugs-brains-behavior-science-addiction/treatment-recovery.
78   [something tangible.]: John and Marcia's relapse, buying the Transition label: JPL.
78   [end up where he belonged.]: Liner notes and credits on the John Larkin LP: John Larkin, *John Larkin*, Transition Records TR 0001, 1986. LP.
78   [almost breaking his fingers]: *VIVA Jam* interview special, 1996.
78   [beneath every fingernail.] Observed in private home video footage of John playing, circa mid-'80s.
78   [*Because you're not enough.*]: *VIVA Jam* interview special, 1996.
78   [drowning above the surface.]: Lung collapse: Interview with Billy and Sharon Larkin, 27 Mar. 2023.
78   [he was there.]: Sobriety date, decision to quit: JPL.

Chapter 15

79   [*I had decided to live instead of die.*]: JPL, unpublished autobiography manuscript excerpt [referred to by author as *Uncovery*], John and Judy Larkin Archive, accessed 2011 and 2023, courtesy of Lee Newman. Lightly edited for clarity.

Chapter 16

80   [several people said back.]: AA meeting attendee, interview Apr. 2024.
80   [*ask and you shall receive.*]: John's arrival at the meeting: JPL.
80   [didn't want to communicate.]: AA meeting attendee, interview Apr. 2024.
80   [Red Hot Chili Peppers.]: Walter Urban's connection to Flea: Flea, *Acid for the Children* (New York: Grand Central Publishing, 2019).
81   [*Perfect for healing*, John thought.]: John's meeting attendance, moving house: JPL.
81   [Then he saw the value in it.]: 'Guide to Sober Dating', American Addiction Centers, 7 Feb. 2024, https://americanaddictioncenters.org/sober-dating.
81   [save face and save your ass at the same time.]: JPL.
81   [shoved all the records into his closet.]: *VIVA Jam* interview special, 1996.
82   ['I did marvelously for where I was at the time,' he said.]: First sober gig: JPL.
82   [*Maybe this time it'll stick*, Billy thought.]: John playing at his parents' anniversary: Interview with Billy and Sharon Larkin, 10 Apr. 2023.
84   [exorcize the pain by exposing it.]: John joining ACA, talking about The Thing: JPL.
84   [act as adults.]: Adult Children of Alcoholics World Service Organization, *Adult Children of Alcoholics/Dysfunctional Families* (Torrance, CA: ACA WSO, 2006).
84   [the whole person I never was.]: Letter from John Larkin to Nora O'Connor, 5 May 1992, JPL.
84   ['Society's very existence depends on the denial of its dysfunction,']: Undated note by John Larkin, John and Judy Larkin Archive.
84   [coming alive, from the inside out.]: JPL.
85   ['This is Judy McHugh.']: Meeting Judy: JPL.

Chapter 17

- 86 [*I have to find out.*]: John's impressions of Judy: JPL.
- 86 [he fascinated her.]: Judy Larkin, *Remembrances of John*, undated document, John and Judy Larkin Archive.
- 86 [I'll find the piano player.]: *VIVA Jam* interview special, 1996.
- 86 [hearing someone extraordinary.]: Judy Larkin, *Remembrances of John*, undated document, John and Judy Larkin Archive.
- 86 ['She dug me, and I dug her,' he said.]: JPL.
- 87 ['This'll never work,']: Sandy Parton speaking at John's memorial, 12 Dec. 1999.
- 87 ['Oil and water,']: Interview with Gregg Pincus, 25 Mar. 2023.
- 87 ['Are you *crazy?*']: Judy Larkin conversation with the author circa 2011.
- 87 [recent drinking binge.] Divorce: Joe Harnell and Ira Skutch, *Counterpoint: The Journey of a Music Man* (Philadelphia: Xlibris Corporation, 2001), Interview with Lee Newman, 13 Jan. 2025.
- 87 [Judy didn't flinch.]: John telling Judy about his past, email from Judy Larkin to the author, 23 June 2011.
- 87 ['Stuttering can do to the soul what cancer does to the body,']: Judy Larkin, undated handwritten note, John and Judy Larkin Archive.
- 87 [minding my own business.]: John moving in with Judy, laying ACA on her: JPL.
- 87 [*I have mine.*]: Judy resisting John's path: email from Judy Larkin to the author, 23 June 2011.
- 88 [no dating and no distractions.]: Death of Bill Larkin, John moving out: JPL.
- 88 [guide and direct him.]: Judy Larkin, *Remembrances of John*, undated document, John and Judy Larkin Archive.
- 88 [start owning my music again.]: JPL.
- 88 ['The land of the unemployed misfit']: Rosanne Welch, 'That Mangy-Looking Joint May Have Great Personality', *Los Angeles Times*, 20 Aug. 1995.
- 88 ['We're going to Berlin.']: JPL.

Chapter 18

- 89 [one of the poorest districts in West Berlin.]: 'Kreuzberg – The Berlin Face of Contrasts', EUSTORY History Campus, accessed May 14, 2025, https://historycampus.org/2022/kreuzberg-the-berlin-face-of-contrasts/.
- 91 [tumbled off the bus at the next stop.]: Arrival in Berlin, exploring the centre, bus ride: JPL.
- 91 [in both voice and trumpet.]: Returning to the Europa Center, playing with the band, making friends with Jimmy and Ingrid: JPL.
- 92 [no ventilation and wild acoustics.]: Nick Paumgarten, 'Berlin Nights', *New Yorker*, 17 Mar. 2014.
- 92 [That changed my whole attitude.]: Zan Stewart, 'Pianist Has Found Right Voicings', *Los Angeles Times*, 21 Dec. 1990.
- 92 [said anything unpleasant to her.]: Annette Heick, '52 Years old and a Pop Star', undated Danish article, 1995.
- 93 [the job came with an apartment.]: Unable to move, Judy's depression, John's gigs: JPL.
- 93 [was all that mattered.]: Interview with Rashidii Graffiti, 16 Oct. 2023.
- 94 [packed up his keyboard, and left.]: Return to the US, John leaving: JPL.

Chapter 19

- 95 [competition was fierce.]: Leonard Feather, 'L.A. Jazz Club Owners Recount Trials, Triumphs', *Los Angeles Times*, 31 Dec. 1987.

96 [her phone and fax numbers.]: John Larkin, *John Larkin Sings*, unpublished recordings, *circa* 1990, John and Judy Larkin Archive.
96 [never having to utter a word.]: Promotion of the tape, John's new gigs: JPL.
96 [incorporate it into his act.] John's elephant analogy, Judy suggesting disclosure: John Larkin, 'Who is Scatman John?', One Voice: International Stuttering Association Newsletter, 6th Issue, Sept. 1996.
96 ['You're *enough*, John.']: *VIVA Jam* interview special, 1996.
97 [He was there because he was good.]: Disclosure, playing too loud: JPL.
97 [His scat – worth hearing,' noted the *Times*]: LA Weekly ad. quoting the *Los Angeles Times*, Thu. 18 Apr. 1991, p. 102.
97 [Scat-man John Larkin.]: LA Weekly Jazz listings, Thu. 27 Dec. 1990, p. 119.
97 [Hello World,' he told Stewart.]: Zan Stewart, 'Pianist Has Found Right Voicings', *Los Angeles Times* (print edition), 21 Dec. 1990.
97 [National Stuttering Project (NSP).]: Interview with Gail Wilson Lew, 6 Aug. 2023.
98 [he knew I stuttered, too.]: Interview with Gail Wilson Lew, 6 Aug. 2023.
98 [a quick shot of stability.]: John moving back in, decision to go back to Europe: JPL.
99 ['It was fantastic,' Stacey said.]: Interview with Stacey Heaver, 28 Mar. 2023.
99 [It's another level of singing.]: Interview with Mike Del Ferro, 3 July 2023.
99 ['I was quite intimidated by his talent.']: Email from Clare Foster to the author, 13 Feb. 2022.
99 ['the fantastic international pianist/singer John Larkin,']: Undated newspaper ad. for the Boeddha Restaurant, Amsterdam.
100 [Just like that, John was fired.]: John's Boeddha gig, being fired: JPL.

Chapter 20

102 [scribbled it down, and hung up.]: Manfred's past, hearing the tape in the car: Interview with Manfred Zähringer, 14 May 2023.
102 [Treudelberg Hotel outside Hamburg.]: Interview with Sabine Nagel-Heyer, 12 Sept. 2024, Interview with Karl Garderer, 19 Nov. 2024.
102 [to expand their options.]: Amsterdam results, German revisit, Spain: JPL, email from Judy Larkin to the author, 27 June 2011.
102 [playing in luxury hotels.]: Pan Agency, putting John in luxe hotels: JPL, interview with Manfred Zähringer, 25 Oct. 2024.
102 [nobody listened.]: Judy Larkin, Facebook post 7 Aug. 2011.
102 ['Same gig. Different clothes,' John quipped.]: Interview with John Morrell, 11 Dec. 2024.
102 [*as good as it gets for a jazzer like me.*]: JPL.
102 ['hardly the venue for John's talent.']: Judy Larkin, *Remembrances of John*, undated document, John and Judy Larkin Archive.
103 [getting John on a record.]: John performing for Manfred, Judy with the tape: JPL.
103 [tape I had concealed in my pocket.]: Judy Larkin, *Remembrances of John*, undated document, John and Judy Larkin Archive.
103 [a commercially viable path.]: Interview with Manfred Zähringer, 25 Oct. 2024.
103 [than ones who could sell]: Interview with Mette Zähringer, 26 Oct. 2024.
103 [listen to it on his drive back home.]: Judy Larkin, *Remembrances of John*, undated document, John and Judy Larkin Archive.
103 ['IT'S FUCKING GREAT' it read.]: Interview with Manfred Zähringer, 25 Oct. 2024.
103 [Manfred decided to do it himself.]: Interview with Manfred Zähringer, 25 Oct. 2024.
103 [sobriety and mental health.]: JPL, reception to jazz pitches: Interview with Manfred Zähringer, 14 May 2023.
103 [where he was in the world.]: Interview with Gail Wilson Lew, 6 Aug. 2023.

104 [medication for her newfound fluency.]: Nora O'Connor, 'There Is Hope', *Letting Go*: The monthly newsletter of the National Stuttering Project: Vol. 12, no. 3 (Mar. 1992).

104 [It will take time for you to realize it.]: John Larkin, letter to Nora O'Connor, 5 May 1992, in possession of Nora O'Connor.

104 ['I'll do whatever you want,' he'd said.]: Konrad Schäfers, Jutta vom Hofe, Claudia Mende, Erhard Hennen interview with John Larkin for the BVSS (Bundesvereinigung Stottern & Selbsthilfe), Nov. 1995.

104 [heart of God via the 12 Steps.]: John Larkin, letter to Nora O'Connor, 10 Aug. 1992, in possession of Nora O'Connor.

104 [Acceptance is the answer to all my problems today.]: Alcoholics Anonymous World Services, *Alcoholics Anonymous*, 3rd ed. (New York: Alcoholics Anonymous World Services, 1976), 449.

104 [long been strained.]: John Larkin, fax to Sharon Larkin, 26 Feb. 1994, Larkin Family Archive.

105 [harder to beat than heroin.]: Interview with Liz Miller, 10 Apr. 2023.

105 [asked for the good news.]: Manfred pitching John to jazz labels: Interview with Manfred Zähringer, 14 May 2023.

105 ['John, don't kill me,' Manfred began. 'But I have an idea.']: John Larkin, interview on *The Mix 95*, Various Artists, BBC Radio International (BBC World Service) Feb. 1996.

105 ['I'm not John Scatman,' he declared. 'I'm Scatman John!']: Suggesting scat and dance: Interview with Manfred Zähringer, 4 Nov. 2023.

Chapter 21

109 ['Oh yeah, sure. Right on, man.']: Undated Scatman John interview, YouTube, https://www.youtube.com/watch?v=aUOKLCktb4g.

109 [came through the speakers.]: Geert Desmet, 'I Bring Out the Child', *Het Nieuwsblad*, 2 Aug. 1995.

109 ['Glamorized electronic imitation,']: John Larkin, undated and untitled memoir note, circa 1991, John and Judy Larkin Archive.

109 [love and acceptance I had been looking for.]: JPL.

109 [*This world is not a safe place for children.*]: John Larkin, undated memoir note, John and Judy Larkin Archive.

109 [Godsend to show me that.]: JPL.

110 [early morning hours.]: '1994 Northridge Earthquake', Wikipedia, last modified Mar. 2025, https://en.wikipedia.org/wiki/1994_Northridge_earthquake.

110 [called friends and family.]: Interview with Mette Zähringer, 26 Oct. 2024.

110 [married in Laughlin, Nevada.]: Clark County Clerk's Office Marriage Records, Clark County, Nevada, accessed 5 May 2025.

110 ['They were a perfect couple.']: Interview with Gregg Pincus, 25 Mar. 2023.

110 ['we still had very little money,' Judy said.]: Judy Larkin, undated handwritten note, John and Judy Larkin Archive.

110 [toasting his future with apple juice.]: Interview with Gregg Pincus, 25 Mar. 2023, wedding photos in the John and Judy Larkin Archive.

110 ['Or we will.']: Interview with Manfred Zähringer, 14 May 2023.

110 ['I knew it was something special,' he said.]: Interview with Axel Alexander, 11 Dec. 2023.

110 [but the first demos were underwhelming.]: Interview with Manfred Zähringer, 25 Oct. 2024.

110 [they're making very special music.]: Interview with Janine Ramond, 12 Jan. 2024.

111 [producer and keyboardist.]: How Ingo and Tony met, their backgrounds: Florian Richter, 'Toni Catania & Ingo Kays: The Producers of Scatman', *Fachblatt Magazine*, July 1995.

111 [technically oriented and worked with keyboards.]: Thomas Berger, 'The Producers of Scatman: Tony Catania and Ingo Kays', *KEYS Magazine*, Aug. 1995.
111 [reinvested their earnings into a studio]: Thomas Berger, 'The Producers of Scatman: Tony Catania and Ingo Kays', *KEYS Magazine*, Aug. 1995.
111 [It was time to get John into the studio.]: Interview with Manfred Zähringer, 25 Oct. 2024; Interview with Axel Alexander, 11 Dec. 2023.
111 [being in the Norwegian Ozarks.]: John Larkin, letter to Harriet Larkin, 22 Aug. 1994, Larkin Family Archive.
111 [The other people were all laughing.]: John Larkin, letter to Harriet Larkin, 15 Sept. 1994, Larkin Family Archive.
111 [The Scatman idea, he said, was a 'go'.]: JPL.
112 [sizing him up.]: Ingo picking up John: Interview with Ingo Kays, 16 June 2023.
112 ['Chameleon-like,' Ingo agreed.]: Florian Richter, 'Toni Catania & Ingo Kays: The Producers of Scatman', *Fachblatt Magazine*, July 1995.
112 [hard for Tony to follow.]: Interview with Tony Catania, 2 May 2023.
112 [catching his breath.]: Thomas Sprenger, 'In Tony and Ingo's Recording Studio, Scatman Takes off His Shoes', *BILD*, 1 Aug. 1996.
112 [espresso machine.]: Florian Richter, 'Toni Catania & Ingo Kays: The Producers of Scatman', *Fachblatt Magazine*, July 1995.
112 [MIDI setup for maximum flexibility.]: Interview with Ingo Kays, 16 June 2023.
112 ['We had nothing.']: Interview with Tony Catania, 2 May 2023.
112 [every imaginable syllable his voice box could produce]: F minor beat and hours of scat-singing, John Larkin, interview on *The Mix 95*, Various Artists, BBC Radio International (BBC World Service) Feb. 1996.
112 [how calm and focused John was]: Interview with Ingo Kays, 16 June 2023.
112 [wasn't so sure about: the rap.]: professionalism, unsure about the rap: Interview with Tony Catania, 2 May 2023.
113 [through the song itself]: John's fear about disclosing his stutter: John Larkin, 'Who is Scatman John?', The Newsletter of the International Stuttering Association (ISA), 6th issue, Sept. 1996.
113 [The text had a message for all the kids.]: Interview with Tony Catania by Jeff Chi, undated.
113 [*Everybody stutters one way or the other*,]: Lyrics from 'Scatman (Ski-Ba-Bop-Ba-Dop-Bop)' by John Larkin (Scatman John). Used with permission.
113 [what we do with those problems that counts.]: Used with permission.
113 ['He had to bend himself to get it done,']: Interview with Ingo Kays, 16 June 2023.
113 [*Just give it a go.*] John saying he was not a rapper: conversation with John Larkin and the author circa 1997, also reported by Tony Catania, interview 16 Dec. 2022.
113 ['Too complicated,' Tony said]: slowing the track down to 100 BPM: Interview with Tony Catania, 2 May 2023; Interview with Ingo Kays, 16 June 2023.
113 ['didn't really fit into the scheme of contemporary pop music.']: Interview with Ingo Kays, 16 June 2023.
113 [resurrect it for a new generation.]: Iceberg Records, 'Scatman John' undated press release, circa 1995.
114 [strange and unsatisfying.]: Interview with Ingo Kays, 16 June 2023.
114 [twenty espressos,]: Interview with Tony Catania, 16 Dec. 2022.
114 ['We had no idea either.']: WDR documentary series 'Unser Land in den 90ern', Ep. 5 broadcast 28 Feb. 2022.
114 ['A laborious but very flexible process,' Tony said.]: Florian Richter, 'Toni Catania & Ingo Kays: The Producers of Scatman', *Fachblatt Magazine*, July 1995.

114 [or in John's case, jazz.]: 'Sampling (music)', Wikipedia, accessed 15 May 2025, https://en.wikipedia.org/wiki/Sampling_(music).
114 ['recognition value,' as Ingo put it.]: Florian Richter, 'Toni Catania & Ingo Kays: The Producers of Scatman', *Fachblatt Magazine*, July 1995.
114 [between 127 and 136 BPM]: Interview with Tony Catania, 2 May 2023.
114 [it was a lot of hard work.]: Interview with Ingo Kays, 16 June 2023.
114 [he had never sung in this form,' Tony said.]: Thomas Berger, 'The Producers of Scatman: Tony Catania and Ingo Kays', *KEYS Magazine*, Aug. 1995.
114 ['Melody, guys, melody,' he insisted.]: Interview with Manfred Zähringer, 26 Oct. 2024.
114 [scat phrase.]: Interview with Janine Ramond, 12 Jan. 2024.
115 [*Just maybe*.]: Interview with Manfred Zähringer, 14 May 2023.
115 [I was so happy.]: Interview with Janine Ramond, 12 Jan. 2024.
115 ['This was, for me, a sure number one,' Axel said.]: Interview with Axel Alexander, 11 Dec. 2023.
115 [maybe no one would steal the idea.]: Interview with Manfred Zähringer, 14 May 2023.
115 [lifted them from the keys to speak.]: John's Jazz Bakery performance: Home video footage, 25 Oct. 1994, John and Judy Larkin Archive.
115 [Annie whispered.]: Interview with Annie Bradberry, 26 Aug. 2023.

Chapter 22

116 ['Scatman' had landed.]: Manfred at MIDEM: Interview with Manfred Zähringer, 25 Oct. 2024.
116 [German charts at number 44.]: 'Scatman John – Scatman (Ski-Ba-Bop-Ba-Dop-Bop)', Offizielle Deutsche Charts, accessed 15 May 2025, https://www.offiziellecharts.de/charts/single/for-date-792068400000.
116 [Somebody else is the judge.]: John Larkin, interview on *The Mix 95*, Various Artists, BBC Radio International (BBC World Service), Feb. 1996.
116 ['Did I really sing that?']: Interview with Ingo Kays, 16 June 2023.
117 ['I'll fax it to you.']: Interview with Janine Ramond, 12 Jan. 2024.
117 [It's very crowded.]: Interview with Manfred Zähringer by Jeff Chi, circa 2021.
117 [aligned with John's ethos.]: Original music video ideas: Interview with Janine Ramond, 12 Jan. 2024; Undated pitch from Chopstick Films, in the possession of Iceberg Records.
117 ['We wanted him in the background.']: Interview with Janine Ramond, 12 Jan. 2024.
117 [He had a great respect for filmmaking.]: Interview with Gregor Schnitzler, 20 Oct. 2023.
118 [He was a genius guy.]: Interview with Tony Catania, 2 May 2023.
118 ['A day full of fun,' he concluded.]: Interview with Gregor Schnitzler, 20 Oct. 2023.
118 ['Nobody played it.']: Interview with Ingo Kays, 16 June 2023.
118 ['This is the worst thing you've ever done,']: Interview with Tony Catania, 16 Dec. 2022.
118 [had he known.]: Interview with Manfred Zähringer, 14 May 2023.
118 [novelty dance hit.]: 'New Releases', *Music & Media*, 7 Jan. 1995, p. 7.
118 [a defining aesthetic.]: Interview with Manfred Zähringer, 4 Nov. 2023.
118 [he looks like *that*.]: Interview with Ingo Kays, 16 June 2023.
118 [The entire package was different.]: Interview with Tony Catania, 2 May 2023.
118 [a set of dentures.]: Judy Larkin Facebook post, 28 Oct. 2012.
118 [joked to his sister-in-law Sharon.]: Interview with Billy and Sharon Larkin, 10 Apr. 2023.
118 [John's jazz background]: Interview with Axel Alexander, 11 Dec. 2023.
119 [younger stars willing to be remade.]: Interview with Janine Ramond, 12 Jan. 2024.
119 [never seen him in a suit.] Interview with George Rivera, 24 Apr. 2023.
119 ['I don't want kids to see me with a cigarette in my hand,']: Interview with Marci Herrara, 14 Apr. 2023.

119 [at his age, rocking the stage.]: First 'Scatman' performance: Interview with Janine Ramond, 12 Jan. 2024.

119 [dozens of times a day.]: Interview with Tony Catania, 2 May 2023; Interview with Janine Ramond, 12 Jan. 2024; 'Garry McHugh – Director and CEO of Young Irish Film Makers', Logan Sounds Off podcast, 21 Apr. 2023.

119 [Norwegian and Danish charts.]: 'VG-lista Topp 20 Singles, Week 5, 1995', Norwegiancharts.com, accessed 15 May 2025.

119 ['You mean I'm on a chart? As a *popstar?*']: John Larkin, interview on *The Mix 95*, Various Artists, BBC Radio International (BBC World Service), Feb. 1996.

119 [John was on the phone chasing him.]: Interview with Manfred Zähringer, 14 May 2023.

119 [it's not going to get any better than this.]: John Larkin, interview on *The Mix 95*, Various Artists, BBC Radio International (BBC World Service), Feb. 1996.

119 [a live on-air conversation.]: Untitled recording, NRK Radio excerpt, Jan. 1995, cassette in the possession of Iceberg Records.

Chapter 23

120 [incredibly quick tongue.]: John's first radio interview: Untitled recording, NRK Radio excerpt, Jan. 1995, cassette in the possession of Iceberg Records.

120 [Denmark's Marienlyst Castle.]: Undated Norwegian press release, 'Scatman John', in the posession of Iceberg Records.

120 ['I felt it was my job as a journalist to address this.']: Email from Hans Christian Andersen to the author, 24 Jan. 2025.

120 [Charleston into dance in 1994.]: 'Doop', Official Charts, Official Charts Company, accessed 6 May 2025, https://www.officialcharts.com/artist/29962/doop/.

120 ['Cotton Eye Joe'.]: 'Cotton Eye Joe – Rednex', Official Charts, Official Charts Company, accessed 6 May 2025, https://www.officialcharts.com/songs/rednex-cotton-eye-joe/.

120 [Smurfs had a techno album out.]: Schlümpfe – Tekkno Ist Cool Vol. 1, Discogs, accessed 6 May 2025, https://www.discogs.com/master/159141-Die-Schl%C3%BCmpfe-Tekkno-Ist-Cool-Vol-1.

120 [they hadn't sung.]: Chuck Philips, 'Milli Vanilli's Grammy Rescinded by Academy', *Los Angeles Times*, 20 Nov. 1990, https://www.latimes.com/archives/la-xpm-1990-11-20-mn-4948-story.html.

121 [something completely new,]: Email from Hans Christian Andersen to the author, 24 Jan. 2025.

121 [when you stutter?]: Untitled recording, NRK Radio excerpt, Jan. 1995, cassette in the possession of Iceberg Records.

121 [it's turned into a positive.]: Untitled recording, NRK Radio excerpt, Jan. 1995, cassette in the possession of Iceberg Records.

121 [he's a stutterer, you idiots?]: Interview with Manfred Zähringer by Cristián Saavedra, 15 May 2023.

121 [over NOT stuttering', John said.]: Larkin, John. 'What? ….Ashamed of Fluency?' Minnesota State University, Mankato, Center for Communication Sciences and Disorders, accessed 6 May 2025, https://ahn.mnsu.edu/services-and-centers/center-for-communication-sciences-and-disorders/services/stuttering/information-about-stuttering/serious-information/from-people-who-stutter-pws/pws-speak-for-themselves/what….ashamed-of-fluency-by-john-larkin.

122 [into the charts on my birthday.]: Interview with Tony Catania, 2 May 2023.

122 ['Have you taken your option?']: Interview with Mette Zähringer, 25 Oct. 2024.

122 [refused to bite: Japan.]: Territories releasing 'Scatman': Fax from Mette Zähringer to Anders Haarder, 24 Jan. 1995, Iceberg Records Archive.

122 [Japan was in.]: Manfred's pitch to Japan: Interview with Manfred Zähringer, 14 May 2023.
122 [best-selling foreign artists of all time.]: 'List of Best-Selling Albums in Japan', Wikipedia, last modified Apr. 2025, https://en.wikipedia.org/wiki/List_of_best-selling_albums_in_Japan.
122 [10,000 copies in its first week.]: Untitled recording, NRK Radio excerpt, Jan. 1995, cassette in the possession of Iceberg Records.
122 [single and an album.]: Fax from Manfred Zähringer to Ingo Kays and Tony Catania, 7 Feb. 1995, Iceberg Records Archive.
123 ['PS: REMEMBER HE STUTTERS.']: Fax from Mette Zähringer to Knud at *MIX Magazine*, 7 Feb. 1995, Iceberg Records Archive.
123 ['Scat Suit' was laid out, waiting.]: Fax from Mette Zähringer to John Larkin, 7 Feb. 1995, Iceberg Records Archive.
123 [#4 on the Danish charts.]: Philip Thomsen, 'He's The Scatman', *BT Magazine*, 10 Feb. 1995.
123 [just in case.]: Interview with Manfred Zähringer, 25 Oct. 2024.
123 ['Rather, a professor.']: Philip Thomsen, 'He's The Scatman', *BT Magazine*, 10 Feb. 1995.
123 [talent is always worth listening to.]: Philip Thomsen, 'He's The Scatman', *BT Magazine*, 10 Feb. 1995.
123 [Half a dozen newspapers and magazines.]: Faxes from Mette Zähringer to various journalists, Feb. 1995, Iceberg Records Archive.
123 [Norwegian paper *Dagbladet*,]: Erik Valebrokk, 'Scatman John', Dagbladet, 17 Feb. 1995.
123 [my age and experience behind me.]: Annette Heick, 'Scatman John: 52 Years Old and a Pop Star', *SE & HØR*, early 1995.
123 [*Eleva2oren* in Denmark]: Fax from Mette Zähringer to K-Tel, 13 Jan. 1995, Iceberg Records Archive.
123 [new Norwegian talk show.]: Stein Ostbo, 'Rounding Success', *VG Magazine*, 17 Feb. 1995.
123 [more for machines than musicians.]: 'Lip Sync', Wikipedia, last modified Apr. 2025, https://en.wikipedia.org/wiki/Lip_sync.
124 [*Scatman cannot be performed live!*]: Fax from John Larkin to Manfred Zähringer, 21 Jan. 1995, Iceberg Records Archive.

Chapter 24

125 [one of the most iconic performances of the song.]: Performance of 'Scatman', NRK1 Norway, aired 17 Feb. 1995.
125 ['The Old Newcomer,']: 'Stuttering to Success', *Abendblatt Evening Paper*, June 1995.
125 ['The Tongue Acrobat.']: 'Scared into Silence', *Aktion Das Magazine*, Mar. 1995.
125 ['Machine Lips']: Kwon Oh-hyun, undated South Korean newspaper, 1995.
126 [artist who could do the same.]: Interview with Manfred Zähringer, 14 May 2023.
126 [one magazine wrote.]: Andreas Güntert, 'Scatman Lets the Syllables Rattle', *CASH* No. 26–30, June 1995.
126 [patience when talking to Scatman John,' said another.]: 'Scatman's World', *Absolute Let's Dance Magazine*, May 1995.
126 ['a severe speech impediment,']: Susanna Ländeniemi, 'Scatman Stammered Himself to the Top', *Iltalheti* Finland, 24 Apr. 1995.
126 ['a nagging stammer']: Paola Buonadonna, 'How Scatman Did the Scooby-Do', *The European Magazine*, May 1995.
126 [was 'suffering' from.]: Popbitz, 'S-S-S-Scatman', *Manchester Evening News*, 24 May 1995.
126 [pestered not to forget.]: Fax from Manfred Zähringer to John and Judy Larkin, 27 Oct. 1995, Iceberg Records Archive.

126 [a smart image.]: Annette Heick, 'Scatman John: 52 Years Old and a Pop Star', *SE & HØR*, early 1995.
126 ['In bed with Scatman,' the article read.]: 'Im Bett Mip Scatman', *Cocktail Magazine*, May 1995.
126 [met with blank stares.]: Description of John in his hotel: 'Im Bett Mip Scatman', *Cocktail Magazine*, May 1995.
126 [shave off his mustache]: Push ups, Vi Unge Magazine, Dec. 1996, shaving: Snurre Snups Søndagsklub show, aired 1996.
126 ['nonsense as his records,' he said.]: Pasi Kostiainen, 'Scatman John Helps Stutterers and Continues to Babble', *Sanomat* Finland, 15 Nov. 1996.
127 [*Gentleman John.*]: Popbitz, *Manchester Evening News*, 24 May 1995.
127 [*Likeable Scatman.*]: 'Scatman's World', *Absolute Let's Dance Magazine*, May 1995.
127 [pouring through the receiver.]: Andreas Güntert, 'Scatman Lets the Syllables Rattle', *CASH Magazine*, June 1995.
127 [song on the radio.]: Email from Steve Larkin to the author, 27 May 2023.
127 ['I'm just trying to help.']: Konrad Schäfers, Jutta vom Hofe, Claudia Mende, Erhard Hennen interview for the BVSS (Bundesvereinigung Stotterer-Selbsthilfe), Nov. 1995.
128 [recording booth.]: 'Official Singles Chart Top 100: 14 May 1995–20 May 1995', Official Charts, UK Official Charts Company, 14 May 1995, https://www.officialcharts.com/charts/singles-chart/19950514/7501/.
129 ['I didn't believe him.']: Interview with Sam Phipps, 22 Apr. 2023.
129 [*Look what we've done,* it said.]: Interview with George and Gloria Rivera, 24 Apr. 2023.
129 [I'm having a great time.]: Philip Thomsen, 'He's the Scatman', *BT Magazine*, 10 Feb. 1995.
129 ['What the HELL?']: Interview with Bob Harrison, 8 Sept. 2023.

Chapter 25

130 [seeing no reason to uproot yet.]: Interview with Lee Newman, 11 Apr. 2024, also photographs from the John and Judy Larkin Archive.
130 [who knows about that,]: Interview with Bob Harrison, 8 Sept. 2023.
130 [back of his closet.]: Judy Larkin conversation with the author, Oct. 1999, *VIVA Jam* interview special, 1996.
130 [Completely different things matter to me.]: 'I'm a Scatland', *Dance Mix Magazine*, 1995.
130 [John told Bob]: Interview with Bob Harrison, 8 Sept. 2023.
130 [fishing for a pretzel in the bowl next to him.]: Undated photo of John at home, John and Judy Larkin Archive.
130 [dance music compatriots were doing okay.]: '7 January 1995', *Billboard* Hot 100, accessed 6 May 2025, https://www.billboard.com/charts/hot-100/1995-01-07/.
131 [*special about her*, John thought.]: Scatman John, 'Scatman's World: Interview CD', RCA, 1995.
131 [*Great stuff.*]: 'Scatman's World', *Absolute Let's Dance Magazine*, May 1995.
131 [The world's in a tragic situation.]: John's opinion of 'Gangsta Rap' and seeing it on MTV: Geert Desmet, 'I Bring Out The Child', *Het Nieuwsblad*, 2 Aug. 1995; Ilkka Mattila, 'The Old Jazz Dude Became the Pop Star Scatman', *Helsinki Sanomat*, 19 Apr. 1995.
131 [We don't need to add more chaos.]: John Larkin, interview on *The Mix 95*, Various Artists, BBC Radio International (BBC World Service), Feb. 1996.
131 ['old bohemian.']: 'Scatman's World', *Absolute Let's Dance Magazine*, May 1995.
131 ['more of the same.']: Interview with Manfred Zähringer, 25 Oct. 2024.
132 [She just sits there.]: Fred Shuster, 'A Worldwide Celebrity … Really', *Daily News of Los Angeles*, 2 Nov. 1995.
132 [Of a land that hasn't any good excuse.]: Used with permission.

132 ['Nobody could get serious after that,' D says.]: Interview with D. Jennings, 21 Mar. 2023.
132 [I had no clue what he was doing.]: Interview with D. Jennings, 21 Mar. 2023.
133 [whenever he appeared in public.]: Based on photographs and video of John Larkin and information from a personal acquaintance in recovery, circa Mar. 2023.
133 [The whole family did.] Interview with Billy and Sharon Larkin, 27 Mar. 2023.
133 [cutout of John from the record label.]: Photo of John with Harriet, 28 July 1995, Larkin Family Archive.
133 [sales in Denmark.]: Interview with Billy and Sharon Larkin, 27 Mar. 2023.
133 [for once in my life.]: Paola Buonadonna, 'How Scatman did the Scooby-do', *The European Magazine*, May 1995.
133 ['I had never seen my cousin Judy so happy,']: Interview with Mike Metzger, 1 Apr. 2023.
133 [she was right.]: Interview with Lee Newman, 11 Apr. 2024.
133 [biggest single of 1995 so far.]: 'Stuttering to Success', *Abendblatt Evening Paper*, June 1995.

Chapter 26

134 [They laughed.]: John in the hotel lobby: Interview with Iris Reimann, 16 June 2023.
134 [for three months.]: 'Top 100 Single-Charts: 27.03.1995 – 02.04.1995', Offizielle Deutsche Charts, accessed 6 May 2025, https://www.offiziellecharts.de/charts/single/for-date-796298400000.
134 [widest-selling album in Europe.]: John's liner notes on the *Everybody Jam* album 1996; also *Music & Media*, 'Europe's Top Cross Border Hits 1995', 18 Nov. 1995.
134 [overflow within weeks.]: Conversation between Judy Larkin and the author, circa 2011.
134 [it happened to me.]: Fred Shuster, 'A Worldwide Celebrity … Really', *Daily News of Los Angeles*, 2 Nov. 1995.
135 [we wouldn't be so frustrated.]: Geert Desmet, 'I Bring Out The Child', *Het Nieuwsblad*, 2 Aug. 1995.
135 [Judy was with him.]: Interview with Ingo Kays, 16 June 2023.
135 [who John was.]: Interview with Iris Reimann, 16 June 2023.
135 [weather forecast.]: 'Welcome to Scatland', BMG *Tracks*, Aug. 1995.
135 [please change rooms?] Interview with Iris Reimann, 16 June 2023.
135 [from car stereos]: Interview with Tony and Ilona Catania, 16 Dec. 2022; email from Ilona Catania to the author, 25 Feb. 2025.
135 [better listen to me.]: Used with permission, WhatsApp conversation with Ingo Kays, 4 Mar. 2025.
135 [as far back as Amsterdam.]: Interview with Mike Del Ferro, 3 July 2023.
135 [things he was really good at.]: Thomas Berger, 'The Producers of Scatman: Tony Catania and Ingo Kays', *KEYS*, Aug. 1995.
135 [through the album sessions.]: John's quirks in the studio: Interview with Ingo Kays, 16 June 2023; interview with Tony Catania, 2 May 2023.
136 [everything.]: Thomas Berger, 'The Producers of Scatman: Tony Catania and Ingo Kays', *KEYS*, Aug. 1995.
136 [like a Eurodance law.]: Interview with Ingo Kays, 17 June 2023.
136 [for the masses.]: Interview with Tony Catania by Jeff Chi, circa 2021.
136 [You can't do that.]: Interview with Ingo Kays, 16 June 2023.
136 [possessed,' it began]: Used with permission.
136 ['Sounds great. Positive!']: Fax from Manfred Zähringer to Ingo Kays and Tony Catania, 4 Apr. 1995, Iceberg Records Archive.
136 [trumpets, saxophones,]: Thomas Berger, 'The Producers of Scatman: Tony Catania and Ingo Kays', *KEYS*, Aug. 1995.
136 [I loved it.]: Interview with Tony Catania, 2 May 2023.

136 [toward changes,]: Interview with Ingo Kays, 17 June 2023.
137 [his breathing.]: Free scatting, John's vocalizations: Interview with Ingo Kays, 16 June 2023; also WhatsApp conversation with Ingo Kays, 4 Mar. 2025.
137 [John had COPD.]: Letter from Dr Mahrer to Iceberg Records, 12 May 1998, Iceberg Records Archive.
137 ['All I need to do is *surrender*.']: John's breathing, lung function, studio break: Interview with Ingo Kays, 16 June 2023; Whatsapp conversation with Ingo Kays, 5 Mar. 2025.
137 [*Walden*]: Reference to Henry David Thoreau's line in *Walden; or, Life in the Woods* (Boston: Ticknor and Fields, 1854): 'The mass of men lead lives of quiet desperation.'
137 [a little easier.]: Gunther Matejka, 'A Loser's Victory', HiFiVizion, Sept. 1995.
137 [stay with them in LA.]: Judy in the hotel: Interview with Iris Reimann, 16 June 2023.
138 [door behind him.]: John leaving the studio: Interview with Ingo Kays, 16 June 2023.
138 [Because all I can do is try.]: John Larkin, interview on *The Mix 95*, Various Artists, BBC Radio International (BBC World Service), Feb. 1996.
138 [full of mutual respect.]: Studio atmosphere: Interview with Ingo Kays, 16 June 2023; Interview with Tony Catania, 2 May 2023.
138 [I ever saw in my life.]: Interview with Tony Catania, 2 May 2023.
138 [take themselves.]: John Larkin, interview on *The Mix 95*, Various Artists, BBC Radio International (BBC World Service), Feb. 1996.
139 [not for them, not for him.]: Interview with John Morrell, 11 Dec. 2024.
139 [woke up in Colorado.]: JPL.
139 [living out of a suitcase.]: Interview with Iris Reimann, 16 June 2023.
139 [traces of cognac in it.]: Interview with Ingo Kays, 17 June 2023.
139 [*There has to be a ballad.*]: Interview with Ingo Kays, 17 June 2023.
139 [reference to stuttering.]: Interview with John Larkin, by Konrad Schäfers, Jutta vom Hofe, Claudia Mende, Erhard Hennen for the BVSS (Bundesvereinigung Stottern & Selbsthilfe).

Chapter 27

140 [John's upcoming album.]: Approach to be in the music video: Telephone interview with Laura Hagger, 19 July 2024.
140 [four million sales worldwide]: John Larkin interview, 'Scared into Silence', *Aktion Das Magazin*, Mar. 1995.
140 ['Like a snowball, like a pandemic.']: Interview with Manfred Zähringer, 23 Nov. 2023.
140 [*How does he do that?*]: John on set: Telephone Interview with Laura Hagger, 19 July 2024.
140 ['70s anthem 'Go West',]: Interview with Ingo Kays, 17 June 2023.
140 ['Soul ain't got no color, man.']: Uncut *VIVA Jam* interview rushes, VHS in the John and Judy Larkin Archive.
141 [human doing]: Used with permission.
141 [as a woman, as a director.]: Video Interview with Zowie Broach, 7 Nov. 2023.
141 [knowing his world exists.]: Original synopsis pitch for the 'Scatman's World' music video by Zowie Broach, copy in Iceberg Records Archive.
141 [another drizzly London day.]: 'Scatman's World' music video scenes: Interview with Zowie Broach, 7 Nov. 2023.
141 [arms thrown wide, beaming.]: Stills of John Larkin during the 'Scatman's World' video shoot, in the possession of Janine Ramond.
142 [But John didn't.]: John's physicality and attitude: Interview with Zowie Broach, 7 Nov. 2023.
142 [A really kind, nice man.]: John's interaction with Laura, Ruth and the kids: Telephone interview with Laura Hagger, 19 July 2024.

142 ['Joyous wisdom,' she said.]: Mic and hat shot, post-production details: Interview with Zowie Broach, 7 Nov. 2023.
143 [sixteen more.]: John at the theme park: Interview with Janine Ramond, 12 Jan. 2024.
143 [I would have given up.]: 'Blitz with Scatman John', *Bravo*, 1995.
143 ['I need her now in every way.']: Fax from John Larkin to Manfred Zähringer, 6 Apr. 1995, Iceberg Records Archive.
143 [in months: a break.]: Judy calling Manfred: Fax from Manfred Zähringer to John Larkin, 6 Apr. 1995, Iceberg Records Archive.
143 [Eddie Cantor and Jimmy McHugh.]: Lee Newman. *Relatively Singing: The Songs of Jimmy McHugh, Eddie Cantor & More*. Original Cast Records, 1995.
143 [very supportive of me.]: Interview with Lee Newman, 13 Apr. 2023.
143 ['but a *happy* stepson.']: Lee Newman, John Larkin's memorial, 12 Dec. 1999.
143 [swapping songs and albums.]: Lee's relationship with John: Interview with Lee Newman, 13 Apr. 2023.
143 [family and my cats,' he said.]: *Entrevue*, late 1995.
144 [leave her in tears.]: Nora O'Connor, 'If the Scatman Can do it, so can I', article in *Letting Go*, the monthly publication of the National Stuttering Association, Feb./Mar. 2001.
145 [whoops and cheers of the crowd.]: John's NSP convention attendance and keynote: Home video footage by Judy Larkin, 1995, John and Judy Larkin Archive.
145 [any kind of fluency.]: Video interview with Daniel Kremer, 17 July 2023.
145 [out there who hear it.]: Home video footage by Judy Larkin, 1995, John and Judy Larkin Archive.

Chapter 28

146 [every other European chart.]: 'Scatman's World – Scatman John', Lescharts.com, accessed 7 May 2025, https://lescharts.com/showitem.asp?interpret=Scatman+John&titel=Scatman%27s+World&cat=s.
146 [climbing any higher.]: Hitparade.ch, accessed 7 May 2025, https://hitparade.ch/charts/singles/23-07-1995.
146 [MTV, VIVA, The Box]: Faxes from Mette Zähringer to various journalists, 14 July 1995, Iceberg Records Archive.
146 [shouting along with John.]: Interview with Laura Hagger, 19 July 2024.
147 [Best Male Artist of 1995]: Brett Atwood, The Eye, 'November Awards Abound', *Billboard*, 28 Oct. 1995.
147 [to talk about it.] *MTV's Most Wanted*, featuring Scatman John, aired sometime in 1995. Exact date unknown. MTV Europe, 1995.
147 [to clone him]: NPN, 'Scatman John' article from 1995 in the John and Judy Larkin Archive.
147 ['I only sleep in my spare time.']: André Blick, 'Scatman John: Greetings to the Swiss Cool Man', 6 July 1995.
147 ['If you don't mean it, it's not.']: John Larkin interviewed on Lista Top 40, Finland, aired on Yle TV2 in April 1995.
147 ['Not me.']: 'Scatman John', *Entrevue*, undated article circa late 1995.
148 [But he was right.]: John's Platinum Party, award story: Interview with Janine Ramond, 12 Jan. 2024; also invitation and photos from the event, seen in the Iceberg Records Archive.
148 [include the track.]: Based on multiple faxes from 1995 in the Iceberg Records Archive, viewed by the author.
148 [music therapy for children.]: Faxes between Iceberg Records and Nordoff–Robbins, 14 July 1995; also Coca-Cola 'Nordoff–Robbins Rock-Cans – 3/6 – Scatman's World',

148 manufactured in Austria for Switzerland, 20 Nov. 1995. Coca-Cola GesmbH, A-Wien, accessed 17 May 2025, https://www.cokecollection.com/index.php?lang=en&pageid=50&canID=7212.
148 [a piece of Scatman]: Based on multiple faxes from 1995 in the Iceberg Records Archive, viewed by the author.
148 ['Goo goo goo Good Humor.']: Fax from Manfred Zähringer to BMG regarding the Good Humor request enclosing the lyrics, 16 Aug. 1995, Iceberg Records Archive.
148 [He does not agree.]: Fax from Judy Larkin to Manfred Zähringer, 22 Aug. 1995, Iceberg Records Archive.
148 [six-figure deal or not.]: Fax from Judy Larkin to Manfred Zähringer, 23 Aug. 1995, Iceberg Records Archive.
148 [no problem.]: Fax from Manfred Zähringer to EMI Publishing, 25 Aug. 1995, Iceberg Records Archive.
149 [final approval of the lyrics]: Fax from EMI Music Publishing to Manfred Zähringer, 25 Oct. 1995, Iceberg Records Archive.
149 [eventually greenlit.]: 'I'm the Good Humor Man' TV ad. aired circa Jan. 1996.
149 [tens of thousands of copies a week.]: Ellie Weinert, 'Scatman John to Show US His World', *Billboard*, 12 Aug. 1995.
149 [because I'm a critic.']: John Larkin interview, *Scatman's World* – Interview CD, RCA, 1995.
149 [rather grisly.]: Stuart Maconie, *Q*, 1995.
149 [positive persona.]: NPN, 'Scatman's World' review, 1995.
149 [advice to be had.]: Michael Smiley, 'Scatman's World', *Vi Unge*, Aug. 1995.
149 [joy to behold.]: Matthias Inhoffen, 'Scatman's World', *Badische Zeitung*, 6 Aug. 1995.
149 ['You are all my children.']: *Scatman's World* album liner notes, BMG/RCA/Iceberg Records, 1995.
150 ['And that' he concluded, 'is a disaster.']: Geert Desmet, 'I Bring Out the Child', *Het Niewsblad*, 2 Aug. 1995.
150 [Over a million.]: Pieter Kops, 'Denmark Dances Across Borders', *Music & Media*, 23 Dec. 1995.
150 [foreign artist.]: Fax from Manfred Zähringer to Musik Markt, 15 Sept. 1995, Iceberg Records Archive.
150 [stalled at #60.]: *Billboard* Hot 100, 4 Oct. 1995 chart, https://www.billboard.com/charts/hot-100/1995-10-04/.
150 [*LA Weekly*.]: Fred Shuster, 'A Worldwide Celebrity … Really', *Daily News of Los Angeles*, 2 Nov. 1995.
150 [Latin clubs]: Phone conversation with Peter Lorimer, 9 Jul. 2025.
150 [Rolf Potts put it.]: Rolf Potts, 'Eurodance Music Ruined My 1996 Arrival in Korea (and Left Its Mark on K-Pop)', RolfPotts.com, 3 Mar. 2017, https://rolfpotts.com/eurodance-music-ruined-my-1996-arrival-in-korea/.
150 [Chicago baseball field]: Dorian Lynskey, 'The 1979 Riot That "Killed" Disco', *BBC Culture*, 22 Sept. 2023, https://www.bbc.com/culture/article/20230922-the-night-angry-rock-fans-destroyed-disco-music.
150 [RCA admitted.]: Fred Shuster, 'A Worldwide Celebrity … Really', *Daily News of Los Angeles*, 2 Nov. 1995.
150 [remixing it.]: '*The Sign* (Ace of Base album)', Wikipedia, last modified Jan. 2025, https://en.wikipedia.org/wiki/The_Sign_(Ace_of_Base_album).
150 [sound more 'American.']: Interview with Tony Catania, 2 May 2023; interview with Ingo Kays, 16 June 2023; also photographs from the session in the possession of Ingo Kays.
150 [holiday sales rush.]: Fax from Manfred Zähringer to John and Judy Larkin, 28 Sept. 1995, Iceberg Records Archive.

151 [vanished from the charts.]: The last chart entry on the *Billboard* Hot 100 was at #98 on 9 Nov. 1995, https://www.billboard.com/charts/hot-100/1995-11-09/.
151 [The US release was scrapped.]: Interview with Manfred Zähringer, 14 May 2023.
151 [Judy said.]: Undated handwritten note by Judy Larkin, John and Judy Larkin Archive.
151 [rejected him again.]: John Larkin interview on MTV Europe, 1995.
151 [Judy said.]: Undated handwritten note by Judy Larkin, John and Judy Larkin Archive.
151 [Michael Jackson came second.]: Fax from Pieter Markus at *Music & Media* to Iceberg Records, 27 Nov. 1995.
151 [John laughed.]: David Glasband at John's memorial, 12 Dec. 1999.

Chapter 29

152 ['Everybody's from Scatman's World!']: John's introduction of the song at various concerts, including in-home video footage from Liquidroom, Tokyo, Feb. 1996.
152 [camera in hand.]: Photos taken of John Larkin by Judy Larkin at the side of the stage, John and Judy Larkin Archiv.e
152 [was content.]: Paola Buonadonna, 'How Scatman Did the Scooby-do', *The European Magazine*, May 1995.
152 ['Or even two times 45 minutes.']: John's tour requests: Interview with Ulrik Hinsch, 1 Nov. 2023.
152 [studio sound live.]: Interview with Steve Brzezicki, 15 Dec. 2023.
153 [Winston (named after Churchill).]: Conversation with Judy Larkin, 1999.
153 [*Johnny Jetlag.*]: Honda S. Jorgensen 'Johnny Jetlag', *Zink*, Dec. 1996.
153 [Steve Hamilton]: Interview with Steve Hamilton, 13 Oct. 2023.
153 ['Very warm.']: Interview with Steve Brzezicki, 15 Dec. 2023.
153 [before fading]: Scatman John: 'Song of Scatland', Offizielle Deutsche Charts, https://www.offiziellecharts.de/charts/titel-details-78535.
153 ['incongruous, to say the least,']: Interview with Steve Hamilton, 13 Oct. 2023.
153 ['A foggy day in London town,']: Fax from John Larkin to Manfred Zähringer, 3 Jan. 1996.
153 [Brzezicki recalls.]: John staying with Steve and his attitude to playing: Interview with Steve Brzezicki, 15 Dec. 2023.
153 [John told them.]: Interview with Steve Hamilton, 13 Oct. 2023.
153 [it was time for the opening night.]: Rehearsals: Interview with Steve Brzezicki, 15 Dec. 2023.
153 [stop the gear from freezing.]: Interview with Ulrik Hinsch, 1 Nov. 2023.
154 [most of them left.]: Kyiv concert: Interview with Steve Hamilton, 13 Oct. 2023; interview with Ulrik Hinsch, 1 Nov. 2023.
154 ['Insanity,' John called it.]: JPL.
154 [it was John.]: Conversation with Judy Larkin circa 2011.
154 [eating caviar.']: Moscow concert: Interview with Steve Brzezicki, 15 Dec. 2023; interview with Ulrik Hinsch, 1 Nov. 2023.
154 [used notes.]: Interview with Manfred Zähringer, 14 May 2023.
154 [onstage in his socks.]: *Kurir*, 29 Jan. 1996.
154 [anyone's guess.]: Hungary concert: *Kurir*, 29 Jan. 1996; Hegedűs Ákos, 'KÉP-regény: Egyensúlyban az élesség,' *Fidelio*, 17 Feb. 2023, https://fidelio.hu/vizual/kep-regeny-egyensulyban-az-elesseg-177565.html.
155 [I didn't know John had a condition.]: Interview with Steve Brzezicki, 15 Dec. 2023.
155 [took him away.]: *Kurir*, 29 Jan. 1996.
155 [put in front of him.]: Conversation with Judy Larkin, 1999.
155 [in his hotel room.]: Interview with Manfred Zähringer by Cristian Saavedra, 15 May 2023.

155 [Look how mean he is …]: Konrad Schäfers, Jutta vom Hofe, Claudia Mende, Erhard Hennen interview with John Larkin for the BVSS (Bundesvereinigung Stottern & Selbsthilfe) Nov. 1995.

155 [holding up lighters.] NPN, 'Scatman, or a Very Fast Singing Tempo', Polish clipping, 1996.

155 [Not once.]: Recording devices, leaving Poland: Interview with Ulrik Hinsch, 1 Nov. 2023.

155 [skipped the nightlife.]: Interview with Steve Brzezicki, 15 Dec. 2023.

156 [He was an incredible musician.]: Interview with Steve Hamilton, 13 Oct. 2023.

156 ['Paul's seat.']: Interview with Ulrik Hinsch, 1 Nov. 2023.

156 [almost two and a half million copies there]: Wikipedia contributors. 'List of best-selling albums in Japan.' Wikipedia. https://en.wikipedia.org/w/index.php?title=List_of_best-selling_albums_in_Japan&oldid=1038213955, last modified 31 July 2021. Note that Oricon totals did not include imports; 2.4 million reported at Genyukai; 'Interview with Scatman John', last modified 5 Oct. 2002, archived at Wayback Machine, https://web.archive.org/web/20021005214909/https://www2m.biglobe.ne.jp/~genyukai/scatman.html.

156 [into the storm.]: Interview with Manfred Zähringer, 14 May 2023.

156 [women wearing hats and mustaches.]: Interview with Steve Brzezicki, 15 Dec. 2023.

156 [such innocent beings.]: Ira Zimmerman, interview with Scatman John Larkin, *Advance for Speech Pathologists and Audiologists Magazine*, 20 Nov. 1995.

157 [John veered off-script.]: John's disinterest in playing the songs straight, solos: Interview with Steve Brzezicki, 15 Dec. 2023.

157 [leaving it all onstage.]: John's Liquidroom performance: Home video footage, 12 Feb. 1996.

157 ['But I can't do this.']: Fax from John Larkin to Manfred Zähringer and BMG, 26 Feb. 1996, Iceberg Records Archive.

Chapter 30

158 [six months]: '3399 Fryman Pl, Studio City, CA 91604', Zillow, Zillow Real Estate, accessed 8 May 2025, https://www.zillow.com/homedetails/3399-Fryman-Pl-Studio-City-CA-91604/20031816_zpid/.

158 [Gold and Platinum records]: Thomas Sprenger, 'In Tony and Ingo's Studio, Scatman Takes Off His Shoes', *Bild*, Aug. 1996.

158 [he is quite exhausted.]: Fax from Mette Zähringer to Bo Sprehn, Domino Film, 13 Oct. 1995, Iceberg Records Archive.

158 [*Journey of Fantasy.*]: Fax from Manfred Zähringer to John and Judy Larkin, 27 Oct. 1995, Iceberg Records Archive.

158 [you had a nickname.]: Undated handwritten note by Judy Larkin, John and Judy Larkin Archive; also conversation with the author circa 2012.

158 [Korea and Japan]: Fax from Manfred Zähringer to BMG Korea, 17 Jan. 1996, Iceberg Records Archive.

158 [Kato-Cha covered 'Scatman (Ski-Ba-Bop-Ba-Dop-Bop)']: '加藤茶 – 加トちゃんのスキャットマン (Kato-chan no Scatman)', Discogs, released 1995, accessed 8 May 2025.

158 [Ultraman gave it a go.]: 'Ultraman – スキャットウルトラマン (Scat Ultraman)', Discogs, released 1995.

158 ['super beautiful.']: Kazuo Hitomi, 'Honami Suzuki's Press Conference', *Syukan Post*, 29 Mar. 1996.

158 [bonus track.]: Recording: Fax from Tad Yoshida, BMG Tokyo, to Marion Hasenohr, BMG Hamburg, 4 Dec. 1995, Iceberg Records Archive; 'スーパーキレイ (Super Kirei) – スキャットマン・ジョン', *Oricon*, released 1996, accessed 8 May 2025. https://www.oricon.co.jp/prof/92569/products/56947/1/.

158 [straight off the road.]: Fax from Manfred Zähringer to Tad Yoshida, BMG Japan, 4 Jan. 1996, Iceberg Records Archive.
158 [over 200,000 copies sold.]: Bergman Tagata, 'Now is the time to know about Scatman John's achievements!' *Excite News*, 13 June 2017; Oricon Inc. *Oricon Weekly Singles Chart Archives, 1996*; Tokyo: Original Confidence, 1996, accessed via official industry data. Sales estimates for 'Su Su Su Super Kirei' (approx. 143,000) and 'PriPri Scat' (approx. 76,000) based on cumulative physical sales (CD and cassette) in Japan.
159 [long-haul flight.]: Fax from Iceberg Records to Warwick Hotel, Paris, 13 Mar. 1996, Iceberg Records Archive.
159 [six million.]: Pasi Kostiainen, 'Scatman John helps stutterers and continues to babble', *Sanomat Finland*, 15 Nov. 1996.
159 [seventh most famous person in Japan.]: Knud Løkke, 'Success and Sushi', *MIX*, 1996.
159 [their normal life.]: Interview with Michael and Laurie Schur, 28 July 2023.
159 [already seen it.]: Interview with D. Jennings, 21 Mar. 2023; interview with Stacey Heaver, 28 Mar. 2023; author's own observations of the car, 1999.
159 [I don't deserve all this"]: Jan Eriksen, 'Danish Company Scores on Scatman', *BT*, 5 Nov. 1996.
159 [pay his own phone bills.]: Fax from Manfred Zähringer to John Larkin, 29 Oct. 1996, Iceberg Records Archive.
159 [early corners of the web.]: Knud Løkke, 'Success and Sushi', *MIX*, 1996; conversation with the author circa 1997.
159 ['John was too shy to talk to him,' Elson says.]: Interview with Elson Trinidad, 10 Apr. 2024.
159 [feelings of a father ...]: John Larkin, undated message circa 1996; 'Scatman's World Wide Web', retrieved May 2, https://web.archive.org/web/20000226140304/http://www.westworld.com/~elson/scatman/scatmsg.html.
159 [He told Iceberg and BMG not to charge]: Fax from John Larkin to Manfred Zähringer regarding a request from Edwin Farr, British Stammering Association, 23 Mar. 1995, Iceberg Records Archive.
160 [straight back to the association.]: Interview with Satoru Hanazono, 30 Aug. 2023.
160 ['A search for what my motives really are.']: Honda S. Jorgensen, 'Johnny Jetlag', *Zink*, Dec. 1996.
160 [*How can I help others?*]: Morten Lind, 'The World's Too Hot to be Cool!', *Volume*, 1996.
160 [imitated his stutter.]: John Larkin interviewed on Lista Top 40, Finland, aired on Yle TV2 in April 1995.
160 [But by owning it.]: Scatman John on Zona+ Mais, broadcast 5 June 1995, RTP1, Portugal.
161 [community of people who stutter.]: Paperwork for the foundation in the Iceberg Records Archive.
161 [he told the committee.]: Email from John Larkin to the International Stuttering Association Committee, courtesy of Shinji Ito, *Stuttering Now*, no. 32 (Apr. 1997).
161 [how to face it.]: 'Interview with Scatman John', Genyukai, last modified 5 Oct. 2002, archived at Wayback Machine, https://web.archive.org/web/20021005214909/https://www2m.biglobe.ne.jp/~genyukai/scatman.html.
161 [opinions are essential.]: Email from John Larkin to the International Stuttering Association Committee, courtesy of Shinji Ito, *Stuttering Now*, no. 32 (Apr. 1997).
161 [has an open mind,' he said.]: John Larkin email to Jaan Pill, 5 Mar. 1997, courtesy of Shinji Ito.
161 [physically abnormal,' he said.]: 'Interview with Scatman John, Genyukai, last modified 5 Oct. 2002, archived at Wayback Machine, https://web.archive.org/web/20021005214909/https://www2m.biglobe.ne.jp/~genyukai/scatman.html.

161 [his PO box.]: Post box at the Studio City United States Postal Service office, 0.7 miles from John's home.
161 ['What if there's another me?' he said.]: Conversation with Judy Larkin in 1999 and also 2011; interview with Manfred Zähringer by Christian Saavedra, 15 May 2023.

Chapter 31

162 ['And fired.']: Interview with Manfred Zähringer, 26 Oct. 2024.
162 [John liked the idea.]: Fax from Eckhart Gundel, Janine Becker (Ramond), and Axel Alexander to Manfred Zähringer, 25 Oct. 1995; fax from John Larkin to Manfred Zähringer, 27 Oct. 1995, Iceberg Records Archive.
163 [Scatman release in months.]: Fax from Manfred Zähringer to John Larkin, 26 Apr. 1996.
163 [the other for editing.]: Interview with Tony Catania, 2 May 2023.
163 [cut the power in protest.]: Interview with Ingo Kays, 16 June 2023.
163 [Tony laughs.]: Interview with Tony Catania, 2 May 2023.
163 [coming home.]: Unnamed Bottrop newspaper clipping, 'New CD Made in Bottrop', 1996.
163 [resonate with them.]: John Larkin, 'Scatman's World Wide Web' message dated 25 Mar. 1996, retrieved 2 May, https://web.archive.org/web/20000226140304/http://www.westworld.com/~elson/scatman/scatmsg.html.
163 [pressure was enormous,]: Lena Storvand, 'S-S-Scatter Again', *Spotlight*, 18 Nov. 1996.
163 [instead of sending us']: Lyrics used with permission.
163 ['We never spoke about politics,' Ingo adds.]: Email to the author from Ingo Kays, 28 Mar. 2025.
164 [I'm not into any politics.]: John Larkin, *Interview with Scatman John*, interview by Matthias Holtmann, Stuttgart: SDR3 (Südwestrundfunk), 6 Nov. 1996, audio recording, ARD-Hörfunkdatenbank, accessed 26 Aug. 2024.
164 [support each other.]: Morten Lind, 'The World's Too Hot to be Cool!', *Volume*, 1996.
164 [outside the studio window.]: John Larkin, *Interview with Scatman John*, interview by Matthias Holtmann, Stuttgart: SDR3 (Südwestrundfunk), 6 Nov. 1996, audio recording, ARD-Hörfunkdatenbank, accessed 26 Aug. 2024.
164 ['One petal at a time.']: *VIVA Jam* Interview Special, 1996.
164 [scat-singing language.]: Interview with Ingo Kays, 16 June 2023, 'Kays & Catania Fax Message', 20 May 1996 to John Larkin.
164 ['I want to catch up.']: Knud Løkke, 'Success and Sushi', *MIX*, 1996.
164 [even for just half an hour.]: Interview with Satoru Hanazono, 30 Aug. 2023.
165 [You need to come here.]: Interview with Tony Catania, 2 May 2023; fax from John Larkin to Iceberg Records and BMG, 26 Feb. 1996.
165 ['Piano Dealer to the stars.']: Jon Thurber, David L. Abell Obituary, *Los Angeles Times*, 14 Feb. 2006.
165 [It was perfect.]: George Litterst, 'Celebrating 30 Years of Disklavier: The History of Disklavier, Part I', *Yamaha Music*, 19 June 2017, https://hub.yamaha.com/pianos/p-history/celebrating-30-years-of-disklavier-the-history-of-disklavier-part-i/.
165 [his mother's place]: Receipt for the purchase of Yamaha DC3II 6'1" polished ebony Disklavier grand piano from David L Abell Inc., dated 11 May 1996, with instructions to deliver the Schafer white spinet to Harriet Larkin.
165 [something to do other than talk.]: Interview with Billy and Sharon Larkin, 10 Apr. 2023.
165 [it was a struggle.]: Interview with Tony Catania, 2 May 2023.
165 [Ingo remembers.]: Email from Ingo Kays, 28 Mar. 2025.
165 ['in the professional way.']: Interview with Tony Catania, 2 May 2023.
165 [bounce back.]: Fax from Manfred Zähringer to John Larkin, 29 May 1996, Iceberg Records Archive.

165 [the reaction was tepid.]: Fax from BMG Tokyo to Manfred Zähringer, 20 June 1996; fax from BMG Hamburg to BMG Tokyo, 3 July 1996, Iceberg Records Archive.

165 ['The lightness of before had disappeared.']: Email from Ingo Kays to the author, 28 Mar. 2025.

165 [So you need to reinvent yourself.]: Interview with Tony Catania, 2 May 2023.

166 [he fumed]: John Larkin interview, Radio AAHs Hollywood, 29 Nov. 1997.

166 [to these kids.]: Fax from John Larkin to Manfred Zähringer, Ingo Kays, Tony Catania, BMG Hamburg, 11 July 1996, Iceberg Records Archive.

166 [They made me a star.]: Thomas Sprenger, 'They Made me a Star', *Bild*, Aug. 1996.

166 [music, please.]: John Larkin interview, Radio AAHs Hollywood, 29 Nov. 1997.

166 [I'm working on it.]: Morten Lind, 'The World's Too Hot to Be Cool!', *Volume*, 1996.

166 [James Earl Jones.]: 'Scatman, Porter Among NCCD Honorees', *ADVANCE for Speech-Language Pathologists and Audiologists*, 14 Oct. 1996.

166 [means the most.]: John meeting James Earl Jones and later comments on the award: Danny and the Scatman, outtakes, 1999.

166 [back into the spotlight.]: D. Krieger, 'Triumphant Procession Through New Orleans', *Popcorn*, 1996.

167 [what was going on.]: Email from Steve Larkin to the author, 27 May 2023.

167 [one magazine wrote.]: D. Krieger, 'Triumphant Procession Through New Orleans', *Popcorn*, 1996.

167 [world that day, he says.]: Email from Steve Larkin to the author, 27 May 2023.

167 ['Everybody Jam!']: Photos taken of the Everybody Jam! shoot, John and Judy Larkin archive.

167 [had before it.]: Lena Storvand, 'S-S-Scatter Again', *Spotlight*, 18 Nov. 1996.

167 [It doesn't get any better!]: Morten Lind, 'The World's Too Hot to Be Cool!', *Volume*, 1996.

167 ['children of all ages']: First heard on 'Hi, Louis' on the *Scatman's World* album (RCA/BMG, 1995) and used many times since.

168 [this is an abomination.]: 'Scatman John: For Me, Drugs Were a Full Time Job', *Entrevue*, 1995.

168 [many others.]: Morten Lind, 'The World's Too Hot to Be Cool!', *Volume*, 1996.

168 [*better than me.*]: Lyrics used with permission.

168 [feelings of inadequacy going.]: *VIVA Jam* 1 hour interview special, 1996.

168 [It can't be.]: Morten Lind, 'The World's Too Hot to Be Cool!', *Volume*, 1996.

168 [smiling on us again,]: Fax from Manfred Zähringer to Michael Schur, 17 Sept. 1996, Iceberg Records Archive.

Chapter 32

169 [bonus tracks.]: 'Scatman John – Everybody Jam!' Discogs, last modified 21 Nov. 1996, https://www.discogs.com/release/1143055-Scatman-John-Everybody-Jam.

169 [had cooled.]: After the *Scatman's World* album in 1995, there were no further Scatman John releases in the UK.

169 ['Of course, I'll do it.']: Fax from John Larkin to Manfred Zähringer, 23 Apr. 1997, Iceberg Records Archive.

169 [officially a nonprofit.]: Fax from John Larkin to BMG Hamburg, 5 Jan. 1997, Iceberg Records Archive.

170 [label was disappointed.]: Interview with Manfred Zähringer, 14 May 2023, Scatman dolls: competition listed on a sticker on the album cover and on promo flyers, in the author's possession.

170 ['I don't think about failure or success,']: NPN, 'Scatman on the Bottle', undated article circa 1996.
170 ['If I can help just one confused soul, I'll show up.']: *Let's Dance*, Oct. 1995.
170 [a collaboration]: Fax from BMG Hamburg to Manfred Zähringer, 20 Mar. 1997, Iceberg Records Archive.
170 [North American promo tour.]: Fax from Logic Records to Iceberg Records, 3 May 1997, Iceberg Records Archive.
170 [he wanted to do it right.]: Fax from John Larkin to Manfred Zähringer, 23 Apr. 1997, Iceberg Records Archive.
170 [They ain't about nothin'.]: Fax from Partnership for a Drug-Free America to Iceberg Records, 21 Mar. 1997, Iceberg Records Archive; PSA aired nationwide on NBC 23 and 25, https://www.youtube.com/watch?v=FhlsEPDMdj0.
170 [no further explanation.]: Fax from John Larkin to Manfred Zähringer, 23 Apr. 1997, Iceberg Records Archive.
170 [older guy fatigue.]: Interview with D. Jennings, 21 Mar. 2023.
170 [national children's network]: John Larkin interview, Radio AAHS Hollywood, 29 Mar. 1997.
170 [on their feet again.]: Conversation with Judy Larkin, 1999.
171 [That meant the world to him.]: Interview with Lee Newman, 13 Apr. 2023.
171 [keeps me alive.]: Honda S. Jorgensen, 'Johnny Jetlag', *Zink*, Dec. 1996.
171 [on trumpet]: Home video footage, John and Judy Larkin archive, and author's own observations.
171 [Cheese restaurant.]: Interview with Joe Celia, 12 Sept. 2024.
171 [the joy of it.]: Unreleased recordings of John's Jazz Workshop, 1997, John and Judy Larkin Archive.
171 [As he always did.]: John Larkin interview on Radio AAHS Hollywood, 29 Mar. 1997.
171 [message could mean.]: Undated handwritten notes by Judy Larkin, John and Judy Larkin Archive.
172 [*Love to you … John*]: Email from John Larkin circa 11 July 1997.
172 [for John.]: John scatting with the sax in Frankfurt: Interview with Ingo Kays and Iris Reimann, 16 June 2023, also WhatsApp messages with Ingo Kays, 7 Apr. 2025.
172 [man of action.]: *Sounds of Frankfurt* Broadcast, Hessischer Rundfunk (HR), 12 July 1997.
172 [important to him,]: Fax from Manfred Zähringer to Wolfgang Weyand, 20 June 1997, Iceberg Records Archive.
172 [turning toxic.]: Ernst Klee, 'How Eugenics Conquered Minds', *De Zeit*, 5 Sept. 1997.
172 [sterilization law.]: Sieglind Ellger-Rüttgardt, 'Special Schools in the "Third Reich." Conformist and Non-Conformist Behavior of Special School Teachers', in *Unwanted Youth in National Socialism. 'Youth Care' and Special Schools in the Rhineland, 1933–45*, ed. Erika Welkerling and Falk Wiesemann (Essen: Klartext, 2005), n.p.
173 [because of it.]: NPN, 'Respect Yourself!' undated article, 1997.
173 [drop Henze's name.]: Institut für Stadtgeschichte Frankfurt am Main. *Umbenennung der August-Henze-Schule in Weißfrauenschule*. Fonds A.46.01, 84. 1997–9, accessed 8 May 2025, https://arcinsys.hessen.de/arcinsys/showArchivalDescriptionDetails?archivalDescriptionId=10187124.
173 [back to his hotel.]: Interview with Andrea Black, 3 Apr. 2025.
174 [*You'll be okay*.]: AOL Instant Messenger chat with John Larkin circa 13 July 1997.

Chapter 33

176 [play him the music.]: Edesio's involvement in the third album, emails from Edesio Alejandro to the author, 7, 11, 12, 13, 14, 15 Dec. 2023.
176 [host might bite.]: John Larkin appearing on *Schreinemakers TV*, RTL, 1997.
176 [path someone chose.]: Scatland Foundation folder and materials, including draft newsletter, John and Judy Larkin Archive, also Iceberg Records Archive.
176 [found a 'way.']: John Larkin appearing on *Schreinemakers TV*, RTL, 1997.
176 [of these events.]: Fax from John Larkin to Manfred Zähringer, 4 May 1997, Iceberg Records Archive.
176 [decided he would.]: Email from John Larkin to the International Stuttering Association, 25 Feb. 1997, courtesy of Shinji Ito.
176 [openly on TV.]: Shinji Ito, 'Remembering Scatman John 4: A Man of Sincerity', Shinji Ito's Stuttering Counseling Room blog, 11 Dec. 2016, https://kituon.livedoor.blog/archives/1808691.html.
176 [non-aggression.]: Email from John Larkin to Shinji Ito and the International Stuttering Association Committee, 18 Feb. 1997, courtesy of Shinji Ito.
177 [chart at all.]: The single does not appear in any available national chart for 1997.
177 [his philanthropy,]: 'Scatman John: The Good Man of the Month' undated clipping from *Petra*.
177 [he acknowledged.]: Email from John Larkin to the International Stuttering Association Committee, 24 Mar. 1997, courtesy of Shinji Ito.
177 [impossible to ignore.]: Conversation with Judy Larkin, Oct. 1999.
177 [schedule is absurd.]: Fax from John Larkin to Manfred Zähringer and BMG Hamburg, 7 May 1997, Iceberg Records Archive.
177 [Toronto and New Jersey.]: Concerts listed in *The Herald News*, 18 July 1997, playing the Polish American Club at midnight and the Abyss Nightclub at 1.30 a.m.
177 [magnificent as a human being.]: Interview with Jan Roeg, 6 July 2023.
177 [refused to play 'Everybody Jam'.]: Fax from Logic Records to Manfred Zähringer, 22 Aug. 1997, Iceberg Records Archive.
177 [separate ways.]: Fax from Manfred Zähringer to John Larkin, 26 June 1997, Iceberg Records Archive.
177 [loved about it.]: Interview with David Helfant, 10 July 2023.
178 [trading ideas.]: Interview with Shane Keister, 12 June 2023.
178 [wiser cousin.]: Unreleased demo, John and Judy Larkin Archive, Iceberg Records Archive.
178 [to meet Shane.]: Interview with Jan Roeg, 6 July 2023.
178 [A whole different sound.]: Interview with Shane Verdi, 6 June 2023.
178 [he announced.]: John Larkin appearance on Radio AAHS Hollywood, 29 Nov. 1997.
178 ['Mambo No. 5'.]: Fax from Andreas Kirnberger to Manfred Zähringer, 9 Dec. 1997, Iceberg Records Archive.
179 [A very special artist.]: Email from Sebastian Roth to the author, 10 Jan. 2025.
179 [your face is.]: Betty Ester, 'Scatman: The Star of the Past Stuttered in Estonia', *Sunday* paper 2 Nov. 1997.
179 ['I'm always tired,' he replied.]: Details of the Lithuanian concerts: email from Vaidas Stackevičius to the author, 30 Mar. 2025.
179 ['Puerto Rican by injection.']: Undated note by John Larkin, John and Judy Larkin Archive.
180 [jazz musician.]: Edesio and John in the studio: Emails from Edesio Alejandro to the author, 7, 11, 12, 13, 14, 15 Dec. 2023.

180 [We understand each other musically.]: Fax from John Larkin to Manfred Zähringer, 5 Mar. 1998, Iceberg Records Archive.
180 [simply go away.]: John's puffiness: Email from John and Judy Larkin to Manfred Zähringer, 15 May 1998, Iceberg Records Archive.
180 [came back glowing.]: Faxes from Manfred Zähringer to John Larkin, 14 and 16 Apr. 1998, Iceberg Records Archive.
180 [broadcast nationwide.]: Fax from BMG Hamburg to Manfred Zähringer, 7 May 1998, Iceberg Records Archive.
180 [into the streets.]: Fax from Dagmar Spremberg to BMG Hamburg detailing the concept for the 'Scatmambo' music video.
181 [Judy was drinking again]: Interview with Stacey Heaver, 28 Mar. 2023; email from Stacey Heaver to the author, 3 June 2023.

Chapter 34

182 [Judy thought.]: John's operation: Fax from Judy Larkin to Manfred Zähringer, 14 May 1998, Iceberg Records Archive; John and Judy Larkin Archive.
182 [was complete.]: Fax from Dr Thomas Mahrer to Manfred Zähringer, 12 May 1998, Iceberg Records Archive.
183 [John will be better than ever!]: John's recovery and negotiations: Fax from Judy Larkin to BMG Hamburg and Manfred Zähringer, 14 May 1998; fax from John and Judy Larkin to Manfred Zähringer, 15 May 1998; John and Judy Larkin Archive; Iceberg Records Archive.
183 [The old John.]: Interview with Stacey Heaver, 28 Mar. 2023.
183 [of all ages.]: Opening line of 'Can You Hear Me', demo in the John and Judy Larkin Archive.
183 [bad dream from hell.]: John's home studio: Faxes from John Larkin to Ingo Kays, 19 Feb. 1998 and undated later in 1998, in the possession of Ingo Kays, John and Judy Larkin Archive.
184 [*Phantom of the Opera*.]: Interview with Stacey Heaver, 28 Mar. 2023.
184 [beautiful to hear you stutter.]: Emails and phone call(s) with John Larkin, 1998.
184 [the organizers.]: Fax from John Larkin to the Danish Stuttering Association, 27 Feb. 1998, John and Judy Larkin Archive.
184 [It's taken a lot of work for both of us.]: JPL.
184 [look at him differently.]: Interview with Barry Mitchell, 10 Apr. 2023.
184 [passport status.]: Fax from Dr Thomas Mahrer to Manfred Zähringer and BMG Hamburg, 22 May 1998; fax from Michael Schur to Manfred Zähringer, 22 May 1998, John and Judy Larkin Archive; Iceberg Records Archive.
184 [left in the dark.]: Fax from Judy Larkin to her lawyer, and Dr Mahrer, 22 May 1998, John and Judy Larkin Archive.
185 [a better job.]: Fax from Manfred Zähringer to John and Judy Larkin, 25 May 1998, Iceberg Records Archive.
185 ['Plan tour w/o killing him.']: Fax from Eckhart Gundel to David Helfant, 26 May 1998, undated handwritten notes by Judy Larkin, circa May 1998, John and Judy Larkin Archive.
185 [using a body double.]: Fax from Janine Ramond to Manfred Zähringer, 23 June 1998, Iceberg Records Archive.
185 [time to heal.]: Fax from John Larkin to Manfred Zähringer, 24 June 1998, Iceberg Records Archive.
185 [listen to them.]: Fax from Manfred Zähringer to Axel Alexander, 26 June 1998, Iceberg Records Archive.
185 [out of the question.]: John's rehospitalization and subsequent tests: Fax from Judy Larkin to Manfred Zähringer and David Helfant, 6 July 1998, John and Judy Larkin Archive.

185 [it's salvageable,' he wrote.]: Fax from John Larkin to Mette Zähringer, 4 July 1998, Iceberg Records Archive.
185 [shot at momentum.]: Animation idea, 'Scatmambo' release: Fax from Manfred Zähringer to John and Judy Larkin, 7 July 1998, Iceberg Records Archive.
186 [to ease the load.]: Fax from John Larkin to Mette Zähringer, 4 July 1998, Iceberg Records Archive.
186 [anything.]: Fax from Judy Larkin to Manfred Zähringer, 10 July 1998, Iceberg Records Archive.
186 ['until it broke down.']: JPL.
186 [There was no undoing it.]: Fax from Iceberg Records lawyer to John Larkin, 3 Sept. 1998, Iceberg Records Archive.
186 [things out.]: Fax from Manfred Zähringer to John Larkin, 3 Sept. 1998, Iceberg Records Archive.
186 [earlier in the process.]: Fax from John Larkin to Manfred Zähringer, 4 Aug. 1998, Iceberg Records Archive.
186 [different story.]: *VIVA Jam* 1 Hour Interview Special, 1996.
186 [memorable]: Fax from Manfred Zähringer to John Larkin, 12 Apr. 1999, Iceberg Records Archive.
186 [for a sick friend.]: Marcia's death: Messenger conversation with Shelley Gilman, 26 Apr. 2023.
186 [pain gets pretty bad,]: Fax from John Larkin to Manfred Zähringer, 31 Aug. 1998, Iceberg Records Archive.
187 ['We had fun every day.']: Interview with Kai Matthiesen, 24 July 2023.
187 [years of smoking.]: Email from Billy King to the author, 17 Aug. 2023.
187 [really there.]: Interview with Manfred Zähringer, 26 Oct. 2024.
187 [better spirits.]: Faxes from Manfred Zähringer to John Larkin, 20 and 21 Oct. 1998, Iceberg Records Archive.
187 [They fell about laughing.]: Email from Billy King to the author, 17 Aug. 2023.
187 [last year of life had begun.]: Home video footage, shot 31 Dec. 1998, John and Judy Larkin Archive.

Chapter 35

188 [wasn't anything fancy.]: Interview with Peter Nicks, 23 Aug. 2023.
188 [silly with me.]: Interview with Daniel Kremer, 17 July 2023.
188 [for a little while.]: John and Daniel laughing, unused footage, *Danny and The Scatman*, 1999.
188 [Pete says.]: Interview with Peter Nicks, 23 Aug. 2023.
188 [oh God, he's great.]: Unused footage, *Danny and The Scatman*, 1999.
188 [Pete says.]: Interview with Peter Nicks, 23 Aug. 2023.
188 [moved on their own.]: Unused footage, *Danny and The Scatman*, 1999.
189 [I could do anything.]: Interview with Daniel Kremer, 17 July 2023; Messenger chat with Daniel Kremer, 13 Jan. 2025.
189 [email and phone.]: Email from Daniel Kremer to Annie Bradberry, 11 Dec. 1999, John and Judy Larkin Archive.
189 [before the final master.]: Interview with Kai Matthiesen, 24 July 2023.
189 [fine with that.]: Fax from John Larkin to Manfred Zähringer, 12 Mar. 1999, Iceberg Records Archive.
189 [express themselves.]: Unused footage, *Danny and The Scatman*, 1999.
189 [miming from start to finish.]: Fax from John Larkin to Manfred Zähringer, 12 Mar. 1999, Iceberg Records Archive.

190 [Sometimes I want to be left alone.]: Unused footage, *Danny and The Scatman*, 1999.
190 [be good to ourselves.]: Morten Lind, 'The World's Too Hot to be Cool!', *Volume*, 1996.
190 [Totally.]: Unused footage, *Danny and The Scatman*, 1999.
191 [on a slide.]: Conversation with Judy Larkin, Oct. 1999.
191 [over the phone]: Interview with Ingo Kays, 16 June 2023.
191 [take care of them.]: Fax from John Larkin to Manfred Zähringer, 11 Feb. 1999, Iceberg Records Archive.
191 [person ever had.]: Fax from John Larkin to Mette Zähringer, 29 Apr. 1999, Iceberg Records Archive.
191 [belief in myself.]: Fax from John Larkin to Manfred Zähringer, 6 May 1999, Iceberg Records Archive.
191 ['You know me.']: Fax from Manfred Zähringer to John Larkin, 7 May 1999, Iceberg Records Archive.
192 [like a monk.]: Home video footage, John and Judy Larkin Archive.
192 [didn't seem to know it had shipped.] Interview with Jonathan Dolan, 1 May 2025.
192 [another label.]: Fax from Manfred Zähringer to Holder Muller, 6 Aug. 1999, Iceberg Records Archive.
192 [might be working.]: Photos of John celebrating with a cake, John and Judy Larkin Archive.
192 [already reached his brain.]: John Larkin, death certificate, 3 Dec. 1999, Los Angeles County Registrar-Recorder/County Clerk, Los Angeles, CA.

Chapter 36

194 [another bar.]: Playing the tree: Interview with Joe Celia, 12 Sept. 2024.
193 [as long as he wants.]: Interview with Gladys Navas, 20 Apr. 2024.
194 [Judy said,]: Judy speaking at John's memorial, tape recording, 12 Dec. 1999, John and Judy Larkin Archive.
194 [Gladys remembers.]: Interview with Gladys Navas, 20 Apr. 2024.
194 [for five hours.]: Judy speaking at John's memorial, tape recording, 12 Dec. 1999, John and Judy Larkin Archive.
194 [what the hell I said to that.]: Interview with Lee Newman, 13 Apr. 2023.
194 [I love you. John.]: Email from John Larkin, circa July 1999.
195 [It was the last thing he ever recorded.]: Final takes of 'Can You Hear Me?', demo recordings, John and Judy Larkin Archive.
195 ['You are getting me all worried.']: Fax from Manfred Zähringer to John and Judy Larkin, 1 Sept. 1999, Iceberg Records Archive.
196 [He's stopped recognizing people.]: Phone conversation with Judy Larkin, Oct. 1999.

Chapter 37

197 [John used to say.]: John Larkin interview on unnamed Swiss TV programme, 1996.
198 [banned in the US.]: Interview with Lee Newman, 13 Apr. 2023; interview with Billy and Sharon Larkin, 27 Mar. 2023.
198 [she'd let it in.]: Interview with Stacey Heaver, 28 Mar. 2023.
198 [not long for this world.]: Interview with Daniel Kremer, 17 July 2023.
198 [John wasn't coming back.]: Interview with Manfred Zähringer, 25 Oct. 2024.
199 [and carry him out]: Interview with Barry Mitchell, 10 Apr. 2023.
200 [watching the screen.]: With John and Judy Larkin at their home, circa mid-Oct. 1999.
200 [waiting crowd.]: Echo Awards ceremony footage, 1996, John and Judy Larkin Archive.
200 [*Just go ahead and stutter.*] *VIVA Jam* interview special, 1996, intercut with Echo Awards ceremony footage.

Epilogue

201 [the open sea.]: John's ashes scattered in 2001: conversation with Judy Larkin, circa 2001; interview with Stacey Heaver, 28 Mar. 2023.
201 [Straight ahead.]: Recordings of John's memorial, 12 Dec. 1999, John and Judy Larkin Archive.
201 [greatest gift.]: Author's own observation as webmaster; numerous obituary clippings in the John and Judy Larkin Archive.
201 [too many memories,]: Ruth Ryon, 'This Move to Las Vegas is a Family Matter,' *Los Angeles Times* (Home Edition), 28 Sept. 2000.
201 [tribute to my baby,]: Fax from Judy Larkin to Manfred Zähringer, 17 Mar. 2000, Iceberg Records Archive.
201 [wait for me,]: Recordings of John's memorial, 12 Dec. 1999, John and Judy Larkin Archive.
201 [age of 83.]: Judy McHugh Larkin Obituary, *Los Angeles Times*, 28 Feb. 2023.
201 [sampled him.]: 'Scatman John,' WhoSampled, accessed 9 May 2025, https://www.whosampled.com/Scatman-John/.
202 [as a tribute.]: 'Scatman & Hatman', Scatman John and Lou Bega, released 13 June 2019, 9122 Records, https://www.9122records.com/scatmanhatman.
202 ['Phenomenal,' he says.]: Interview with Manfred Zähringer, 14 May 2023.
202 [as a family.]: Interview with Lee, Christena and Heston Newman, 13 Apr. 2023.
202 [bought the grand.]: Conversation with the Larkin family, 27 Mar. 2023.
203 [he writes to me afterward.]: Email from Steve Larkin to the author, 27 May 2023.
203 ['We need to play his songs.']: Interview with Anita Blom, 24 Dec. 2023.
203 [*If you stutter, you're not alone.*] The National Stuttering Association, https://www.westutter.org/.
203 [open, and accessible, she says.]: Interview with Heather Grossman, 17 June 2024.
203 [Stuttering Foundation]: Email from Jane Fraser to the author, 3 Sep. 2023.
203 [stuttering organizations around the world.]: Conversation with Judy Larkin, circa 2001.
204 [Eventually, it rises.]: Mentioned in unused footage, *Danny and the Scatman*, 1999.
204 [could write such a book.]: John Larkin, undated memoir notes, John and Judy Larkin Archive.
205 [he was no saint.]: Konrad Schäfers, Jutta vom Hofe, Claudia Mende, Erhard Hennen, interview with John Larkin for the BVSS (Bundesvereinigung Stottern & Selbsthilfe), Nov. 1995.

INDEX

Please note: Page numbers with a capital P before them refer to plate numbers found in the central section of the book.

2 Unlimited 109

Abell, David L. 165
Ace of Base 150
acid *see* LSD
Ackerman, Chuck 22
Ackerman, Paul 22
addiction
    alcohol 22–7, 59–65, 68–9, 77–8
    amphetamines 33–4, 42–4, 58
    attempts to stop 53–4, 62–5, 76–97
    cannabis 63–5, 77–8
    cocaine 64–71
    heroin 36–7, 69–71, 76
    and isolation 104
    LSD 40–1
    medical 184–5
    morphine 184–5
    overdose 69–71
    relapses 65, 68–9, 77–8
    smoking 17–21, 105
    ten-year sobriety 167–8
    twenties 33–52
adolescence 17–31
Adult Children of Alcoholics (ACA) 83
adverts 148–9, 158–9
advocacy 149–50, 159–61, 160, 171, 172–3, 176–7
Afro Cuban music 178, 179–80
ages
    8th grade graduation 3
    childhood P1–3, 5–6, 9–16
    eighteen P4
    fifties P10–16, 103–105, 109–201
    five years old P2
    forties P9, 65–103
    nine months P1
    teenage years P4, 17–31
    thirties P7, 52–65
    twenties P5–6, 31–52
Ain't Misbehavin' 95
Akai sampler 114
Akasaka 63
alcohol 22–7, 59–62, 68–9, 77–8
    attempts to stop 62–5
    cruise ship contracts 65, 68–9
    Delirium Tremens 68
    drunk driving 61–2
    relapses 65, 68–9, 77–8
Alcoholics Anonymous (AA) 69, 76–7, 79, 80–7, 89, 98–9, 104–5, 132–3, 139, 184, 194
Alejandro, Edesio 175–6, 179, 186
Alexander, Axel 110, 115
Alexandra Hotel, The 111
algebra 24
All Blues 171
All Saints Catholic School 5–6, 13–16, 19–20
alter egos 59
    see also Scatman John
America
    Everybody Jam 170, 177
    Scatman's World 150–1
    see also locations within America …
American Institute for Stuttering 203

America Online (AOL) 169
American Speech-Language-Hearing Association (ASHA) 166
amphetamines 33–4, 42–4, 58
Amsterdam P9, 98–100
Andersen, Hans Christian 119–21
Angel Dust (PCP/phencyclidine) 60–1
Angelo, Gus 29–30, 35, 50, 56
Angel's Flight 74
anger 138
Animal Sounds 65–6
Anne 24–5
Annie Glenn Award 166
antipsychotics 58
Arista 150
arguments, Marcia 59
Arkin, Alan 27
Arkin, Bob 27
Armstrong, Louis 18, 29, 91, 139, 164, 166, 167
Arnold, Buddy 76–7
arrests 27, 61–2
ashes 201
As Time Goes By 103
Atkins 61
attempted murder 27–8
August-Henze-Schule 172–3
award party 147–8

bail 28
bands
    cruise ship contracts 64–5, 68–9, 81–2, 102–4
    De Vons 42
    first 22
    Fred 54–7
    gigs at Marty's 33–4
    God's Children 48–50
    Groove-Fuss P5, 37
    John Larkin Quartet P9, 72–4
    Johnny Larkin Combo 29–30
    Magnolia Jazz Band 91–2
    Marshal Hooks & Co. 51
    Mayo Tiana Septet 31–2
    The Norsemen 30–1, 35
    Oingo Boingo 65–7
    Scatman's World tour 152–7
barbiturates 43–4
Barker, Bruce 171

Barry, Julian 171
Beatles, The 2, 39, 102, 153
Bebop 10, 36
Beck, Nancy 23
Bega, Lou 202
benzedrine 33, 42, 58
Berlin, Germany 88–93
Berlin Wall 89
Best, Tim 153–5
Beverly Bowl, Montebello 35
Biden, Joe 2
Bild 166
Billy *see* Larkin, William
birth 9
bisexuality 47
Bla Bla Café 55–6
Black, Andrea 173
Black Narcissus 156
Blom, Anita 203
Blue Dolphin Studios 74
Blunt, Emily 2
blizzards 9, 11
Blue Dolphin Studios 74
BMG Ariola Hamburg 110–11, 142–3, 147–8, 162, 166–7, 185
BMG Tokyo 122
bobbahn 142–3
Boeddha, The 99–100
Bonnafaunt, Bob 54–7
Bottrop, Germany 112–15
Bradberry, Annie 115
'brain cell situation' 170
British Stammering Association 174, 184
Broach, Zowie 141
brother 9–10
    and bullies 14
    living with 54
Brubeck, Dave 18
Brzezicki, Steve 152–5
BT newspaper 123
Budapest, Hungary P17, 154
bullying 14, 25
Bundesvereinigung Stotterer-Selbsthilfe (BVSS) 127
Butterfield, Paul 77

cabinetmaking 21
Cacayorin, Philip 72–4
Café Moskau 92

248 INDEX

California, El Sereno 9–11
Calling Out 176
cancer 183, 185, 190–200
    death from 201
    diagnosis 190–2
    final days 195–200
cannabis 63–5, 77–8
Cantor, Eddie 39, 90, 92, 143
Can You Hear Me? 183, 195
car crashes 61–2, 70–1
Carla, Sister 13
Catalina Island 201
Catania, Ilona 135, 165
Catania, Tony P12, 111–15, 118, 122, 135–9
Catapres (clonidine) 81
Catholic doctrine 13, 15–16
   Mass 15–16
   sexuality 24–5
cats 130
Cavett, Morgan 74
Celia, Joe 49–51, 193
Central Sound Recorders 71–4
Charley's Place 73
chart positions
   Scatman 119
   Scatman's World 146–7, 151
Cheli Air Force Station cafeteria 19
Chez Alex 93
Chopstick Productions 117
Chickadee Song, The 187
childhood P1–3, 5–6, 9–16
children
   at the house 170–1
   safety of 109
choir 28–9
Christus factus est 28–9
chronic obstructive pulmonary disease (COPD) 137, 143, 152, 155, 157–8, 165, 170–1, 177, 180–7
Clarence 33–5
clave 32
clonidine 81
Club Hollywood, Estonia 179
Coca-Cola 148
cocaine 64–71
CODA 87–8
codeine 63–4, 66
Cokes, Ray 147

Coldwater Canyon 70–1
college years 26–32
Coltrane, John 36, 147, 172
Come Back Inn 55–6
Commerce Hyatt 84–5
commercials 148–9, 158–9
communion 15–16
Connie 37
Corea, Chick 72
covert stuttering 121, 174
crime 20, 24, 26, 27
   attempted homicide 27
   drunk driving 61–2
   criminal damage 26–7
Crouch, Stanley 37
cruise ship contracts 64–5, 68–9, 81–2, 102–4
Crutcher, Rusty 68–69
Cuban music 179–80
Cussia, Vic 25
Czech Republic 169

Dagbladet newspaper 123
Damien 60
Dana Anglia 102
Danny and The Scatman 188–9
David 11
dealing, cocaine 64–8
death
   John 201
   Judy 204
   Marcia 186
Del Ferro, Mike 99
Delirium Tremens (DTs) 68
Denmark 122, 123, 148
Dennis 27
dentures 118
depression 31, 40, 93–4, 171
De Vons 42
diagnosis of cancer 190–2
Disco Demolition 150
Disney 170
divorce 96
documentary 188–9
domestic violence 60–1
Don Bosco Technical Institute, Los Angeles 20–21
Doop (band) 120
DoRo Film 166

Dragon Man 69–71
Dream Again 186–7
drinking 22–7
drunk driving 61–2
Dunn, Paul 153–5

Earl Jones, James 166
earthquakes, Northridge 110
East LA College 26, 27
East Los Angeles 48–52
Echo Awards 2, 199
Eco Park studio 179
Edesio's Dream (renamed *Dream Again*) 186
eighteen years old P4
eighth grade graduation P3
Eletta, Sister 5–6, 13
Eleva2oren 123
eleventh grade 24–5
El Sereno, California 9–11
Enterprise Studios P11, 150
Entrevue magazine 147
Eric 51–2
Espinoza, Jimmy 29, 32, 34
Estonia 179
Eurodance 123–4, 136, 150
Europa Center 90–1
European Magazine, The 133
Evans, Bill 36
Everybody Jam! (album)
 chart positions and sales 169–70
 concept and themes 162–164, 168
 recording 163, 165–66, 168
 release and reception 169–171
Everybody Jam! (single)
 in America 170, 177
 recording and naming 164, 166
 release 168–9
 promotion of 168, 171
 video shoot 166–7
Everything Changes 139
evictions 76
expulsions 21, 26–7
extreme weather 9, 11

Fabulous Baker Boys, The 102
faith 15–16
fan-made websites 159

fan mail 134, 161
Farmdale Elementary School 11
Farrell, Joe P9, 72–4, 76–7
father 9–10, 14–15, 17–18
fear of death 194
fedora 119
feeling people 18
fetishes 51–2
fifties P10–16, 103–105, 109–201
final days 197–200
Finland 160
first band 22
first job 19
Fitzgerald, Ella 18, 29
Flea (bassist) 80
Flint, Shelby 74
flute 30
Flyers, The 103
football team 25
Forrest, Dick 171
Foster, Clare 99
forties P9, 65–103
frajos 17
Frankfurt, Germany 169–173
Franklin High 27
Fraser, Jane 203
fraternities 27
frat parties 26–7, 29
Fred (band name) 54–7
'freed stuttering' 29
FroggyLand, Jazz and the Blues 11
Front Line Films 140

Gad, Tobias 187
Game Over Jazz 139
gang members 27
Gangsta Rap 131
Germany 101–3, 127, 155, 166
Get Back 153
Gilman, Marcia P7, 57–80, 96
 arguments 59
 children 60, 75–7
 cocaine 64–71
 codeine 63–4
 death 186
 divorce 96
 eviction 76
 marriage 59–60

meeting 57–9
proposal 59
recovery attempts 74, 76–7
separation 76–7
violence 59, 60–1
girls, teenage years 22–7
Gladys 193–4, 195
Glave, Chuck 34, 193
Glenn, Annie 166
Glico, Pucchin Purin 158
God's Children 48–50
'going fluent' 190
'Going Out' 77–8
gold disk 147
Good Humor 148
Graffiti, Rashidii 93
Granada Hills, San Fernando Valley 31–2
Grand Prix award 160
Gretchen 89–90, 92, 93
Groove-Fuss P5, 37
Grossman, Heather 203
Gruber, Freddie 34, 36
Gundel, Eckhart 115, 185
guns 27

Hagger, Laura 140–2
Hair 44–5, 48
Hall, John 30
Hamel, Damien 60, 67
Hamel, Hersh 60
Hamilton, Steve 152–6
Hanazono, Satoru 164
Hans 99–100
Happy Birthday 41, 55
Harnell, Joe 70
Harrison, Bob P9, 72–4, 129, 130
Hartmann, Jon 68
hashish 44
hat 119
health decline
cancer 183, 185, 190–200
COPD 137, 143, 152, 155, 170–1, 177, 180–7
hospitalization 180–3
Heaver, Stacey 98–9, 180–1, 183
Hegedűs, Ákos 154
Heick, Annette 123
Heit Nieuwsblad 131

Helfant, David 170, 177
heroin 36–7, 69–71, 76
Hewitt, Gary & Jackie 56
Hey You! 150
High School 20–6
Hill, Lauryn 170
Hi, Louis 139
Hinsch, Ulrik 152–5
hippie lifestyle 39–52
Holiday, Billie 10, 39
homelessness 131–2
home purchase 143
home studio 171, 183, 188–9, 195
hospitalization 182–3
housekeeper 193–4
Humax Pavilion Shinjuku complex, Tokyo 156
Hungary P17, 154, 169
Hungexpo, Budapest P17, 154
hypnosis 10

Iceberg Records P13, 101–3, 105, 122, 135, 147
Iguana Café 88
imitations of stuttering 148
Ingram, Luther 51
Intercontinental, The 102–3
International House of Pancakes, The 43
International Stuttering Association (ISA) 161
interviews 66–7, 97
advocacy 160, 171, 176–7
Gangsta Rap 131
Journey of Fantasy 164–6, 166, 169–71
Scatman 119–27, 133
Scatman's World 146–7, 149–50, 158–9
Invisible Man, The 166
Island Princess 64–5
Ito, Shinji 176

Jackson, Michael 147, 151
Jacobs, Darryl 53
Japan P16, 122, 150, 156–7, 158–9, 164, 169–70
Japan Stuttering Genyūkai Association 160
jazz 18
college years 29–32

INDEX 251

East LA 48–52
see also bands
Jazz Bakery 115–16
Jazz Jam (Changed to *Everybody Jam!*) 164, 166
Jazzology 164
Jennings, D. 132, 170
Jewish ancestry 92–3
John Coltrane 74
John Larkin LP 78, 81, 130
John Larkin Quartet P9, 72–4
John Larkin Sings 95–7, 101–3, 110
'Johnny Jetlag' 153
Johnny Larkin Combo 29–30
Johnny Trenard 59
Johnson, Nils 95
John-to-John conversations 136–7
Jonathan, with (Marcia's grandson) P8
Jones, Marlin 72
Jorgensen, Honda 160
Journey of Fantasy (changed to Everybody Jam! Album) 158, 162–5

Kafafian, Eddie 70
Kaiser Wilhelm Memorial Church 90
Kanebo Cosmetics 158
Kato-Cha 158
Kaunas, Lithuania P19, 179
Kays, Ingo P12, 111–15, 118, 135–9, 172, 183
Keister, Shane 178
Kelce, Jason 2
Kelce, Travis 2
KEYS Magazine 136
King, Billy 187
King George VI 2
KISS 170
Konakai 30–1
Korea 158
KPFK Radio 66–7
Kremer, Daniel 145, 188–9, 198
Kurír (newspaper) 154
Kursinski, Mr. 26
Kyiv, Ukraine 153–4

Lamar, Kendrick 2
Larrance, Steve 65–6

Larkin, Bill 9–10, 14–15, 17–18
Larkin, David 54, 110
Larkin, Harriet P3, P7, 9–10, 12, 17, 20, 83–4
Larkin, Jillian 202
Larkin, Judy *see* McHugh, Judy
Larkin, Marcia see *Gilman, Marcia*
Larkin, Sarah 202
Larkin, Sharon 26, 31, 54, 59, 82, 104, 133
Larkin, Steve 54, 127, 166–7
Larkin, William (Billy) P1, 9–10, 14, 54, 202–3
Lasonio, John 81, 171
Last Night I Dreamed 73
LA Weekly 150
legacy 201–2
Lennox, Annie 131
Let it Go 168, 177
Letting Go (NSP Newsletter) 103
licensing requests 148–9, 163
Listen to the Scatman 201
Lithuania P19, 179
Liquidroom (Tokyo) 156
Loen, Norway 111
Lofgren, Mr. (Lofty) 19–20
Logic Records 170, 177
Løkke, Knud 164
Lorimer, Peter 150
Los Alamitos 61–2
Los Angeles 33–88, 95–8, 110, 159
Los Angeles Times 88, 97
loss of virginity 24–5
Lotus, The 66
Love Boat, The 64–5
Love Cry 73
Love Me Tender 158
Love Scenes from Planet Earth 178–80, 179–80, 185
LSD 37–8, 40–1, 45–7, 58
Lunaria's 96–7
lung function tests 137

Maconie, Stuart 149
Magnolia Jazz Band 91–2
Major League III 178
major swelling 180–3
Mambo Jambo 136

Mambo No.5 178
Maria 34–5
marriages
    Judy P10, 110
    Marcia 59–60
Marshall Hooks & Co. 51
Marty's 33–4
Masquerade Room, The 35
Mass 15
math 24
Matthiesen, Kai 185, 188, 189
Mayo Tiana Septet 31–2
McCartney, Paul 156
McHugh, Jimmy 39, 115, 143, 202
McHugh, Judy P10, P20, 39, 85–105,
    109–204
    Amsterdam 98–9
    Berlin 88–93
    car crash 70–1
    commitment to 96
    death 204
    depression 93–4
    during recordings 137–8, 142
    during video shoots 142
    early days 87–8
    and Eloise 198–9, 204
    Jewish ancestry 92–3
    John's cancer 195, 198
    marriage P10, 110
    meeting of 85–6
    relapse 181, 184
    separations 88, 94–8
McPherson Avenue 9–11
McVinnie, Duke 54–7
media appearances 66–7, 97
    advocacy 160, 171, 176–7
    Gangsta Rap 131
    Journey of Fantasy 164–6, 166, 169–71
    Scatman 119–27, 133
    Scatman's World 146–7, 149–50, 158–9
medical addiction 184–5
Mellaril (thioridazine) 60
Merlin McFly's 67–8
Metelitsa (club) 154
methadone 37, 76
Methedrine 43
Metzger, Mike 133

Mexico City 178
MIDEM 116
Miller, Jim 81–2, 88
Million Dollar Theatre, The 10
Milli Vanilli 120
Misfit, The 44, 73
Mitchell, Barry 184
Mix magazine 164
modern therapy for stuttering 203
money and success 159
Monk, Thelonious 34, 36, 101
Monterey Road, Pasadena 27
Montreux Palace Hotel 105
morphine 181, 184
Morpho 154
Morrell, John 102
Moscow, Russia 154
Most Wanted 147
mother P3, P7, 12, 17, 19, 83–4, 104–5
Mount Wilson 193
MS Stardancer 81–2
MTV Europe 146–7
Muñoz, Carli 65
Music & Media magazine 118, 150–151
music bungalow 26
Musicians Alcoholics Anonymous 80–5
Musicians' Assistance Program (MAP) 170
My Funny Valentine 74

Naima 74
Nancy 42–4, 48
Napster 194
National Stuttering Association (NSA) 203
National Stuttering Project (NSP) 97–8,
    103, 115, 143–5, 188
Navas, Gladys *see Gladys*
Nevin, Father 15–16
Newman, Christena Rich- 202
Newman, Heston 202
Newman, Lee P16, 133, 143, 194, 202
New Orleans, Louisiana 166–7, 170
Nicks, Peter 188–9
Nome, Petter 125
Nordoff–Robbins 148
Norsemen, The 30–1
Northridge earthquake 110
Norway 119–21, 123

NRK radio 119
nuns 5–6, 13–15

obstructive pulmonary disease 180–3
O'Connor, Nora 103–4, 144
oedema 180–3
Oingo Boingo 65–7
On the Sunny Side of the Street 91
Only You 136
opiate withdrawal 81
overdose 69–71
oxygen tanks 152, 155

Pan Agency 102
Papel, Mark 40–1, 43–4
parents P3, P7, 9–12
    and bullies 14–15
    childhood relationship with 17–18
    and childhood sexual assault 12, 83–4
    rebuilding of relationship 104–5
    return home to 31–2
    and smoking 17
    and stuttering 15
Parker, Charlie 9, 34, 36
Patricia (song) 179
Paula 35
Paul, Billy 140–1
Paul, Robin 30
PCP *see* Angel Dust
Pedrini Music 29
People of the Generation 163
Petra magazine 177
Peverada, Johnny 19
peyote 58
phencyclidine *see* Angel Dust
Phipps, Sam 'Sluggo' 65–7, 129
piano
    college years 29–32
    first band 22
    and flirting 23
    gift of 19
    initial interest 18
Pincus, Gregg 110
Pitchford, Eloise 127–9, 146, 169, 171–4, 183–4, 186, 191–2, 194–200, 204
platinum disk 147–8
Poland 155
police 24, 26, 27, 61–2

politics 163–4
Popkomm 110
Popstar 138
Portugal 160
'pot only' rule 63–5
Potts, Rolf 150
Prado, Pérez 178–9
Price, Ruth 115
PriPri Scat 158
promo tours 138–9, 164–5
proposals, Marcia 59
Provenzano, Sam P6, 50, 53
public education 149–50, 159–61, 160, 171
Pucchin Purin 158
Puerto Rico 65

Queen (band) 156, 166
questioning, of sexuality 47
Quiet Desperation 131–2, 137

Radio AAHS 170, 171, 178
radio performances 66–7
Ramada Hotel 112–15
Ramond, Janine (Becker) 110, 114–15, 117, 119, 142–3, 147–8
rape 12, 45–7, 83–4, 168
Ravenhall, John 187
Real McCoy 130
Re-Bachelorization Headquarters 36
recordings
    Animal Sounds 65–6
    Everybody Jam! 166–171
    John Larkin Quartet 72–4
    John Larkin Sings 95–6
    Journey of Fantasy 162–5
    Scatmambo 175–6, 179–80, 185
    Scatman (Ski-Ba-Bop-Ba-Dop-Bop) 112–15
    Scatman's World 135–9
    Take Your Time 186–7
recovery (see sobriety)
redemption 15–16
Red Hot Chili Peppers, The 80
Rednex 120
relapses 65, 68–9, 77–8
Relatively Singing 143
Respublika magazine 179
return home 31–2, 53–4

254 INDEX

Return to Forever 72
reviews 97, 118
Rich-Newman, Christena 202
Riemann, Iris 134–135, 137, 172
Rivera, Bobby 14, 23, 30, 42, 129
Rivera, George 30
Rivera, Gloria 30
Robinson, Prince 82
Roeg, Jan 170, 177
roller coasters 142–3
Rondo 123–5
Rosen, Richard 95
Rossacher, Hannes 166
Rotterdam, The 68
Rowan & Martin's Laugh-In 39–40, 70
Route 66 44, 153, 160
Russia 154

Sabu 49–50, 61
Sakamoto, Kyu 157
safety of children 109
sampling 114, 153
San Fernando Valley 57
Santa Monica Civic Auditorium 28
Scandinavia 119–22
Scat Daddy 178
Scatland *2, 135*
Scatland Foundation, The 161, 171, 176, 203
Scatland Studio 171, 183, 188–9, 195
Scatmambo 175–6, 179–80, 185
Scatman & Hatman 202
Scatman (Ski-Ba-Bop-Ba-Dop-Bop)
  chart positions 119, 134, 140
  initial hearing of 116–17
  live performances 124–5
  press for 119–27, 133
  recording 112–15
  release 119–30
  video shoot 117–19
Scatman John
  initial planning 109–11
  naming 105
  Scatman 112–15
Scatman's World (single)
  chart positions 146
  lyrics and themes 140–41
  recording 135

release 146
video shoot 140–2
Scatman's World (album)
  in America 150–1
  chart positions and sales 149, 151, 156
  concept and themes 131–132, 134–5, 137, 139
  liner notes and dedication 149
  reception 149
  recording 135–9
  release 146–50
  tour 152–7
Scat Suit 126
scattering of ashes 201
scatting, initial 29–30
Schaefers, Konrad 127
Schnitzler, Gregor 117–18
school visits 172–3
Schur, Michael 154, 159
Seeger, Gary 49–51, 69
Sehr, Kai 180
self-talk 137
senior B crew 26
senior year 25
separations, Judy 88, 94–8
sexual assault 12, 45–7, 83–4, 168
sexuality
  Catholic doctrine 24–5
  fetishes 51–2
  questioning of 47
  and shame 42
Sharla 55–6
Sharon 82–3
Sheeran, Ed 2
Shelley 60
Sheri 60, 75–7
shoeless feet P17, 154
shotguns 27
Shut Your Mouth and Open Your Mind 163
Sigma Theta Chi 27
Silent Generation 168
Sing Now! 136
Sin with Sebastian 178–9
Sinsinawa Dominican Sisters 13–15
skepticism, about stuttering 120–1
Skibb, Martin 102
Smiley, Michael 149
Smith, Mimi 50

smoking 17–21, 105
Smurfs, The 120
snow 9, 11
sobriety 76–7, 79–85, 104–5, 167–8, 184
social commentary 137
Softly as in a Morning Sunrise 73
Song is You, The 101
Song of Scatland 139
Sorry Seems to be the Hardest Word 187
Sounds of Frankfurt (festival) 169, 172
soundchecks 156
South Korea 162
speedballs 69–71
spirituality 189
Stackevičius, Vaidas 179
Stax Records West 50–1
Steal the Base 178
stealing 20
Steve (friend) 27
Stewart, Zan 97
Studio City 55–6, 81
stuttering
    advocacy 149–50, 159–61
    bullying 14
    Catholic doctrine 13
    disclosure of 97, 113, 149
    fathers' reactions 15
    hypnosis 10
    imitations of 148
    modern therapy 203
    performances 97
    skepticism 120–1
    and stigma 160–1
Stuttering Foundation, The 203
stuttering pride 160–1, 172–3
suicide attempts 75–7
Sukiyaki 157
Superior Vena Cava Syndrome 183
Surratt, Al 35
surrender 81, 137
Su Su Su Super Kirei 158
Suzuki, Honami 158
swelling 180–3
Switzerland 105

Take Your Time 186–7, 189, 191–2
Talented Artists Management (TAM) 42
Tarzana 54–7

Taylor, Cecil 66
Technotronic 109
teenage years P4, 17–31
teeth 118
temper 138
tenth grade 22–4
ten-year sobriety 167–8
Tharla, Sister 13
theft 20
The Thing 12, 45–7, 83–4
thirties P7, 52–65
Thomsen, Philip 123
throat singing 55
Tiana, Mayo 31–2, 37
Time (Take Your Time) 133, 139
Toronto, Canada 44, 47–48
Tokyo, Japan 156
Tokyo Stuttering Association 164
Tony (Miali) 23, 32
Totten, Michael 71–4
touring P12, P17, P19, 152–62
Transition (label) 78
Treudelberg Hotel 102
Trinidad, Elson 159
Tyner, McCoy 56, 66, 159
twenties P5–6, 31–52

Ukraine 153–4
Ultraman P16, 158
uncovery 79
Urban, Walter, Jr. 80–1, 83

vandalism 26–7
Vangelis 134
Varga, Diane 96
Venice Beach 55–6
Verdi, Shane 178
video shoots
    Everybody Jam 166–7
    Scatman (Ski-Ba-Bop-Ba-Dop-Bop) 117–19
    Scatman's World 140–2
Vietnam War 43
Vilnius, Lithuania 179
violence 27, 59, 60–1
virginity, loss of 24–5
Vi Unge magazine 126
VIVA Jam 168

256   INDEX

Wallat, Jimmy & Ingrid 91–2
Waller, Fats 80, 95, 101
Warsaw, Poland 155
Wattstax festival 51
weather 9, 11
websites 159
weddings P10, 59–60, 110
(We Got To Learn to) Live Together 163
Welcome to Scatland 136
Well You Needn't 95, 101, 162
Wert, Chuck 19
What a Wonderful World 153, 155, 157
White House, the 11–12, 46–7
Williams, Steve 153–5
Wilson, Bill 69
Wilson Lew, Gail 103, 115
Winery, the 57–9
Winston (dog) 158–9, 191
women
    Connie 37
    Judy McHugh 39, 85–105, 109–204
    Marcia 57–80
    Maria 34–5
    Nancy 42–4, 48
    Paula 35
    Sharla 55–6
    teenage years 22–7
Wonder Palms Hotel 35
Wong, Ed (Edward) 189–90
Woodrow Wilson High 22–7
Woodward, Clark P9, 72–4
Wurlitzer 49, 54, 57

Yankovic, 'Weird Al' 171
Yoost 99
Young, Noah 65–6

Zähringer, Manfred P13, 101–3, 105, 109–11, 113–15, 116–17, 122–4, 143, 148, 162, 178, 186, 195, 198
Zähringer, Mette P13, 110, 122–3, 148, 158
Zastoupil, Curt 30
Zombie (Cranberries song) 131